MW01487608

What Does George Clooney Have That I Ain't Got?

- Keefer Stories -

Kip Keefer

What Does George Clooney Have That I Ain't Got?

BDI Publishers

ISBN: 978-0-9970445-0-8

FIRST EDITION

BDI Publishers
Atlanta, Georgia

Acknowledgments

Many thanks to the following individuals. Their collective efforts have turned this idea into a reality. My sons, Case, for inspiration and encouragement and Clayt for invaluable technical and logistical support that made this initiative possible. Cathie Blair and Traci Keefer, for continuing support. My lifelong friend Brent Darnell, and his team at BDI Publishers. Brent provided the pathway, direction and motivation to make this idea, a reality. Leda Dimperio for constant assistance, coordination and facilitation of events. Leah Karol and Laura Eason, through their collective photographic and artistic talents, crafted the miracle of my Hollywood transformation. All of my dear friends, especially Joe, Jim, Mark and Steve. They are not only the biggest fans of Keefer Stories, but played amazing parts in so many moments of my life. Jennifer Harben Wallace for her uplifting support, spirituality, resplendence and incomparable heart. And Terre Quillian, a brilliant bright light in my life. Her wondrous perception and reinforcing recognition provided the most vital component for completing this book, restoration of faith and belief in myself.

Introduction

What Does George Clooney Have That I Ain't Got?

Keefer Stories

OK, I suppose you're asking the obvious question, who is Kip Keefer and why would I possibly be interested in his stories? Certainly it is a viable, logical query?

In many ways, Kip Keefer is a typical modern day male. However, my journey and experiences have always been and continue to be, anything but ordinary.

This collection of the tales, perceptions, lessons learned, philosophies, comedies, heartbreaks, near misses, adversities, and mayhem, will hopefully entertain, enlighten and enrich you. There is little doubt that there will be many things too, in these pages, that readers will identify with. It is a classic American story with twists and turns, laughter and sadness. Childhood, family, friends, love and romance, fatherhood, vocations, country, humor, historic reflections and madcap mishaps, all presented in vivid, unfiltered detail.

Like so many others, I have found myself caught up in the phenomenon that is social media. In observance of that and my active participation as a Facebook poster, I am referring to the sections of this book as posts instead of chapters. And I will use actual Facebook posts to introduce the subject matter that will follow.

In the tradition of the late, great American writer and humorist Lewis Grizzard, I am adopting a format of autobiographical and interspersing entertaining stories. I hope to honor his memory and celebrate his brilliance.

For many years, gatherings with my closest lifelong friends have always resulted in my being asked to tell and retell the endless inventory of "Keefer Stories." Now it's your turn to hear them. I hope you find this collection relatable, entertaining, enjoyable, heartwarming, humorous, and thought-provoking.

Post 1

What Does George Clooney Have That I Ain't Got?

"Fame is fleeting, Obscurity is forever."

I'm sitting here waiting to watch Jeopardy (Alex Trebek, Canada's greatest export ever) and the end of one of those dreadful entertainment shows is on. Too bad they weren't around during The Inquisition. These programs with their unabashed, frothing, shameless, groveling glorification of Tinsel Town celebrities are nauseating enough. Toss in the way it is presented exuberantly with stomach turning pseudo-enthusiasm by plasticized hosts, and you would have had a dandy torture device. It would only take minutes to convert a non-believer forced to watch endless episodes of these hype fests and they would have been willing to do anything to make it stop. Either that or their heads would have exploded like the alien invaders in Mars Attacks after hearing Slim Whitman and Gene Autry yodeling.

To be perfectly honest, I really wasn't paying any attention to the show's content. As usual, I was pecking away on my iPad posting yet another brilliant thought or observation for my legion of fans to enjoy. The very last story on the show was about the Golden Globe Awards and a lifetime achievement honor presented to George Clooney. Well, let me say this about that, I am a George Clooney fan and an admirer of his work. I have no problem with the report, even though it was some contrived award they drummed up to give to him. It was the bubbly follow up, obviously to fill the last 15 seconds of the show that the effervescent program hostess babe unleashed that broadsided my attention and served to cream my corn. Coming back to her at the conclusion of the video feed (I have no idea who she was), but she was a pretty standard issue for these types of gigs. I would estimate that she was early 30s, beautiful, tall, shapely (of course) and had probably been in the hair and makeup chair for a three-hour session prior to taping the 10 or 12 minutes that she would be on camera. Poised at her anchor desk, she gazed longingly at the camera and simply sighed. Then she uttered these words:

"If there was a lifetime achievement award for being "Hot" he would've been awarded for that a long time ago."

To which, I wittily, instinctively, reflexively said out loud in an agitated tone, this intelligent, knee-jerk response ... "Oh, barf."

The reference to "hotness" by women in describing a man is a particularly irritating "hot" button issue with me. The origin of that resentment probably stems from the fact that I have never been referred to as "hot" unless I was ...

A. Spending longer than a minute and a half indoors at my mother's house in Florida in the middle of summer. It is a Turkish steam bath absent the fat men in towels.

B. Had just consumed an entire bucket of five-alarm chili.

C. Performed the ultra-rare feat of mowing the lawn on a 100-degree day of southern humidity.

D. Lost a bet on an agonizing, improbable photo finish on a horse race I knew I surely had won.

E. Internally combusted and burst into flames.

Males that women generally consider "Hot" almost always fall into one of these categories ...

A. Pretty Boys. Men who are cute like a girl.

B. Guys with lots of $$$$. It is amazing how the Hot Quotient skyrockets in correlation to wealth. Fame in this category only turns up the heat. Cash is obviously smoking hot!

C. Foreigners

D. Bad Boys and Anti-Heroes. No matter how heinous and disgusting these social miscreant douchebags are, many women find them irresistibly, hotly attractive.

Please don't misunderstand me; I am not trying to suggest that women are totally superficial. Certainly men are better known for that less than admirable trait. However, in the interest of fairness, the practice of assessing another person strictly on looks is not gender exclusive. Then you toss in other factors totally unrelated to appearance and the formula goes from superficial to silly rationalization of one seeing what they want to see. My views on the subject, contrary to how many might interpret this, are not based on sour grapes or jealous resentment. Sadly, it's just one of those aspects of modern life that chalks up to … "It is what it is."

George Clooney and I are both in our 50s. If he takes a stroll on a red carpet, women of all ages, scream, swoon and faint. If I took that same path, those same women would yawn, look away and pretend I was invisible. Is George Clooney that incredibly good looking or am I homelier than a Pekingese turned backward with his butt shaved?

I have looked at ole George in comparison to myself. We both have a head, face, neck, shoulders, arms, ten fingers, ten toes, torso, midsection, posterior, legs, and feet. I presume we have been issued comparable unseen parts. Two eyes, one nose, two ears, mouth, and chin. I am taller than him, he's slimmer than me. So I am calling it a tie so far. Hey, I call them like I see them!

I have no choice, in the interest of fair and accurate assessment to declare George the runaway winner in the skin quality and hair categories. However, I think it's pertinent to point out that a whole team of people maintains HIM like a Rolls-Royce Silver Shadow. He is buffed, polished, snipped, clipped, nipped, tucked and perfected on a daily basis. By all reports, when there was concern that the superstar's dazzling smile was losing its luster, no problem! Let's just fill his mouth with new teeth. Pearly white, bright and shining, dental implants. In this era of emphasis and hysteria for all things natural and organic, do I score any points for being 100% genuine, natural completely reliant on my own grooming and completely unaltered? Let me go ahead and answer my own question, certainly not.

How else is George better than me? Well, millions of dollars, worldwide acclaim, fame, fortune and an astounding new wife. She is an international star in her own right. An attorney who gallivants about the globe intervening in crisis resolutions and humanitarian efforts. Obviously, Georgie gets a big checkmark for those significant categories. It would certainly be safe to say, in all of these areas, what we have on our hands is an absolute mismatch, a blowout.

I am unwilling to concede, however, that Clooney's indisputable advantage emanates from superior intellect and God-given abilities greater than my own. Paths to those promised lands and twists of fate are illuminated in varying ways from a number of different directions. George was delivered a huge key to instant access on the road to success by being the nephew of a very prominent star and singer from the 1960s, his aunt, Rosemary Clooney. I give him total credit for making shrewd career decisions and ascending to his current level of monumental stardom. However, I don't feel inferior to him in any way in terms of mental abilities, wit, humor, kindness and consideration as a human being, or in comparison of our respective skill sets. Now if you are doubled over laughing at my assertion that I have every bit as much talent as George Clooney, I am most happy to entertain you. Here's another zinger for you... Surround me with all of the support and collaborators that George deals with on a daily basis in every aspect of what he does, and I am absolutely certain that my abilities would translate into comparable, if not even greater quality results. I truly believe I am more gifted creatively, and a better speaker, writer, and humorist. And, I know that I am a nicer person. And, unlike George, I am not rude, sullen and boorish when I have had too many belts of firewater, as he has been known to do. Not only do I not imbibe excessively and embarrass myself, I seldom drink at all.

So, let's review. Obviously the female population has spoken loudly and clearly ... George Clooney is Hot, and I, Kip Keefer, am Not. I submit to the court of public opinion, however, this important question: Would my temperature reading not dramatically rise if I too was a world famous actor, jet-setter, and celebrity? Alas, I am not any of those things. So yes, George clearly has something major that I certainly do not have.

But hold on ... not so fast my friend! I have one last hold card to play in this high-stakes showdown. While I may have set new standards in underachievement, I did manage to produce and star in an ongoing smash hit. The script I penned led to the introduction of a pair of remarkable sons, and they are two of the finest human beings ever to set foot on this planet. (Okay, I'm just a tad biased.) Here's the thing ... Offer me the chance to swap my incomparable blessing of fatherhood for all of the women, adulation, private jets, gala awards dinners, amenities, privileges and unfathomable riches, and my answer would be instantaneous: Thanks but No Thanks! George may grasp golden statuettes to hail his greatness, but for me, although there is no red carpet hoopla, every single day I am the recipient of the most gratifying of lifetime achievement awards, and they are walking around, not sitting on a shelf. There is nothing more rewarding than watching my boys forge their paths and accomplish extraordinary things. Any real father will tell you, anything you have ever done or accomplished pales in comparison to thrilling to your children's successes.

So deal with it George, Kip Keefer has something amazing … that you ain't got!

Glance and a Nod

For many years, I was living a dream. Lovely homes in suburbia, beautiful wife who was an incredible mother, and two remarkable, heaven sent sons. In September 2001, everything took a terrible turn. I was suddenly and unexpectedly served with papers suing me for divorce. My family and what we had all together built was being seriously altered. My relationship with my sons was far, far and away the most important thing in my life. The harshest reality, of no longer being permitted to live in the same household, My House, rocked me to the core.

Making matters worse, it was the period of the only career crisis of my life. I had one job offer, and it was far away from Wichita, Kansas where my children lived. To keep things afloat, I would have to accept the position of general manager at Tucson Greyhound Park in Arizona.

The incredible bond I had with my firstborn son, Case, was built on so many things. Undeniably one of the core elements of that foundation was our shared devotion and love of sports. It extended into all areas of anything sports oriented. We talked about sports, we collected a wide array of items, we watched games and anytime we could, anywhere we were, we went to all kinds of games. Memories of sitting in stadiums and arenas all over the country with my wide-eyed best sports buddy are incredibly cherished images. To think back and realize that those were the building blocks of the extraordinary career and immense talent he displays today, is unbelievably gratifying. However, the shared experience of Case's actual participation in a number of sports was indescribably, incredibly important and strong. From the time that he was a little boy, playing the earliest introductions of basketball and baseball, I had been there every step of the way. Practices as well as games. Rituals of post-game celebrations and meals. I was his coach on many of those teams. What a wonderful platform it was to subtly introduce and instill, through our experiences, important life lessons. Implantation of values and the art of successfully relating to others.

When he was eight years, he began playing football. He instantly loved the game and everything associated with it. We had moved to the Birmingham area where football is as important sociologically as anything in the state. In other words, even third and fourth graders putting on helmets and shoulder pads is serious business. Most of the young men who played for the Clay Cardinal team were kids who had grown up together and knew each other well. I had told Case that first day that the way to make yourself noticed was to impress the coaches, and even the other kids, at the very first opportunity. The old mouthwash commercial had delivered back then a valuable message that had always stuck with me for many years, "You never get a second chance to make a first impression." I had told him, "They will most likely have you run a lap to warm up before practice." I suggested to him to use his maximum effort and try and be the first one to finish, ahead of everyone else. I stood there and watched in awe as my amazing boy sprinted to the front of everyone else and outran them all. He arrived back to the coaches well in advance of the rest of his teammates. He was noticed immediately and praised profusely. In the first five minutes of his first football practice, he had distinguished himself. And that wasn't just for show, from that point forward, throughout his entire football career, that effort never diminished.

It would amaze his mother during the games when at a critical point, where a key play was needed, I could shout encouragement such as, "We need a big-play Casey, get them in the backfield." Almost without fail that's exactly what he would do. Cathie would say, "That is so amazing, you say it, and he does it."

All throughout his childhood years and into his seventh and eighth-grade middle school football seasons, any thought of missing a game was inconceivable. I did miss one game during his youth career when I was dispatched to Iowa of all places to arrange a simulcasting deal with an Indian casino. Bad weather delayed my return. Other than that, I saw every one.

It was his freshman year in high school when the upheaval occurred. There were a limited number of 9th-grade games usually held on a Monday or Tuesday in the early evenings. I had seen the first couple of contests before having to report for duty in Tucson. I missed two games but was able to come home for the third. There was only one more scheduled at the end of October. Regrettably, I was not able to be there.

On that Monday evening after his game, I received an excited call from him telling me he had big news. I assumed it was related to the game he had just played. Of course, a report on that action was on the agenda, but he had called with bigger news. Even though he was now in high school, his effort and commitment were still being noticed by coaches. The varsity team had made the state playoffs and were hosting a first round game the Thursday night of that same week. Before the freshman game that evening, Case and only one other 9th grade player had been selected by the coaches to dress out and added to the roster for the Varsity playoff game. It was a huge deal. The best part of it was, he knew how significant that would be for me to learn and how much I would appreciate what he had accomplished. It was extremely gratifying to understand how he relished sharing it with me above all others.

After the initial excitement of the big headlines, my heart sank. The game was 72 hours and 860 miles away. There was no practical way for me to be there. I also remembered at that instant, a meeting of the Arizona Racing Commission was scheduled that same morning in Phoenix at 10 AM. One of my major job responsibilities was to represent my track at those meetings, and this was the first one that had been conducted since I had started the job. I told Case that there did not appear to be any chance that I could make it. He said that was fine, that he had no chance to play anyway. I hung up the phone elated and deflated. I was so proud of what he had accomplished and sick that I wasn't going to be there to enjoy it with him. From a practicality standpoint, it made perfect sense, but based on our history, bond and special relationship, the notion of missing it was an intolerable injustice.

The thoughts of not being there gnawed at me all night. Early the next morning, I was sitting at my desk on my computer desperately searching for a way to pull this off. The meeting would be starting at 10, Phoenix time, 11 AM central. There was already an hour not in my favor to overcome. I checked early afternoon flights for Wichita and was disappointed to find that none were available that would get me into town until the game was at least halfway over. Still that was better than not going at all. I happened across a flight that was going to Oklahoma City that actually if everything went perfectly, would work. I booked the excessively costly short notice flight, reserved the rental car at OKC and suddenly harbored high hopes.

My presentation and participation in the meeting went well that morning and expediently. I dashed to the airport in time to catch the early afternoon flight. Hustling to the rental car counter, that pickup went off also without a hitch. I had just enough time to speed the two hours and 15 minutes up Interstate 35 which turns into the Kansas Turnpike and make it to Wichita before game time. Everything had to go perfectly, and remarkably it did. I walked into the stadium at 7:15, the timing could not have been better.

On the far right-hand corner of the field, was the pathway from the locker room back in the main school building where the team came up, assembled, were introduced, and ran on the field. Immediately looking that direction, I saw the mass of blue and white clad Wichita Collegiate Spartans making their way toward the entry gate. I sprinted along the fence line to get as close to the entry point as possible. There were at least 40 players standing together, some jumping about, anticipating the signal to run under the goalpost and on to the field serenaded by blasting music and raucous cheers. I didn't know what number Case was going to be as I scanned furiously amongst the group to try and spot him. Of course, all the players were wearing their helmets so my search was concentrated more on height and size. I also figured that he would be in the back half of the group since the established older players would be taking the lead. Incredibly, just like a scene from a Hollywood movie, a player turned his head just at the instant that I was examining him to see if he was my son. Eye contact was made, and there was no doubt that recognition from us both registered in the most fleeting of seconds. Now he was a big, important varsity football player for the first time. He was certainly not going to do anything ridiculous or uncool like waving to his dad. He had not expected me to be there, but I doubt seriously he was surprised. The exchange that did occur was far more significant and one of the greatest lasting images that will forever reside in my memories. A tiny smile was clearly visible to me under his facemask, and at the exact same instant, we both gave one another the slightest acknowledging nod. In the next second or two, the team charged onto the field.

In that fragments of a mere second or two, the miracle of everything that had happened leading up to that fleeting instant was flooding through my mind. The incredible circumstances that had resulted in my marriage and formation of our family, bestowment of the miraculous, greatest gift I could ever have received, an amazing son with which I would have the most inseparable, close-knit connection of my existence, and the remarkable bonus blessing of a second magnificent, equally as extraordinary son. Even in that time of current strife and heartbreak, the emphasis was solely on what was succinctly most significant and important. What I had, and what I had experienced was well worth any of the hardship and pain that came along with the deal. All of that swirling in my brain was then also mixed in with the great relief I suddenly felt to have not missed such an irreplaceable, important moment. It is difficult to explain, but I can tell you amazingly, I felt totally cognizant of the significance of what had just occurred. I wandered out a little further towards the edge of the woods and am not ashamed to admit, that I, a grown man, let out a torrent of emotion and stood there with tears filling my eyes.

My little boy in that instant was taking the first steps toward becoming a man. The mutual glance and the subtle nod was certification and affirmation of everything we had done and experienced together and how much it had all meant to us both.

Undeniably, it was also something else extremely significant. It was the dawning of a brand-new era and chapter. That simple exchange was an important, once-in-a-lifetime, rite of passage. It was private exclusive territory and communication that exclusively could only be conveyed, and fully appreciated, between a father and his son.

KEEFER STORY

New And Improved

Progress and innovation are concepts that make something great even better. If enhancement can be achieved, copying or duplication are not as desirable or necessary. The continuing evolution of electronics for instance, as each newer model improves on the original and its direct predecessor. This concept can certainly be true of successive generations as well. To confirm that thought, may I present the new and improved copy of ... me. That would be my son Clayt.

With every passing day, it becomes more and more apparent that my second born son in so many ways is a remarkably similar re-creation of myself. The fact that I recognize this is highly insignificant when compared to his acknowledgment of that fact. I was tremendously surprised when he said to me recently, "There is no doubt, I am just like you."

To start listing our common traits would be a daunting undertaking due to how many examples can be cited. The best attributes we share are the way we treat other people and make them feel good about themselves. I have always been aware of my own politeness and consideration of others. I marvel at Clayt's skills and his emphasis on those same traits. We both have a capacity for being at our best when the situation demands it. And, in the areas in which we become extremely interested, we are motivated to pursue knowledge, competence, accomplishment, and success.

Unfortunately, the similarities also extend to some negative qualities. We are procrastinators, we are uncomfortable with the allocation of time to things we are not actively immersed in, and we do not like being forced to follow the rules and guidelines established by others. And then there is the exhibiting of frustration. It is particularly profound in situations where we do something in a poorly thought out or haphazard manner. We have very little tolerance with ourselves if we display any ineptitude whatsoever.

It is tremendously gratifying to me, however, to point out that this remarkable kid surpasses me in a number of outstanding categories. His intelligence and aptitude are a major upgrade to mine. He is a modern-day renaissance man. His skill set includes the ability to design and build things, and his wide-ranging interests extend to pursuits like cooking. My older son Case was always tremendously attentive, dutiful and a constant, loyal, implicitly trusting inseparable sidekick. Clayt on the other hand, has always not only marched to his own unique tune, but he has fiercely and unyieldingly done things uniquely his own way. His range of interests as a child were all over the board and not influenced by anyone except his own fascinations. But something amazing was happening during that entire period of his self-choreographed personal growth. He was soaking in everything from the people around him he loved and was influenced by stealthily constructing an awe-inspiring depth and character. All of this amalgam of watching, listening, absorbing and learning blended with his own determined inner self and formed a remarkable, ever-evolving product.

Some parents would've been appalled at the latitude that we extended to Clayt from the beginning. As a preteen, he took to calling us, Cathie and Kip. There were some people who pointed out that was a sign of some sort of disrespect. We knew better! His tremendous inner belief and self-assuredness as to who he is created an individual who was not comfortable assuming a role of pretentious and disingenuousness. As his parents, we recognized that any approach that suited his comfort zone was best for his own development as a person. Besides, his respect and love for us were never in question. This was not a rebellious child whatsoever in the traditional sense. His only revolution was his absolute determination to be himself.

Here's a great example and a favorite story of many of my family and friends. In the summer between Clayt's eighth and ninth grade years, we were in Atlanta. On a visit to the newly opened Georgia Aquarium, he and I were standing, marveling at the giant tank in that facility which featured hundreds of species of exotic undersea creatures. Suddenly, a massive Ray entered this panorama of wonderment. He glided along effortlessly through the watery canvas. I said with great reverence and excitement to then 13-year-old Clayt, "Look at him, it's like he's not really moving at all but he is gliding right along. It's like he's just perfectly aerodynamic."

Clayt took a step back, looked at me incredulously and replied, "Aerodynamic? Really, does it look to you like he is floating on air? I think what you meant to say was, hydrodynamic."

Of course, I knew immediately he was absolutely right and admitted that my choice of words had definitely been inaccurate. As he turned to walk away, I saw a subtle shaking of his head and clearly heard the audible mumble he muttered, "Idiot." I would venture the guess that most fathers would not be receptive to their young son calling them an idiot. But I wasn't offended and didn't feel disrespected in the least. He was simply doing what he always did, calling it like he saw it.

His college career has taken six years to complete. He has approached that at his own pace. Established parameters and other people's timetables are just never going to be congruent with his distinctive methodologies. Well, that might annoy a lot of people; I've always found myself secretly rooting for him to uncompromisingly hold on to his unrelenting approach. Again, he is taking basic concepts that I have always embraced an emphatic step forward.

I like to think that if I would've had the same sort of guidance, understanding, opportunities and support that Clayt has benefited from, that I might be a far different person and improved version of myself. However, there probably is no greater satisfaction than feeling gratified that through Cathie and my efforts, our boys have been able to grow up to be individuals and enjoy the freedom, and abundance of self-confidence, to set the course of their choosing. That is not limited to just personal and career choices they make, but literally to who they are and aspire to be. I believe the key is really simple, it comes with understanding that parenting is not about control. Emphasis on creating restrictions and constantly trying to be a corrective or protective force ultimately is not a successful strategy. These are your children, they are part of who you are and giving them the credit that they have the capacity to learn and grow effectively using the gifts that their parents and God have given them, makes far more sense. It comes down to simply providing information that alternately, perhaps even at a point far down the road, leads to good decision-making. And most importantly, instilling the confidence and comfort that you know and have faith in their talents, intellect and ability to navigate brilliantly their own life's journey. With the proviso, of course, that on that journey, you are always there if ever needed.

I have been rather rigid in my assessment of myself in the pages that follow. Certainly, there have been all too many missteps, and it feels in so many ways I have underachieved. I fully comprehend that I could have accomplished so much more. But in the arena of fatherhood, I am willing to pat myself on the back and feel very secure in the fact, that I have done the job very well that I set out to do.

Post 2

Through My Eyes

"It never ceases to amaze me. Despite the fact that I have had the monumental setback of vision impairment, at this stage of life it seems to me that I am seeing things far more clearly than anyone I know."

I thought a good place to start on this journey through my rather interesting lifetime foray would be discussing my current situation. I am now in the latter stages of my 50s. While that fact is ominous enough, I also have another major issue to deal with other than just advancing age. Basically, at this point in my life, my vision is diminished to the point where it's very difficult to see. My condition is a strange one, which is consistent with every other aspect of my existence. There is nothing wrong with my eyes, my problem lies in my optic nerves not being fully functional. For those of you who may not have paid attention in biology or anatomy class, the optic nerves are basically the transmission centers in the back of the eye socket that receive the visions from the eyes and send those signals to the brain for interpretation. I had a structurally defective set up of my optic disc which is basically the junction of all the nerves and vessels that service that particular area. As I gravitated into my 50s, blood flow to that area became more and more constricted. It was particularly exacerbated at night when my blood pressure would drop to levels where that area of my body was not receiving adequate blood supply. The tissue that forms the optic nerve basically starves for oxygen and leads to it becoming largely dysfunctional. Without getting completely technical in the explanation, I can see things that are very bold and clearly defined like this current writing on my iPad. Anything abstract is distorted. My peripheral and field of vision are both dramatically reduced and severely limited. Which means that it's not wise, even dangerous, for me to operate a motor vehicle. As you can well imagine, dealing with this issue was a real life changer, and in no way a positive one.

In May 2009, I was privileged to attend my eldest son Case's graduation from college at the University of Kansas. One month later, I was in Austin, Texas, chairing a meeting of the rules committee for the sport of greyhound racing. On the third morning there, I woke to a distressing situation. The vision in my left eye had been consumed by more than three-quarters of its surface by a mysterious black shelving effect. Upon returning to Birmingham, it was announced to me that I was suffering from a condition in that eye, known as, NAION. That stands for, Nonarteritic Ischemic Ocular Neuropathy. For the next two years, I lived with completely diminished sight in my right eye but was functioning very well by just having full use of my left. Then, in April 2011, during a visit to Florida, I woke up with similar symptoms in my good eye, the left. My neuro-ophthalmologist in Birmingham said there was nothing that could be done. I sought out the leading expert in the country on that condition, he was based at the University of Missouri. I traveled there twice at great expense, and he tried a bit of an experimental treatment, but alas, it proved futile.

Thankfully, not being a nuclear physicist or brain surgeon, the major compromise to the acuity of my vision has not dramatically affected my ability to make a living. My role as a manager, bureaucrat, broadcaster, and writer are still well within my range of abilities. I am proud to say that I really didn't emotionally collapse or freak out over what had occurred, I simply stepped back and formulated what I thought was going to be a reasonable response and plan of action.

The biggest adjustment was going to be accepting the fact that for the first time I was going to have to make two major changes in my previous approach. Number one, having been the ultimate fly by the seat of my pants guy for many years, having to deal with the spontaneity that's been taken away by my condition required some degree of planning and organization to be put in place. If I was required or wanted to be somewhere at a certain time on a certain day, I had to think ahead and make arrangements to make that happen. Since 1973, anytime I wanted to go somewhere, all it required was grabbing the keys, jumping in the car, and heading that way. Now, life was going to be dictated and different. As far as possessions and lifestyle, organization became critical. You could not just haphazardly lay down your glasses, keys or any other personal items because that would lead to disarray, inconvenience, and frustration at the point that you needed to access those things again. Systems needed to be devised to facilitate order. Perhaps being the least inclined to be the obsessive/compulsive person on earth, it proved to be a daunting adjustment.

The second major factor was coming to grips with the fact that my primary principle of life throughout my days on this planet, my self-reliance, would be significantly altered. I am not a person who likes to ask anyone for anything. My role in virtually every relationship I've had throughout my life has been to be the provider, the facilitator, the person who makes things happen. Selflessness, not selfishness, was the way that I always rolled. Suddenly, I found myself in a position where the involvement of others was going to be critical for me to maintain my lifestyle. As I analyze the situation, the seeming curse actually began to feel like a potential blessing. The answer was simple, find someone at a point in their life that wanted to become a part of something special. A friend, collaborator, partner, lover, and companion, someone to join my team. With that special someone on board, the day-to-day goals and drive to have the lives we both aspired to would be tremendously enhanced for us both. I began to think of the possibilities, all of the things that could be made possible that even in my fully sighted years had not been. The concept of push me/push you seemed like a phrase dipped in magic itself. Suddenly, this issue seemed to me to be a veritable fire swiftly lit under my dormant backside. I reconciled the thought that with adversity comes opportunity. And the thought of being with someone special, that could help me make it all come together, was a very enticing prospect. For a time, I even started to think that what had happened to me was going to turn out to be a miraculous blessing, a wake-up call in disguise.

I was never concerned with the fact that I was seeking someone to pencil into the unfolding drama that was my life. I dismissed any feelings of selfishness for the fact that my track record was well established. This cohort, my partner in crime, was going to be in a position to benefit and enjoy the spoils of our success every bit as much as myself. And, I was sure, that anything this key person to the equation contributed, I would give back and exceed 100 fold.

Alas, the best-laid plans of mice and men, well you know the rest. Either that person that I thought for sure would be on the immediate horizon of my destiny does not exist, cannot possibly be real, or I have not looked in the right places. Other than brief interactions with several outstanding candidates, the impending miracle has been a giant flop. In general terms, there just aren't a lot of people milling around out there who are waiting to get involved and occupy the copilot seat in someone else's life. I assumed they would be plentiful, I was wrong.

The results of the past four years have been for the most part devastating. With my validation as a human being already challenged by my new reality, my fruitless search and heartbreaking disappointments when I thought I had found that salvation, have served to deliver a debilitating blow. To be lost and searching is one thing, but when seemingly no one really cares or exerts any effort to try and deliver you, mentally and emotionally it feels like your viability as a person has been rescinded. You are required to report to the motor vehicles department once a year to renew and validate your automobile tags. The equivalent to accomplishing those tasks as a human being is successful, enriching, joyful contact with others. So many days and nights in the last four years have been gut-wrenchingly lonely, joyless, loveless empty hours.

In the early years that the Atlanta Braves had moved south at the same time that my family did, I spent endless hours listening to games on the radio and later television. One of the Braves' broadcasters, Ernie Johnson Sr., a former pitcher for the Braves in the major leagues, always included the following statement in his broadcasts that baffled me. He would say something to the effect of, "And to all of our great fans that are Shut-Ins, I want to wish you all the best." I remember thinking almost every time he said that, what in the hell is a shut in? Were they like people in nursing homes? I never really understood. On many days and nights in recent years, I found out the harsh answer to that question. In many ways, I had become one of those aforementioned folks ... A Shut-In.

Being a people pleaser, entertainer, and most of all, a resounding, prototypical extrovert, the assignment of frittering away hours on end by myself is a most harrowing, horrible experience. So many times, I tried to recalculate the situation and come up with alternative ideas on how to deal with my situation. Putting together a project wish list was easy. However, I was haunted by a central theme that I had never been able to escape from during my entire life cycle. I am a classic procrastinator and am very poor at the concept of self-motivation. I require an audience, pathetic, maybe? But that's just the way it is. I am a walking contradiction, capable of doing virtually anything if encouraged and counted on. But totally paralyzed and powerless to forge ahead on my own if there is any uncertainty whatsoever that my accomplishments won't be acknowledged. This classic internal tug-of-war, coupled with the situation I found myself in, created a most unsatisfactory, unproductive period. And, my initial solution to simply find somebody to help drive the ship of progress, prosperity, and fulfillment, lingered in my head as the most viable pathway out of this real and self-imposed wilderness. After all, surely fate and divine providence had a plan to make all of this make sense?

When my vision was affected, and the implications became clear, it was not something that I thought was going to be a total obstructing roadblock on my journey down the path to contentment and happiness in my remaining years. After all, everyone has issues. Some, of course, are far more severe. Terrible diseases, cancers, tumors, etc. Many people I know have serious back, knee and other physical ailments that cause them tremendous pain and discomfort. It's just the bill that comes due in life when you're lucky enough to continue to advance in age. The card I was dealt, involved my vision, and while that was a pretty bitter pill to swallow, I accepted it and rationalized a number of ways to deal with it. However, now with perspective that has developed over a significant period of time in dealing with it, I have arrived at a sobering conclusion. Obviously, I am still alive despite what happened to me physically. However, it can be argued very convincingly that what occurred has been in some ways a death sentence for me. That is because the person that I was is no longer with us. Today, I am clearly someone different than I was four years ago. My belief systems have changed, my perceptions have been forever altered. The way I regard my fellow beings is completely different than it was before. But I really don't have time to lament and mourn the passing of my previous self; it is way past time to quit analysis and reassessment and start moving forward.

Despite the setbacks and disappointments, in so many ways I am vastly advanced from where I was previously. In terms of my talents, potential contributions, and capacity to enhance, enrich, enlighten and entertain others, I am poised at a peak that is an all-time high. In what ironically is not just an analogy, straining to see through the smoke and fog that my condition has created in my actual vision and from my emotional viewpoint, those things that I live for and have always strived to achieve are still standing. Life is already a path of uncertainty that is strewn with objects that can easily cause an annoying stumble or even a major fall. That abstract concept has become my reality. Of course, in either circumstance, it would be far easier to be guided down the pathway. But others solitarily navigating that territory are almost exclusively preoccupied with negotiating it in their own ways to fulfill their own needs. So what are the choices, standing still waiting is an unproductive and unfulfilling approach. Still, that seems to be to most the safest strategy, standing still. Fear of change, avoidance of unease, withdraw to an inner self-secure sanctuary may work for the many, but it is impossible for me. Someone in my position particularly is dismayed and disgusted when people take that approach. Literally and figuratively, blessed with vision, they should be able to see far better. My vision is certainly compromised, but my view has never been clearer. You have to forge ahead, even if there are potential pitfalls and danger. Because standing still and warily cowering with uncertainty over the prospect of the unknown is indefensible. That bunker mentality may be employed in some unfounded self-preservation effort to stay alive and dodge further damage, but by no means is that really living. Regardless of how one finds themselves removed and dormant, whether it be self-imposed exile, lack of mobility and access, or debilitation of any kind, one thing never stops, TIME! Undeniably, we only have an undetermined amount of it. After all this, for the first time in my life, I feel a resounding sense of urgency to utilize every moment of my allotted time to its utmost potential. Ironically, I guess you could say, I have truly, finally "seen" the light!

KEEFER STORY

Fountain Drink

In March 2012, I was attending a convention in Las Vegas for the racing industry. It was less than a year since I had experienced the devastation of developing my optic nerve issue in my left eye. For the two years since the incident occurred on my right side, vision from my left actually sharpened. I was able to function normally in all things as I had previously. Being affected on both sides was an absolute game changer. Thankfully, the damage on the left was not as severe as the right, and I blessedly retained some degree of sight.

I had approached my affliction and the limitations it brought about with determination not to allow it to define me or significantly slow me down. I was anxious to partake in any and all previously routine travels, events, and activities.

I had been to Las Vegas so many times over the previous 20-year period that I had a tremendous comfort zone and confidence in my ability to get around successfully there. That, of course, was beginning with arriving at the airport, retrieving my bag and arranging transportation to the hotel via taxi. The headquarters for this meeting was the fabulous Bellagio Hotel. After checking in and attending the first two days of meetings and events, everything was going swimmingly. People who knew me well were aware of my issue but the majority of the attendees had no idea.

Prior to heading west, I had talked to my pal, Jim. It was a tremendously exciting time for him and his beautiful wife, my also long time dear friend Craige. In just a couple of months, their first grandchild was due. In the next couple of weeks from that time, a baby shower/party was scheduled to celebrate the impending arrival. Jim had come up with a unique idea for a gift. He had grown up in metro Cincinnati and had been a Reds fan since birth. His earliest baseball hero, who plied his trade at a classic, vintage ballpark, Crosley Field, was none other than Charlie Hustle, Peter Edward Rose. When Jim and I first met and started hanging out in the early 70s in Atlanta, our mutual love for baseball was one of our strongest bonds. I was already a Pete Rose admirer. He played the game with an intensity and dedication that was unprecedented. Every time he stepped on the field, regardless of the situation, he played every inning like it would be his last. Jim soon converted me into a super Rose fan. We were able to see the Reds when I came to town to play the Braves, and also on our frequent trips to Cincinnati. Those were the days of the big red machine, a team consisting of one of the best everyday lineups ever assembled.

Jim was interested in acquiring a classic Pete Rose photograph or poster and having it framed. Even though his son Adam and lovely wife Lauren had already found out this was going to be a little girl, Jim was undeterred. He reasoned that it would be most appropriate to immediately apprise her of her heritage and the legend that is Pete Rose. After all, this is the man in all of baseball history who has collected more base hits than any other man who ever played the game.

The true sweetener to the deal which would make it incredibly special, would be not only to present the framed masterpiece but also have it personalized and signed by the man himself. As far as executing that mission, who you gonna call? Certainly not Ghostbusters. That's right ... Sing it with me, Kip Keefer!

At nearby Caesars Palace, in their fabulous Forum Retail Shops, there was a high-end sports memorabilia store. Pete Rose had made an arrangement several years before with the owner of that particular shop to spend considerable time there for the purpose of autographing items pertaining to him purchased at the store. It was an odd set up that I had made note of several times in the previous couple of years. As you walked down the corridor and came upon the shop, a TV monitor mounted on the far corner of the front window showed a rather poor quality, closed circuit shot of the small room, presumably within the confines of the business, where Pete was stationed on a metal folding chair in the event he was present on that day. The view had very much the look of an interrogation room. Rose would be sitting there patiently waiting for someone to come in.

I had encountered Rose a number of years before at the Caesar's Palace race and sports book. He was sitting with a couple of guys betting horses on a weekday afternoon. I knew we had two very good mutual friends, so I started the conversation. He had maintained a close association for many years with a man who served as one of my earliest mentors in the racing business, Jay Black, the late, longtime publicity director at the fabulous Derby Lane track in St. Petersburg, Florida. For many years, the Reds' spring training was there, and anytime Rose wasn't playing baseball, you could bet your bottom dollar, the aptly named Charlie Hustle would be at the track. Jay always fixed him up with whatever he needed. He also had played with and against my former next-door neighbor and friend Denis Menke. We talked back-and-forth throughout the next couple of hours as we handicapped the races and ventured a few investments. His speculations were slightly more ambitious than my own. I was betting $25-$30 a race; he was using those same denominations with the addition of considerable zeros. Around $2500-$3000 per race. The hilarious kicker to that story is, about a week later, ironically at Jim's house, reading the sports section there was an article speculating on Rose's chances of being considered for the Hall of Fame again. The article pointed out that if he was trying to change his image, he wasn't helping matters by being spotted recently betting on sports or horses at Caesars Palace, with some, "unknown associates." Jim and I laughed and reveled in the fact that I was one of those nefarious shadowy figures.

After wrapping up the final day of the racing meeting agenda on a brilliant, bright, sun-splashed, desert Wednesday, I set out for the short walk up Las Vegas Blvd. from Bellagio to Caesars. Despite the considerable glare, which is a major problem with my particular vision issue, I was able to dodge the other pedestrians, successfully cross streets and nimbly avoid curbs, fire hydrants, and any other obstructions along the way. I arrived at the entrance to the Forum Shops and stepped inside to the ornate, marble-floored, meticulously maintained area. As previously mentioned, the concept of local knowledge, and a mental picture of places you have visited before frequently are tremendously helpful when your eyesight has been compromised. However, that knowledge, coupled with a very slow adjustment from my available vision stepping in from the ultra bright sidewalk to the fashionable mood lighting of the foyer, would prove to be a hazardous combination of factors.

To access the hallway in the shops where the memorabilia store was located, walking to the left side of the area and riding the escalator up to the next level was the route. I was well aware of the veritable lay of the land and quickly glanced to my left catching a faint image of the base of the escalator some 30 or 40 yards away. As I began purposely striding in a direct march toward that area, I started thinking about whether or not Rose would even be there. Now my eyes had locked on to the desired destination, the escalator. What happened in the very next stride is difficult to explain but became a defining moment in my coming to grips with the fact, that just walking around was no longer a routine operation.

Literally, in one step I was walking, the next step … I was face down in cold water. My mental picture of that entry area had failed to register or remember that the escalator rose up to the next level over a spectacular fountain. To further add to my peril, my already impaired vision had been rendered even more ineffective by a tardy adjustment to coming in from the glare of the outside. Looking up and certainly not expecting anything to be in my path, I had completely missed the fact that a knee-high wall ran around the entire perimeter of the fountain/escalator area. In full stride and without any warning, I had walked directly into the wall striking it just below the outermost portion of the front of my right knee. It had literally cut my lower legs out from under me and launched me into a perfect parallel position where my next step was not a step at all, but recognition that my entire head and torso area were immersed in H2O.

My lower legs, which had willingly surrendered the rest of my body to its watery submergence, were the only parts of me that were dry. They both lay perched upon the offending wall from roughly my knees all the way down to my feet. The rest of me was thoroughly drenched. It's amazing how fast you can react even when something is completely unexpected. I would love to see footage of my unplanned swan dive, particularly the part where I remove myself from my damp predicament. I can remember quickly looking around and seeing only a couple of people that had apparently witnessed this bizarre occurrence. No one said a word, and I did not give them much opportunity. As soon as I was standing, dripping copious amounts of water on the shining floor, my overpowering instinct was just to get out of there as fast as I could. I retreated in the same direction that I had entered just a moment or two before. I had already splashed, now I followed that up with splishing and sploshing as I walked. There are some subtle benefits of not being able to see well. Such as reactions of others to a soaked man, his entire head and upper body dripping wet, on one of the busiest streets in the country. I felt great relief being outside on the sidewalk, under the bright sunshine. Suddenly, it didn't seem to matter much that I was so soggy. I had nothing to wipe myself off with, so I opted to sit on a nearby bench and let the warm breeze and sunshine work its magic. At that point, I realized that my phone was likely ruined, the cash I carried soaked and my wallet and its contents significantly wet. And as I sat there, I had the first indication that where I had banged my leg into the wall was a pretty sensitive spot. There was a dull pain, more disturbing, strange sensation of numbness (which remains to this day) starting from the lower corner of my knee and extending well into my calf area. I suppose it was the equivalent to striking a blow to your elbow's funny bone. That's an appropriate description since the whole incident was an uproarious, comedy of errors that could only happen, to ... Guess Who?

After 10 minutes or so, I decided to make the sad retreat back to the Bellagio. The Pete Rose mission had literally been washed out on this sunny day. My unscheduled dip had certainly put a serious damper on my plans. Suddenly, with a single step, the trip that had gone so "swimmingly," was all wet.

I am happy to report that the next morning, without any further mishap, I was able to make it to the store. The reassuring sight of a slightly disheveled baseball legend sitting in his isolation chamber on the television monitor was extremely uplifting. I browsed through the store and found what I believed to be the perfect item. A large photograph of Rose at first base after singling for hit number 4,192. With that knock, he passed Ty Cobb in all-time hits. The photo is of him standing with his arms outstretched, holding his batting helmet acknowledging the crowd's thunderous reaction. I purchased the item and was ushered into the back room for my audience with Pete.

He wasn't particularly animated or bubbly that morning, but we had a nice conversation. I reminded him of our commonalities and previous encounter, and he was polite enough to act like he remembered. He diligently signed the photograph after I explained to him who the principles were that initiated our session. Pete Rose is a man who is rather brash and not prone to be easily touched by sentiment. However, he did seem to appreciate that one of his greatest fans, dating back to the early 60s, was enlisting him to participate in the joy of celebrating his first grandchild. He wrote, "To Hadley, Best Wishes from your Grandpa Jim's favorite player. Pete Rose, the Hit King."

I was not able to attend the party, but my former wife did go and delivered the special item. It was reported back to me that it was a tremendous "Hit," and forever more the story that goes with it, even adds to its value. After all, even with the inexcusable, never-ending snub of the Hit King's banishment from baseball and the Hall of Fame, at least, this Rose memorabilia item is historically enshrined in another notable archival institution. It will always be a part of a Keefer Story.

Post 3

Where It Begins

"Nostalgia is the conversion of dreams into comforting, pleasant remembrances, even if they never came true."

Early in the year of the Lord 1956, a handsome young man about town in the Washington DC area was pondering his future and seeking his destiny. William Walston Keefer turned 21 that February 2, and little did he know that the year to come was going to be filled with a life-defining set of developments.

He was the only child of his mother Julianna, who bore him at the tender age of 18. Her parents had immigrated to this country from Czechoslovakia as a young married couple, even arriving and being processed at Ellis Island. Her father was a carpenter by trade, and for a number of years after the birth of their son Ralph and daughter Julie, they traveled around the eastern United States settling where work was available. In an interesting twist of fate, Juliana was actually born in Birmingham, Alabama in June 1917. The US economy was booming, and with the onset of World War I, there was a great deal of manufacturing job opportunities. Birmingham was the Pittsburgh of the south, a major steel producing community. In the early 1920s, the Fisher family moved to the Washington DC area and settled there permanently.

In 1929, the stock market crashed along with the US economy. By 1934, as the Depression continued, Juliana married William Harold Keefer, an aspiring young businessman in Washington DC. Shortly thereafter, Bill Keefer made his appearance on the planet. Of course, in that era, traditional families were by far the rule and hardly ever the exception. My grandfather had a difficult time in that depression era of finding a solid, promising job. It also seems that when he did find employment, it did not last for very long. Ironically, it was my grandmother who became the career person in the family. Now you have to keep in mind that in 1940, there were very few women who left their homes and went to work. A friend had let my grandmother know there was an opportunity for some part-time work with the federal government. She immediately distinguished herself and was rewarded with a full-time offer with the Department of Commerce. Starting as a secretary, she quickly worked her way up the ranks and became a financial analyst. The effects on her marriage to the original Bill Keefer were destructive. Her success and his failures took its toll, and he turned to the bottle for solace. Over the next seven or eight years, a stormy pattern of discontent and discord resulted.

In the meantime, young Bill Keefer became more or less the responsibility of my grandmother's mother, Andula. She was a no-nonsense, salt of the earth, Czechoslovakian immigrant, and later, officially an American citizen, fulfilling the dream of living in this country. When America became involved in World War II in December 1941, it changed so many lives, and the Fisher/Keefer family was not exempted. My father's uncle, my grandmother's brother, Ralph Fisher went into a special Army unit and was assigned to northern Italy. His heroism and bravery quickly resulted in him being promoted to captain. In an intense battle on a hillside against the Nazis in 1943, Captain Ralph Fisher, U.S. Army, was killed in action. His outnumbered force that he was commanding was slowly losing the position on the hillside they were trying to hold. He ordered the evacuation of his men in conjunction with the arrival of air support that he had requested. As the Germans advanced, The captain did not vacate the position himself. In essence, the fire he had ordered upon the advancing Germans who were overrunning his position resulted in the decimation of that attacking force but also rained down the hellish fusillade that would bring an end to his own life. The heartbreak of his death was devastating. His memory throughout my childhood was ever present. His Medal of Honor and service photograph were pridefully displayed on the family mantle for decades.

The war eventually ended, and life in Washington went forward. He soon was of age to start attending high school. His study habits were haphazard, and his conduct was also less than exemplary. My grandmother, her marriage now in complete disarray, decided the best thing to do would be to send him to a disciplined, military/boarding school. Young Bill found an imposed structure and flourished in that environment. He starred in high school football and displayed promising characteristics for a potentially bright future. During this period, my grandmother had become romantically involved with a government worker colleague, a married man, named Wayne Chambers. Their attraction was undeniable, and soon both took steps to end their respective marriages so they could be together. Shocking and scandalous behavior for the early 1950s. Their value as employees overrode the violations of established codes, so Wayne was transferred to the Department of Interior, quieting the storm clouds of violated protocol.

My Dad, a well-connected young man, benefited from strings being pulled to gain him admission to Duke University. The Blue Devils were a football powerhouse in that era, and it was my dad's intention to go there as a walk-on and make his mark on the gridiron. But the life of a walk-on proved overly difficult as did the demands of academic excellence. And when no one was looking over his shoulder directing activities, things went awry. After just his freshman year at Duke, Bill Keefer had had enough of Durham, North Carolina. He returned to Washington to reunite and hang out with high school friends and perform a series of odd jobs over the next couple of years. Then that fateful day arrived when he was introduced to a bright blue-eyed, young girl from West Virginia who was working for Coca-Cola. Her name, Saralyce James.

By her own admission, 20-year-old Sara, who had literally come down from the hills of West Virginia to the big city of Washington DC, didn't know very much about anything. She had come to town to live with her Aunt Alice and had landed a job with Coca-Cola as a secretary. It did not take long for executives there to start getting the enchanting, young beautiful blonde involved in photo shoots and appearances for the brand. She has been raised in the most humble and rural of circumstances imaginable. She had grown up near Clarksburg, West

Virginia, on the top of a remote little mountain called Hephzibah Hill. Her mother, Della, was one of 11 children born to a couple of German immigrants named Brumage. Her father, Charles James, did odd jobs and was a bit of a drifter. He was not a regular provider, and by all accounts was rarely sober or civil throughout my mother's young life. Her half-sister, Nina, the product of Della's first marriage, was 18 years her senior. She had three other older full siblings, Margaret, Danny, and Dick. At the conclusion of high school, when she had the opportunity to move to Washington to seek work, to her credit she took it and never looked back. Virtually every relative and family member had lived their entire lives and died in the mountaineer state. In fact, few, seldom if ever, traveled elsewhere.

The courtship was a whirlwind, and the marriage took place in December 1956. My mother was dazzled by the seemingly sophisticated and dashingly handsome Bill Keefer. She thought he looked a lot like an iconic figure of that time, Elvis Presley. Although it was not a result of any sort of plan, immediately Sara was pregnant. In October the following year, 1957, William Kip Keefer was the result.

As has been the case back in military school during his high school days, now Bill Keefer had structure and clearly defined lines that he had to honor. He landed a sales job with the Johnson Wax company, Pledge, Raid, Glade, Bravo a Floor wax, etc. and purchased, with the help of his mother, a charming suburban home in the Washington suburb of Rockville (and before you ask, no, the Flintstones and the Rubbles were not our neighbors).

It was in that house that I would live for the first 8 1/2 years of my existence. But I also spent an awful lot of my time at this fantastic estate that my grandmother and her husband Wayne had purchased right on the Chesapeake Bay in Annapolis, Maryland. It was the ultimate paradise for a kid. And I relished going there and running wild in the gigantic yards. I endlessly explored the catacombs of the undiscovered rooms in the basement and even on the dock where they kept their boat in the bay.

Those were truly the best days! I would awaken and my great grandmother, who I named Kiki when I barely could talk (in her heavy accent she would say Kippy, and I would answer Kiki), would fix me breakfast and make sure I had plenty of what she called "fruit juice." I think it was a mixture of orange, grapefruit, and apricot? But every morning we were in Annapolis, I would dutifully drink my juice and eat whatever she prepared. I knew the sooner I finished, the quicker I could get outside and have my run of the place. Kids today can't even conceive that being outside and making up your own forms of entertainment was the only option that you had back in those days. Unless it was severe weather outside, and I'm talking wrath of God stuff like tropical storm winds and lightning, you went outside and stayed there all day long.

I became totally obsessed with football at an early age because that was my dad's greatest love. Every firstborn son desperately wants to bond with his father. By the time I was in first grade, I was a walking encyclopedia about players in the NFL, particularly the Colts and the Redskins. We lived just outside Washington in the heart of Redskin territory. But on those weekends we were in

Annapolis, that was Baltimore Colts area. I knew every player and every player's number. The televised games were rare, usually only the local team on Sunday. With two gigantic yards in the front and back respectively, I would go out and play an entire game by myself matching the Redskins against an opponent each week. I would call signals, hand the ball off to myself, and then throw myself to the ground when the imaginary defenders brought me down. I would throw passes and run to catch the ball that I had just hurled playing quarterback and receiver. And all throughout the action, I did thorough play-by-play and color analysis of every event in my games. When halftime rolled around, I would head into the vast basement that had a couple of tiny little back rooms that I assume were originally designed to be some sort of dressing quarters. They had bright, multi-bulb lighting around mirrors, and it looked like the perfect place for a network studio. I would draw helmets and post imaginary matchups of other games going on in my league, tape those papers on to the mirror to simulate a scoreboard, and give halftime score updates and details on these imaginary out of town

My initial school years were basically uneventful. While I grasped the concept that Dick, Jane, Sally and Spot were trying to convey, I don't remember it being particularly alluring. I instantly loved any kind of history or geography and hated any kind of math. In addition to my sports obsession, I also became a bit of a singer and performer, which I know will come as a tremendous shock to many of you. I became proficient in several Peter Paul and Mary songs, mainly Puff the Magic Dragon. In first and second grade, it was not unusual for me to be called on to perform that song with several of my classmates at various school functions. Thinking back, I believe that many of my teachers were intrigued and/or impressed with the fact that I was not the least bit intimidated by being on stage. I actually enjoyed and embraced it.

Being a young student in Washington DC produced my everlasting earliest memories. On Friday, November 22, 1963, as I ambled down my street, Hunters Lane, after a day of first grade academic excellence, and came upon my house, I saw my mother sitting on the top step of the front porch weeping uncontrollably. Naturally filled with angst to see my mother in such a state, I ran to her side and frantically tried to comfort her. When I asked her what the matter was, she looked at me with tears streaming down her face and said simply, "They've killed the president!" That was pretty heavy information for a six-year-old to process, but I remember it so vividly I can almost describe every detail. By that time, my sister Kristy had been born in April 1961. She was napping and missing these tumultuous events. I remember being frustrated because she would never wake up, and I was anxious to have somebody to share the news with. Not surprisingly, at two years old, she did not seem to care very much.

Earlier in that first-grade year, we spent an awful lot of time in school on evacuation drills, and what I now realize was a ridiculous waste of time. That, of course, the squatting under desks in a fetal position while covering your head with your arms between your knees. Of course, that was a result of the tensions with Cuba and the missile crisis precipitated by our Russian friends.

It's laughable now to think that assuming those positions would've had any influence whatsoever in our capacity to survive. When faced with vaporization, I probably would prefer to be comfortable.

The best thing about going to elementary school in Washington is the field trips. Talk about outstanding venues to visit. I don't know that it was ingrained in me or I simply had the capacity to understand it, but being an American to me was the greatest gift a person could possibly be blessed with. I loved the museums, monuments and historical places. I can remember a second-grade field trip to the Lincoln Memorial standing at the base of the steps gazing up at father Abe poised on his majestic throne-like chair and being absolutely consumed with pride and awe. In the third grade, on a trip to Ford's theater, gazing upon the very spot where Lincoln had been assassinated by the delusional, misguided famous actor John Wilkes Booth, I was deeply affected. It may have been a result of the traumatic experience of being in Washington and watching the entire Kennedy saga unfold.

Of course, my other crystal clear memory of my childhood in Washington were those unbelievable, almost miraculous opportunities I would get to go to Redskin games with my dad. My grandmother bought my father season tickets every year to the Redskin games. One of the highlights of our year was the week before the season started my mom and dad would host a party with all of my dad's raucous buddies to get ready for football. Optimism always ran high, this was going to finally be the Redskins' year. Sadly, it never was, the Skins basically sucked year in and year out. I can't describe to you the feeling of pride and excitement I had when my dad would parade me down in front of all of his gathered group to basically allow me to show off all of my football acumen and knowledge. During the season, I would usually be allowed to attend two to three games. My mother would decline the opportunity to go, I think predominantly knowing that I really wanted to attend. And for that five year period, I always got the opportunity to go to the game right before Christmas time because that's when Santa would appear at the half.

The time, of course, was the mid-60s. The civil rights movement and campus unrest in the form of protests over the Vietnam War was in full force around the country. However, in my little vacuum of a world in Maryland, I was totally clueless of what was even going on. I remember one game against Philadelphia when coming home my dad's station wagon needed gas. He had four or five friends crammed in the car so I naturally was in the way back by the tailgate. We pulled into a station downtown, and I still remember the distinctive ringing of the bell when the car would run over the wire to alert the attendant that somebody was at the pumps. My dad, never the most patient of individuals, and most likely agitated to an extra extent by the alcohol he consumed during the game began honking his horn when the gas station employee did not materialize. Finally, after three or four minutes, an elderly black gentleman in overalls came ambling out of the Esso Station building. As he approached the vehicle, I remember my dad saying something that I really didn't understand, "What is this, is this a colored only station?" The man responded, "No sir, fill it up?" At eight years old, it was the first time that I realized that there were a schism and a separation amongst people. I didn't see color in those days; the Redskins had Bobby Mitchell, Charlie Taylor, and other great black players. They were every bit as much my heroes as Sonny Jurgenson and Paul Krause, white stars on the team. In later years when I became cognizant of what had been occurring in the country that I had been too young and sheltered to be aware of, that experience at the gas station always resonated in my mind.

At the conclusion of the school year when I wrapped up the third grade, life as I knew it was getting ready to take a very distinctive, new direction. As we embarked on the summer of '66, our family consisted of my mom, dad, myself and a sister and brother, Kristy Kay and Charles Kerry.

My sister was the prototype model perfect child. She was soft-spoken, sweet and extraordinarily well-behaved. She was an adorable little blonde and did everything anyone asked of her. Naturally, she always made straight A's. Particularly annoying was her penchant for eating anything and everything that was put in front of her. So predictably I got the constant peppering of, "Why can't you be a good eater like your sister?" My picky eater status made my life a living hell. Especially on those occasions of visiting my grandmother and her intimidating, constantly critiquing husband Wayne. "Eat your Brussels sprouts, take a bite of that radish, rutabagas are delicious." … Aargh! "Look, Kristy has cleaned her plate, what a good girl. She ate every bite of the goat droppings we fried up for her. They were good too, weren't they honey?"

On some inspired weekends, my dad would perform his culinary magic and create this hodgepodge of grossness referred to in the family as "Farmers Breakfast." Basically, it consisted of haphazardly scrambled eggs, potatoes chopped up, giant pieces of onion and cut up frankfurters. Individually, none of the ingredients were that appalling but mixed together it was the most unattractive, unappealing dish imaginable. Since this was his creation, a great rift developed between us anytime he concocted it. I would stubbornly hold my ground and refuse to eat the mishmash. He would forbid me from leaving the table and threaten me with expulsion from whatever fun activity was planned on that weekend day. In a short time, the plate full of garbage would grow stone cold, then it was absolutely inedible. I am proud to say I never acquiesced and gave in. Like modern-day progressive politicians, I learned to wait them out by stalling and shuffling my food around my plate. Most of the time, they would lose interest and give up. Of course, I was also expert on days that I knew farmer's breakfast would be served, to hoard some extra napkins in my pocket and skillfully, stealthily extract handfuls of my allotted portion, wad it up in the napkins, then nonchalantly return them to my pockets.

Of course, that system was not foolproof. At a holiday gathering at my grandmother's, there was great excitement at the presence of a fabulous new dish that night on the table, stewed tomatoes. I would've much preferred to gobble down the goat droppings that we discussed earlier. Of course, a spoonful of the delicacy was dished up on my plate, and I stared at it in horror at the prospect of touching my other food. I skillfully executed my usual hazard removal plan. Alas, they say there is no such thing as the perfect crime, there's always a detail that even the most cunning of criminal minds overlook. That evening, the flaw in my plan was the fact that I was wearing white pants. Upon being excused from the table, as I stood up, two giant red blotches in the area of my thighs appeared for all to see. The dastardly stewed tomatoes had revealed my devious little secret by soaking through my very white britches. Of course, my step-grandfather could not resist, bellowing out this declaration, "Looks like you really enjoyed those tomatoes!"

Over the period of the next 45 years, my, and later my children's, reluctant eating habits prompted my grandmother to launch into the same story she told every time in support of the joys of developing a taste for horrid foods. The oft-repeated anecdote involved my dad as a young boy and his disdain for liver and onions. One summer, after being sent to camp in Vermont, my dad returned home to Maryland, and one of his initial questions to my grandmother allegedly was, "How come we never have liver and onions?" At camp, when that was all there was to eat on certain nights, he had developed a love of his formally most hated food combination. Despite the fact that I heard the story over 100 times over all those years, it never changed the way I felt about what I liked and did not like.

In the early to mid-60s, the sleeping giant in the Southeast, a burgeoning community called Atlanta, was coming into its own. The powers that be with the SC Johnson company saw fit to promote their bright, promising young salesman, WW Keefer to district manager in this rising Mecca of the South. So my parents actually boarded an airplane in Washington and flew to the modern jewel that was the Atlanta Airport. Their search for the homestead of our new lives in this new land ended up being focused on a suburb that was just emerging northeast of the city. Their selection was a house that had just barely begun to be built in the Chamblee/Dunwoody area right on N. Peachtree Rd. Three blocks from I-285.

When they returned to Maryland, the first thing my dad asked me was, "Who plays shortstop for the Atlanta Braves?" Of course, being the baseball card baron and expert on all sports that I was at the ripe old age of 8 1/2, I declared Woody Woodward and Denis Menke. My Dad looked at my mother and said proudly, "I told you he'd know." Then, he informed me that Denis Menke was my new next door neighbor. For a sports fanatic rising fourth grader, it was like hitting the ultimate jackpot. Major-league baseball players lived in houses, in neighborhoods? And better yet, next door to me? Just like the Keefers, the Braves had just moved during that off-season from Milwaukee to Atlanta. It was the first major league sports franchise in Atlanta and for that matter in the South. As excited as I was, little did I know just how awesome that was going to be.

We arrived in Atlanta in July 1966. For the first three weeks in town, we had to live in the Holiday Inn over off I-85. We moved in at the beginning of August just before the school year began. The elementary school for our new neighborhood was a good distance away at Hightower Elementary over closer to Doraville. My third-grade year was not a great academic success in Washington at Holiday Park elementary. The teacher was a crabby, humorless woman named Ms. Rabold. Even at that early stage of life, I needed to be inspired to produce results. Let's just say me and the old bitty simply did not click. She had tried to push me through intimidation, basically I never budged. Apparently the result was that I was not terribly productive in the quality of my work which was reflected in my grades. The wise minds that ran the higher academic beacon of learning known as Hightower decided that perhaps I would be a good fit in the lowest level fourth grade class. Not to glorify myself but just state the facts, it was a very poor assessment. My original classmates in the South were an interesting collection of some folks that while very nice, let's just say their intellectual capacity was glaringly limited and even minuscule. I was an instant hit, a major rock star in my first couple of days. My legions of classmates would've followed me anywhere. Alas, all good things have to come to an end. Not even halfway into the first quarter of the school year, I was shifted from the intellectually challenged group to the class consisting of the elite young minds of the era, at least, those in that area, in the fourth grade.

The years between 1966 and 69 were some of the most uproarious in American history. But our growing bedroom community continued to see a constant influx of people from all over the country converging on Atlanta. My life was centered around the Dunwoody North Driving Club, the community pool which was just at the end of the short path behind my house on the other side of the woods. Despite having very little experience with swimming, I showed a certain aptitude for it and immediately was signed on with the swim team there. My sports participation up to that point had been a solo enterprise, so it was great to be part of an organized activity. I wasn't much of a fan of 6 AM practices but learned to live with it as a price of a poker kind of proposition. I also was introduced for the first time to youth sports. I was playing Little League football, basketball, and baseball. I wish I could report that I was a superstar at that early stage, but that would be a colossal exaggeration. Truth be told, I was a rather late bloomer, and even at the stage of sixth and seventh grade, my playing skills did not match my enthusiasm for participation.

Our family had also become immediate friends with the Menkes next door. Denis was an awesome guy who always was tolerant of my star-struck awe in his presence. Before long, that ill ease began to change as my parents spent time at their house and vice versa. Jean Menke was also very nice to me. In the summer of 1967, it was pretty common for her to take me to at least one home game in just about every home stand. It was almost too good to be true. This continued through the 1968 season. In the era of Vietnam protests, campus violence and unrest and the gut-wrenching assassinations of Martin Luther King and Robert Kennedy within a two-month period, my life as a young man in Atlanta, Georgia could not have been any better. The summer Olympic Games in 1968 were held in Mexico City. They were scheduled later in the year to avoid the oppressive summertime heat. The games were actually held in late October which correlated with my parents and the Menkes mega Halloween cookout and party. Being right at the end of the baseball season, many of the invited guests were luminaries from that world.

As the party rumbled on in the backyard, I watched the Olympic Games in my living room surrounded by big league players. I was 11 years old, hanging out with Joe and Phil Niekro, Clete Boyer, Denny Lemaster and Pat Jarvis.

But as we learn as we advance in age, nothing lasts forever, at least not the good things. A month or so after that party, the announcement was made, the Braves had completed a blockbuster trade with the Houston Astros. Denis Menke was a Brave no more.

A major change took place in those years with the building of both Peachtree High up the street about a block and the completion of Chesnut Elementary. The front doors were perfectly aligned with mine on North Peachtree. As an incoming seventh grader, I was in the first graduating class in the history of that school. I flourished in that year, despite the fact that I was at one time suspended for three days. My heinous offenses, which occurred on back-to-back days, were writing an unflattering song about the music teacher and then to avoid a ridiculous disciplinary measure of keeping us after class after school for misbehavior, I logically climbed out a window and scurried across the street home. They called my mother in and threw the book at me. My desperate, reckless offenses could not go unpunished. I thought my song deserved an A for creative effort. All I did was alter the lyrics to the song we were learning, You're A Grand Ole Flag. It never contained the name of the teacher who ultimately confiscated the inspired copy. But I suppose she assumed that it was dedicated to her, to which she would be, correct! Here is how it went …

You're a grand old flag, you're a damned old hag,
And forever in the hate will you stay,
You're the emblem of the things we are sick of,
The home of the dead and the graves,
Every heart turns blue when it looks at you,
And there's never a boast or brag,
May all my classmates hear real good,
Keep your eyes off the grand old bag!

Despite the trauma, in June 1970, I was a proud member of the graduating class of Chesnut Elementary. Next stop, the big school up on the hill, Peachtree High.

KEEFER STORY

MY DAD … A Great "Unfluence."

Last year, on Father's Day, I found myself seriously reflecting on the meaning of that concept and how it relates to my personal experiences as a son and father. I would like to tell you a story. It is about the special relationship between a father and his son. The remarkable bond between a dad and his firstborn male child. The dynamic that materializes in their journey together. The imparting of fraternal wisdom and guidance and a fervent desire to establish camaraderie and shared experiences. These are the foundation and building blocks that establish belief systems, core values and even greatly influence future pathways. Much of this may sound like common sense; however, the means that determine the results can come from a surprising, diverse, unconventional array of directions.

My early childhood memories are playing in my neighborhood and weekends at my grandmother's massive house and vast wonderland on the edge of the Chesapeake Bay. I clearly recall as a six-year-old, my mother weeping for the slain young president in Dallas on that fateful Friday. And, I remember idolizing my dad. His passions were Washington Redskin football and horse racing. By the time I was seven years old, I knew every player, pored over the schedule and watched every game, living and dying with each snap. The Redskins were horrid, but my dad and I shared the experience. He had season tickets, given to him annually by his mother. He usually went to games with his friends, but my expertise and enthusiasm eventually earned me an opportunity to go to home games most of the time. Our other thing, horse racing. Going to the tracks in the DC area on a Saturday, Laurel or Bowie was a huge deal. A couple of times a year, we took a train up to the Shenandoah Valley and went to the races at Charles Town. It was the ultimate quality time with my father. I could read a racing form before I mastered the adventures of Dick, Jane and Spot, and the enthralling kids' news sources, The Weekly Reader and Highlights.

There was a champion horse that I absolutely loved named Kelso. I saw him win a race in person, and just a month or so later was thrilled to see him win again in New York via black and white TV. That fall in 1965, my dad sprung the ultimate surprise. On a Thursday, he showed up at lunch time at my school and checked me out. The reason, Kelso was running that afternoon at Laurel in a race known as The Washington DC International. Heady stuff indeed for a third grader. Kelso won, I spent a weekday afternoon with my dad. It was one of the most memorable days of my childhood, heck, and my life.

A few months later, my father was offered a promotion that would require relocation to the South, to Atlanta. I had just become aware of the existence of such a place because of the Braves' relocation that spring from Milwaukee. My folks traveled to Georgia to find a house. Upon returning my dad asked me, "Who is the shortstop for the Braves?" I said, Denis Menke. He looked at my mom and said," I told you he would know," looking back at me he said, "he's your new next door neighbor." Another moment I will never forget.

Dunwoody North was instantly awesome. The pool, our massive backyard, Tenneco on the corner and a big league player next door. I quickly made friendships and my father's career demanded much of his time. Between his job and partying in the neighborhood, our time together dwindled. I was introduced to Little League, but my dad was rarely present for my games. I was a decent swimmer for DNC. One meet, the first my dad attended, I floundered badly in a race because I raised up to make sure he was watching. By 7th grade, I was seldom home, always out playing something, somewhere. My dad was increasingly a rare visitor and his work was not the only culprit. The sexual revolution was in full swing, and he had no intention of missing it.

I watched my parents' marriage implode. I didn't know the issues, but it did not matter. Eventually, my dad's uncontrollable spirit and desires, like Wild Fire in that song, busted down his stall and was lost. Three days before my first day at Peachtree, August 1970, my dad left us to move to Buckhead and pursue without obstacles his new lifestyle.

Except in Hollywood, divorce then was not widespread. I was horrified, mortified, ashamed, and most of all embarrassed. I told no one; I was in denial. The bill of goods parents try to sell, that it has nothing to do with you, well, they were peddling something I wasn't buying, then or now. The selfish choice he made was to leave his family, his marriage, and ME! My dad, my former idol, and our relationship didn't have enough standing or merit to rival his narcissism. For the most part, our time was up. We were basically estranged for the next couple of years. I wanted nothing to do with him.

Adulthood brought new perspective and a modicum of forgiveness; however, the dynamic was something altogether different. While he voraciously pursued an adolescent, all-consuming lifestyle, I assumed the role as the mature, level-headed, voice of reason. He had been promoted and transferred to Memphis in 1973. After Peachtree, I attended college in Memphis and lived with him. Over the next few years, we were together in various living arrangements as I pursued opportunities in Memphis and for a year when he was assigned back to Atlanta. During that period of years, there were two more failed marriages, numerous relationships with a variety of women, excessive drinking and smoking, reckless gambling on anything and everything, and basically a never-ending quest for self-gratification. I found myself becoming the antithesis of Bill Keefer. The irony was, his "unfluence" in that wacky, unconventional era proved to be extremely influential in molding the person I was becoming.

I spoke to my dad today, Father's Day, 2015. He is NOW 80 years old. He has grudgingly slowed down in the last couple of years ... but hasn't stopped. Rum and vodka still flows, the smokes still burn, and his judgment melts away when he encounters a pretty smile. Just a year ago, a woman in her 30s feigned interest in him long enough to steal several thousand dollars and his car. Just the latest in a string of stories. However, despite all his shortcomings, there is not a mean bone in his body. He has chosen to run roughshod through life and roll the dice at every turn. My friend, Mark Random said a few years back, "If Bill Keefer can make it to 75, there is hope for all of us."

When you have a father whose two enduring lessons imparted were ... Knuckle down, buckle down, Do It, Do It, Do It, and Women are like buses, stand on the corner and another will come by, you must look deeper for substantive lessons. So these are a couple of the better examples of what my relationship with my dad gleaned. I have made a living in the racing business and broadcasting. Predominantly sports and advertising. I was a general manager of a track at 36. I was doing radio, writing and voicing commercials in my early 20s. Those accomplishments came early and easily. I had a 20-year head start in training and preparation for those opportunities resulting from trying to bond with my dad. And cautionary tales learned from his antics? ... Well, those were incredibly educational. Especially in my own fatherhood career. Understanding that being a successful father involves putting the emphasis on your kids and not yourself is the key. The fortification and confidence they received from knowing their needs came first, yielded secure, self-assured, bold personalities. My dad taught me that, by what he did not, perhaps could not provide. But teach me? You bet he did!

Post 4

Patriot Games

"Adolescence... what a fascinating, challenging, confounding time. You are desperately trying to find yourself but have no clues of where to look. The process involves necessary rebellion at the same time as grudging acceptance of the inevitability of conformity. It is simply miraculous that anyone emerges from it successfully."

Patriot Games

By the time the end of summer rolled around and it became time to make the big step up to the high school, things had changed in my world again. The confining stall that contained my father's wilder will was finally kicked in and his bolting of the conventional course ensued. The sexual revolution of the early 70s was upon us, and my colorful father had no intention of missing out on it. My folks repeatedly fought during that final year, and twice my mother actually tried to load the car and leave, of course, with the three of us kids in tow. Both times, I refused to go. Not out of loyalty to my father, I was already disgusted by the little bit of what I knew. I just failed to see what would be accomplished by getting in the car with no plans and just driving to some undisclosed location. I believe psychologically; I hated the discord and could not come to grips with why this kind of disheartening drama had to be introduced into my life. My dad had become involved in a torrid affair with a voluptuous blonde bartender downtown. Running off in a frenzy and leaving the security of our house didn't seem like a very viable idea to me. It's a sad development when a 12-year-old has to be the adult in the house. My parents divorced shortly thereafter. For the next four years, I had very little involvement with my father.

The day I started at Peachtree High School, in August 1970, I was 12 years old. I had not yet reached puberty, and I weighed about 125 pounds and probably stood less than 5 foot 4 inches tall. What a genius set up it was. There were juniors and seniors who were already 18 years of age. They possessed driver's licenses, engaged in amorous activities, shaved, displayed muscular builds and body hair. These were my schoolmates, ha-ha. And suddenly, I was cast into a world where I was surrounded by seemingly grown up women. Girls wearing makeup and brassieres. To say that environment was intimidating for a very young man/boy is perhaps the understatement of all time. And I didn't get off to a great start. On my very first day upon entering the classroom, I saw a young lady so vibrant and beautiful that my young mind was overloaded on the spot. This was eighth-grade English, so I knew that this was actually a contemporary of mine. I stealthily went down the row and slipped into the desk just behind hers. Awestruck, I watched her for several minutes until a wave of students entered the room. She excitedly waved to a person who was obviously a friend and gestured for her to come in her direction. She wheeled around and gestured toward the desk where I was seated and told her friend to sit there. Then she said words that I'll never forget, "I'm sure this little boy won't mind moving to another desk." The saddest aspect of that is, I probably replied yes ma'am. In retrospect, it was a fitting preview of my future life encountering the wondrous, magnificent, and treacherous opposite sex. Traumatized by immediately being dismissed as some kind of child by a classmate, for the next two years, I didn't look at or speak to anyone of the female species. Humiliation runs deep!

Any negatives associated with constantly feeling threatened with physical harm by the grown men I was matriculating with or the unbelievable feeling of inadequacy surrounded by girls vastly advanced on the maturity scale ahead of my stunted development, were leveled out that first Friday afternoon when I attended my very first pep rally. It was the ultimate sense of community and belonging. Sitting there on those wooden bleachers, it just seemed inconceivable that I could be part of something so massive, exciting and amazing. The band blasting away their tunes, The various classes displaying their school spirit chanting and roaring wildly, the beautiful, perfect cheerleaders, resplendently adorned in their very short skirts and emphasizing their very prominent curves. They looked like they had been dropped to the gym floor from the loftiest levels of heaven. And the football heroes wearing their jerseys. Our school's warriors preparing for battle that very night. To say I was fired up, inspired, excited and invigorated to be alive that afternoon on my walk home from school would be a serious misrepresentation. I did not get to attend that first high school game. My mother had to work, and by the time she got home, she was too tired to take me. For the record, Peachtree lost to neighboring Chamblee that night, which was a sobering, disappointing blow. It seemed inconceivable that such a perfect storm of emotion and inspiration did not result in an on the field triumph. One of many lessons learned in a young life.

Of course, undeterred by my lack of size and strength, like every red-blooded eighth-grade, All-American boy, I went out for football. I was certainly not big enough or remotely bad enough to warrant any playing time whatsoever. We had over 80 8th grade Patriots on the squad coached by a basketball coach, that's right basketball, Fred Franks. An excitable young coach named Jimmy Parham was his assistant. EIghty-five kids, two coaches, just perfect. Several of our overgrown, early maturing players quickly targeted me for bullying and abuse. They would come and arbitrarily knock me to the ground, not during a play, just while I was standing there. Another of their favorites was to have someone crawl behind me and push me over them. They also enjoyed sticking various weeds and flowers in the holes of my helmet unbeknownst to me. It was a different era, that kind of teasing was not even particularly frowned upon. It was jungle law basically, survival of the fittest. And at that stage, I was hardly a match for these older, or at least, much more mature, deep-voiced, muscle-bound cretins.

Things do have a way of working themselves out. After the second game of our rigorous five-game seasonal schedule, I had not seen the field in the first two contests. My 13th birthday fell on Wednesday afternoon that week, and of course, football practice was scheduled as always. Despite my less than stellar experience to that point, I had not missed one minute of any practice game or required activity. My mom had offered an evening out to celebrate my birthday that included pizza and a movie. I told her that I did not have to go to football practice that day so the plans were made. We dined regally at a newly-created food establishment called Pizza Hut. We then enjoyed the theater big screen, taking in Clint Eastwood in Kelly's Heroes. The next morning in school, I was accosted by several of the fellows that enjoyed tormenting me. Ironically, the leader of the pack of jackals would turn out later to be one of my best friends on earth. But at that point, Mark Random took unbridled joy in making me miserable. He demanded to know why I had not been at practice the previous day, and I told him it was my birthday and I had other plans. He told me that Coach Franks was furious and that he had kicked me off the team. Right after school that day, as was my usual routine, I ran down to my house, but this time, I did not put on my football pants, cleats and undershirt to return to practice. I bagged up all my equipment and embarked on the slow condemned man's trudge of shame to turn in my gear. I summoned up my 13 years and one day of manhood and knocked on the coach's door. I profusely apologized for missing practice the day before and asked if he would possibly reconsider and allow me to stay on the team? No doubt, I was most likely tearful as I made my contrite appeal. Franks looked at me quizzically. He stood up, walked to the door and called for Coach Parham. He asked him, "Is this fellow on your defense?" After six weeks of practice and two games, the head coach had no idea who in the hell I was. To his credit, Coach Parham admitted that I indeed was a member of his defensive squad. They briefly discussed my heinous offense of missing the previous day of practice and told me to not let it happen again. That afternoon in practice, now a controversial, notorious, but suddenly recognizable figure, I was actually called on to participate in part of the day's scrimmage. And on Saturday, game day, against Shamrock High, I actually saw game action at safety. In my six or seven plays, I did absolutely nothing, but I was on the field playing for my beloved high school. And following that, I actually played in each of the last two games. In the season finale against Sequoyah, I even timed a late jump on the pile to look like I had participated in the tackle. As I came off the field, Coach Parham patted me on the helmet and said good job. It was a transcendent moment of validation. I had not only suited up for the 1970 8th grade Peachtree Patriots football team, but I had also recorded a highlight moment and was acknowledged with an atta-boy for it. Seriously, it was a growing and learning experience because it would've been very easy in light of the circumstances, to simply quit, but I stuck it out to the end.

The other major development of eighth grade was meeting Jim Heavern. Our teaming up in a physical science class presided over by Ms. Hudson, turned into a monumental event in the course of history in the Peachtree/Dunwoody area. Individually, we were two smallish obscure, behind the scenes guys. Together, we became an immediate collective force. Jim's intellect and depth of sports knowledge were on the same level as my own. In a very short period of time, we were organizing activities and games between our neighborhoods; we also began blazing a trail which would lead to organizing and defining a wide variety of aspects that would affect numerous friends and classmates over the years.

Jim was the oldest of seven children and lived on iconic Cherry Hill Ln. The Heaverns were natives of Northern Kentucky, in the Cincinnati suburbs. I was immediately enamored and became immersed into the structure of the large brood that resided there. With my family in disarray, it was comforting to be part of such a large and vibrant family unit. I immediately became close with all of Jim's brothers and sisters, four boys and two girls and with the colorful leader of the band, his quirky, funny dad, Jim Sr. and the remarkably relaxed matriarch Marilyn.

By the time our sophomore year rolled around, my eighth-grade antagonist Mark had moved back from living during our ninth grade year on Saint Simons Island in South Georgia. But now, I was more developed, confident and mature. My next encounter with Random proved to be one that sparked our longtime friendship and added a third musketeer to our growing group. Our bond with Mark was twofold. One a love of the newest discovery we had made, Atlanta Flames hockey. And two, and most importantly, Mark was already far in advance of us in his ability to interact and befriend girls. He was a must add to our group based on those criteria.

Random's birthday in 1973 came along months before mine and Jim's. That, of course, also made him an invaluable member of the team. A whole New World was opened to us by the miracle of mobility. We went to every game, participated in any and all activities, and embarked on the wonderful task of actually beginning to grow up. That summer, inexplicably, our parents all decided that we would be allowed to take a one-week road trip to Cincinnati; Heavern and I were 15, Mark, 16. We got as far as Chattanooga before we started having car trouble. Random's older model Dodge Dart developed radiator issues. We were forced to stay overnight while repairs ensued, and by the time we paid up and were once again merrily on our way, our collective money supply had dwindled down to next to nothing. We made it to Cincinnati and blessedly Jim's grandfather, a classic personality, prominent attorney and very wise man, Lawrence Drahman, took pity upon us and refinanced our sagging economies. The way he determined our net worth at lunch that first day was simply to ask each of us individually how much money we had on our persons. Famously, the responses went as follows, organized Jim, pulled out his wallet and revealed he had approximately $20. I dug deep into my pockets and produced about $11. Now it was Random's turn. Nonchalantly, he sifted through some change in his hand and declared he had about 57 cents. After laughing heartily at our saddest sack status and telling us he didn't think we were going to get very far for the next week on that amount, he helped us out. He infused our travel enterprise by giving Jim money for our basic expenses.

We stayed with his other grandparents, Jim's dad's folks, and basically had the time of our lives. My former neighbor Denis Menke by that time was playing for the powerhouse Cincinnati Reds. He left us tickets to several games at Riverfront Stadium. Our days were spent exploring the area and going to different landmark places that Jim wanted us to see from his childhood. As mentioned, Mark already had the appearance of a very mature young man, which had been the case even back in the eighth grade. The day before we left town, Mark went into a store and actually bought a case of beer. We also managed on that trip to go to a nightclub, The Brass Ass, where obviously we would not have been welcomed if proper scrutiny had been in place. It was not a strip bar but more like a burlesque type place with scantily clad women and an atmosphere that can best be described as a little bit sordid. The trip was all part of an undeniable, welcome transition. Our junior year which was soon to begin was definitely our coming-of-age period.

Suddenly girls were not just in the background, they were in starring roles in everything we did. I was able to receive my license in October, and Jim followed in November. Suddenly, we were all free to terrorize the village on our own terms. A neighbor of Jim's down the street, Joe Lipham, was now a part of our inner circle. Prior to hanging around with us pretty much full-time, Joe had an interesting collection of friends including some of the more notorious hoodlums in the school. The uniqueness of our group, however, was that we were not really ostracized or in opposition to any of the other cliques in the area. While not being close to the thuggish or geekish element, we were certainly not enemies. Our group's influence grew, and suddenly there were multitudes of people going down the hockey games, participating in our various leagues, including our remarkable street hockey league. At its height, we had five teams, schedule, organized playoffs and even statistics. The games were played on the weekends at Kingsley elementary school long ways on their three basketball courts. Our team, the

Peeler Pucks, successfully prevailed over a variety of stern challengers. The Street Fighting Men, Kingsley Jets, and Dunwoody Brewers were all formidable competitors. Jim, Mark, Joe and I were the core group that made our team go. But we had other great additions as well. Two of Jim's younger brothers, Dan and Tom, Cherry Hill residents Dave Smith and his brother Doug, Brent Darnell, Mark's longtime friend Phill Linderman, and an exceptional athlete named Mike Patton.

Despite having no ice skating experience, of course, we tackled playing ice hockey as well. My organizational skills and determination soon had us enrolled in a high school hockey league. We even had ultra-cool red white and blue Peachtree hockey jerseys with our names on the back. Surprisingly, we were very competitive, largely because the aforementioned Patton turned out to be an absolute demon on ice. Playing the game for the first time in his life, by season's end, Mike had scored an incredible amount of goals and by far led the league in every statistical category. The first time we ever assembled to practice, we had rented the rink from 2 to 4 AM on a Saturday/Sunday morning. Naturally, I padded up in my street hockey goalie equipment, most of it makeshift and not very protective, and put on ice skates for the second time in my life. Thankfully I had some aptitude for blocking shots because I sure wasn't very good at skating. At one point, I had wandered out of my net, and in my anxiety to get back in position had gotten moving too fast and did not know how to stop. Desperately, I grabbed a hold of the heavy metal post on top of the net which resulted in it spinning around and falling on top of me. I was pinned underneath it like a rodent caught in an elaborate trap. The handful of guys who knew how to skate properly, and stop correctly, skated in quickly intent on christening my ineptitude properly by sliding to quick stops and spraying me with multitudes of the cold ice chips as I lay there helplessly. It was highly entertaining, even if I was the butt of the joke.

Following basketball season that junior year, the fifth member of our merry little gang became a full-fledged fixture. Steve Hardy seemed to be an unlikely candidate to join our crew. Until that winter when we started to corrupt him, he had been a straight-laced, determined, dedicated, independent individual focused solely on basketball. Through sheer driving hard work, Hardy had made himself into a star hoops performer and one of the best pure shooters that any of us had ever seen. Not to paint the picture that he was a glorified goody two shoes, just extremely dedicated to being the best player he could make himself. Riding with Hardy in his 4-barrell station wagon was very similar to climbing into a NASCAR rig in terms of the speed of the experience. Steve prided himself on breaking records for arriving at venues, such as downtown to the Omni for games. Captain Kirk on the Starship Enterprise could order Major Scott to execute warp speed. Hardy reached that level every time he fired up the car. His approach and work ethic paid off big time as he played college basketball at Dekalb and Coastal Carolina. In the summer of 1974 he diversified, and expanded his thinking from long range jump shots and music, adding girls, beer, hanging out and having fun to the mix.One girl in particular seized his attention, cheerleader Betty Ann Brinkley. They have been married now for close to 40 years, and enjoy one of the most successful marriages imaginable As for our merry band of men, he fit in perfectly. Our core group was complete. And it remains intact now some 45 years later.

An additional cast member that should be noted, contributed significantly to our successful, rollicking good time that was our junior year. We had the very good fortune of befriending a wonderful spirit who delighted in our attitude and shenanigans. The remarkable fact was, she was a senior. Kim Hoover not only had a whimsical, adventurous personality and fabulous sense of humor, she also worked in the Peachtree front office. With an insider we had indoctrinated serving on the other side across enemy lines, we were truly open for business. She had the ability to make our names disappear from absentee reports and perhaps even better, could legally finagle paperwork that officially checked us out of school.

One memorable Tuesday, we had made the decision early on that we were going to find something better to do than spend the day in the hallowed halls of Peachtree High. Random, Jim, Kim and I busted out of the joint early that morning. It was Ferris Bueller's Day Off, years before that film was made. In fact, we actually played out a scene that had not even been written yet in Hollywood. Heading straight to my house, we got on the phone contacting Dunwoody High School. Kim's sister Nancy was a junior there and like her sister was zany and fun. Kim was able to negotiate Nancy's release from her school day, simply by claiming she was her mother and that she had an appointment. I have such fond memories of watching Nancy gleefully striding down the front walkway at Dunwoody High and climbing in with us into Mark's trusty Dodge Dart. Her prison break made our traveling party complete. What a day we had. We headed to Marietta and the Iceland ice rink. The Atlanta Flames were conducting a 10 AM practice that morning. We watched it all through the glass right down on ice level. We then went downtown and hung out at the new CNN Center and had lunch. It was just a perfect day and the lovely, charming and hilarious Hoover sisters were the perfect partners in crime.

Our senior year arrived in the fall of 1974 following a summer of nonstop fun activity. I returned to football after my significant hiatus, and it was one of the best decisions I ever made. I was still rather undersized, and as mentioned earlier, my slow blooming self still was not at full capacity. I was listed at 5-9, 170 pounds, a fleet-footed wingback, backing up our star receiver, my 8th-grade tormentor and excellent bud, Mark Random, at the position.

I didn't play all that often, and deservedly so. I wasn't very good. In my defense, there was no effort to develop my skills or find a niche on the team where I was productive. Early on in kicking drills, I did show some aptitude for taking proper angles and blocking punts. Twice in one week of practice, I made plays of that variety. As the first game approached and assignments were made, I was not included on the punt return team. That told me two things, number one, it really didn't matter what you accomplished during practice, and two, most likely, our outstanding coaching staff wasn't even really paying attention. That did not come as a great surprise, it was blatantly obvious that our coaching staff was far from outstanding.

The week of our first game, Wednesday practice would be our final full contact tune-up. In a scrimmage, I lined up at wingback and was responsible for running a slant pattern, which is a short pass route where you angle to the middle of the field. I came off the ball and ran my pattern. The quarterback threw the football toward me, but it sailed and went high. I jumped and stretched out trying to reach the height to gather it in. That turned out to be a most regrettable mistake.

Football in 1974 was a much different game than it is today. Player safety and protection of "defenseless players" was not a major focal point as it is today. In fact, defensive players were urged and encouraged to deliver savage blows to vulnerable receivers. Many defensive backs kept their personal statistics for "knockouts." One of the nicest guys on our team happened to be a defensive back and a good friend of mine, Kenny Godsey. On the football field, Ken played the game aggressively and was well renowned as a big-time hitter. With me all stretched out up in the air, I was an inviting target. The blow he delivered that day was so solid it was heard in adjoining counties. Seismic measuring devices registered it at earthquake monitoring stations. In one instant, I realized the ball was way over my head, and in the next megasecond, I was slammed into head-on by a speeding beer truck. Like a boxer, who had been hit by an unseen haymaker, I was down. I tried to draw a breath, but the air that had been in my body had already by that time exited the atmosphere. I saw this brilliant bright light, and a group of deceased relatives beckoning me forward. Incredibly, in less than a minute, miraculously systems were restored and my lungs reopened for business. The coaches seemed relieved when I was able to stagger to the sidelines and get off the field so the practice could resume. Godsey told me later on that it was one of the best hits he ever delivered. How touching that it was reserved for me. Needless to say, my route running over the middle from that point forward was far more cautious, and I never again dared leave my feet and jump on a football field.

The next afternoon, the day before our first big game, we were having a simple tune up practice wearing only T-shirts, gym shorts and helmets. I was lined up in the receiver group. The quarterbacks were making throws to us as we ran our various patterns. At one point, we were running a simple 10 yard out route, where you run hard straight for 10 yards, plant, and then break to the outside to receive the ball. I was just behind in-line our all everything, super stud, alpha male, Mr. Peachtree, Ken Davis. I had gone to school with Ken since elementary days. He was a grown, polished man by the time he was 14. The girls swooned over him, the coaches fell all over themselves to make sure he was happy and healthy, ready to go. Despite all of his luster, he was actually a pretty genuinely good guy. I liked him and despised him at the same time.

Davis took off running, reached the 10-yard spot and stopped to make his cut. Screaming in agony, he crumpled to the ground. There were no defensive players or contact of any kind. When he planted and turned, his knee simply shredded. The day before, when I had been bludgeoned, there was at best a cursory response as I lay writhing on the ground. With Davis down, a massive crowd ran to his aid. Every coach looked crestfallen and devastated.

Of course, in those days, there was no such thing as a cart standing by to handle catastrophic injuries. To my best recollection, five or six people hoisted him up and carried him, like a vanquished gladiator, to the faraway locker room facility which was perched atop a daunting, steep hill. The next morning, we learned the harrowing bad news. Ken had torn ligaments and was done for the season. I sincerely felt bad for him, as mentioned, he was a good guy and his future prospects as an athlete, which were promising, suddenly were jeopardized.

In the locker room that night before taking the field for our season opener against Dunwoody, the new high school recently opened in our neighborhood that had been filled by half of our former classmates; Coach Turner gathered us for a pregame speech. The theme was basically finding the collective strength to overcome adversities. He talked about the ironies of life. Unexpected events, such as this very week in practice. "How is it possible that one of our players took one of the hardest hits imaginable and is sitting here dressed out and ready to go. Then the very next day, simply participating in light drills, in shorts, one of our players, an extraordinary young man, goes down with a devastating injury. Yes, it was an immense loss to our team." Now being rather cerebral and having a well-developed knowledge of sports speak, I knew exactly what the point of that sermon was. It was basically, there is no justice; we must accept it and overcome it. Or in other words, it should be this guy who sucks who's sitting here suited up that got knocked out, not, God forbid, our superstar player. It was so heartwarming to be a key component in the coach's stirring speech. It was so effective, that it, combined with our anemic offensive system and embarrassing lack of proper preparation led to us being dealt a humiliating defeat by our upstart new rivals.

There are several amusing football anecdotes from that season that you will be able to find in the "Keefer Story" that follows this chapter. The team wound up a disappointing four and six. We had a number of very competent players on the defensive side of the ball, and an offense so inept that scoring points was almost a miraculous event. There were literally 15 to 20 players that did not participate, who were some of the more skilled athletes in the school. Just two years after our senior campaign, under the tutelage of the new coach T. McFerrin, who had replaced the nitwit we had, went deep in the state playoffs and establish the school as a powerhouse during his entire tenure.

One quick additional story that I include because it served as a profound life lesson, influencing my ability to interact successfully and hopefully positively impact people, occurred late that season. With just a couple of weeks left and a team with a losing record, football practice becomes a rather listless and arguably useless exercise. By that juncture of the season, everybody has nagging injuries and enthusiasm has been greatly diminished. The significant drop off in the exuberance category, was not limited to just on the field mediocrity. Those of us still without girlfriends, who had not benefited from our football notoriety and fame, had to sadly face the truth. It's not who you are or what you're doing, it's what you look like. Anyway, I digress. At that point, the limited scrimmaging that is conducted is simply for the offense to practice a play or two put in for that week's game plan. Whatever warm bodies remained standing were plugged into play defense against the first team offense. Their job was to provide passive resistance disguised as trying to stop the play. Our defensive line was decimated by injuries, so guess what, I was tabbed to line up at defensive tackle for a series of plays. Across from me on the line was our team's largest human, Kent Roach. He started and played every game at the right tackle position. Outweighed by more than 100 pounds by my 6 foot 5 counterpart, I was basically blasted off the line in the first two plays like a leaf propelled in hurricane-force winds. Before the third pummeling, Coach Roy Garnet pulled me aside and simply said, "Keefer, what are you doing?" I wittily replied, "Being destroyed by Roach, Coach." (I actually laughed out loud at my own quip) then went on to say, "What do you expect? He makes two of me."

Garnet was kind of a homespun good old boy, whose expertise was not in football; instead, he was the school's baseball coach. I guess he was picking up a few extra bucks helping out as an assistant on the football staff. He never seemed keenly interested or particularly knowledgeable about the game, but he was a good guy and everybody liked having him around. On the very first day of summer practice, as we stretched before calisthenics, one of those ear piercingly loud, supersonic formations of planes roared by just overhead. Garnet stepped back and looked at the sky, watching the incredible speed on display. I said to him, "Coach, it looks like you are into aeronautics?" He looked toward me and with an embellished twang in his tone simply replied, "Yep, it's a jet."

So now, he had a reply to what I had just said in our current conversation. In almost a whisper, so no one else would hear, he said, "He is slower than molasses in January. Come off the ball quick, step in between him and the guard, and use both your hands to push the side of his head toward the end of the line. Then shoot right through there." On the next snap, I did just what he described. My quick jump and forceful push opened a sizable gap. It was a pass play, and within three steps, I was right on the quarterback KC Rankin. Whistles blew to stop the play, and two of the coaches immediately began to harangue the bewildered Roach, demanding to know what in the hell just happened. Meanwhile, I trotted back to the defensive huddle fresh off the best play I had made all year. I made eye contact with Coach Garnet and nodding, he quietly said," There you go." Lining up for the next play, I tried it again, and I was pancaked to the ground and pinned to the earth like a rag doll. That was the price to pay for making the biggest guy on the team look foolish.

Where had those simple instructions and encouragement been all year from any of the coaching staff? How about other short phrased ideas that could've been presented to me that may have actually made me a decent, contributing player. It was a valuable lesson. To this day, I try to be intuitive and pay close enough attention to pass along seemingly simple concepts that can make a difference for others. It is especially an effective tool in parenthood, teaching, management, and coaching. Positive reinforcement, encouragement and just reiteration of basic principles can surprisingly make a tremendous positive difference.

It was time for a different season. No pads, no helmets, just ridiculously short shorts that when you look at them today in old footage or photographs, look comical. The previous summer, I had worked hard in the hopes of hooping it up on the Peachtree basketball team, my senior year. My close friends, Steve Hardy and Dave Smith, were going to be the two top performers on the club. The graduation of a number of excellent performers from the previous year had left the roster a little thin. I participated all summer in the basketball program, showed up for every workout and game. But when the season rolled around, for whatever reason, Coach Franks let me know that I was not going to be suiting up. It was particularly disappointing considering that the year before he had always given me every assurance that there would be a spot for me the next year. All during that junior season, I lugged around this gigantic camera, the earliest versions of video, and shot every game from high in the bleachers, home and away. That included a trip to the Decatur recreation center for a raucous Saturday night game against Decatur high school. They were a skilled, all-black team led by star point guard Michael "Mad Dog" Maddox. The game was an absolute blowout; we were defeated before we ever settled in. I assumed my usual position high in the bleachers but word quickly circulated amongst the crowd that my presence meant the game was being televised. The entire evening I had to stand, lean, sway and gyrate to try and record images on the court because of the constant parade of people jumping in front of the camera waving wildly thinking they were on live TV. Midway through the second half, with the score getting uglier all the time, I was able to film a most amusing ritual executed by the crowd at large.

The jam-packed gathering presented quite an energetic, choreographed dance routine which literally rocked the building. Along with the dance, several versions of the following lyrics were sung/screamed at the top of their lungs ...

Peachtree we love ya,
Peachtree we love ya, because you always give your all,
Peachtree we love ya,
Peachtree we love ya, but you just can't play no ball!

As that junior year in basketball wound down, I found myself in a most interesting role one Friday night at Tucker High School. The morning of the opening sub region playoff game, Coach Franks received the sad news that his wife's father had drowned in some sort of fishing accident. Obviously, he had to leave immediately with her, which shifted the head coaching responsibilities that night to an assistant, the head B-team coach, Bernard Roy Adams. Coach Adams was a very competent, extremely successful, basketball coach. His ninth and 10th-grade teams had won an astounding amount of games over the last three or four years including one long epic winning streak. However, Coach Adams was, putting it mildly, a tad high strung. Now suddenly cast in the role as the head man, in his varsity coaching debut, in a district playoff game no less, not surprisingly Roy was visibly unsettled and nervous.

Coach Franks loved his video equipment and kept it locked in impenetrable quarters in the depths of his office. There was no retrieving it for the game, so Coach Adams told me to just sit on the bench with the rest of the guys. Astonishingly, once everyone settled down, I was in the third seat down the row, a position that would normally be filled by an assistant coach. It was Adams, then occupying the next seat was eighth-grade coach Dee Childress. He was a very tall, soft-spoken, mild-mannered fellow who looked completely out of place and ill at ease in this setting. Throughout the opening half, things were not going well for our team. Coach Adams was sweating profusely furiously, wiping himself constantly with the towel which he clutched with a death grip in his hands and occasionally even chewed on. He had coached all of the current players during their careers coming up the ranks, but this was the first time that he had been asked to coordinate their efforts at this high-level. Tucker had a large athletic frontline and were exploiting our man defense repeatedly by dumping the ball down low and executing pick and rolls down to our baselines for short scoring opportunities. One of their forwards, in particular, was on fire and never seemed to miss. But the execution of their offense and the set ups he was receiving yielded easy scoring opportunities through short shots or even wide-open layups> Just before the end of the first half when that same player banked in yet another jumper, I mentioned to coach Childress, sitting next to me, my observation that perhaps we needed to employ a zone defense and pack in the lane area, which would force them to have to extend the range of their shots. At that point in the game, their outside shooting prowess was not even known. They were getting all easy stuff inside. Amazingly, Childress immediately leaned into Coach Adams, who was kneeling on the floor on one knee. I heard him ask, "What do you think of the idea of us going to a zone?" Incredibly, Adams immediately called for a timeout. He gathered all the players and informed them that we were going to go to a 2-1-2 zone defense and force them to start shooting the ball from the perimeter. As I shook my head in disbelief, Russell Colton, a senior player on the team seated on my other side said to me, "Looks to me like you might be coaching the team." I was glad there was a witness. We stayed in the zone the majority of the game but wound up losing a one-point heartbreaker. So I guess I must grudgingly admit that my record as a high school basketball coach was 0-1.

After Franks reneged on his promise to give me a square shot at making the team, he threw me a bone and gave me an assignment that I welcomed probably just as much. Perched on a stage just behind the far goal in the PHS gymnasium, was my new broadcast position. I became the public address voice of Peachtree basketball that season and had a blast doing it. I was given no instructions, and no guidelines were imposed upon me. Looking back, that was pretty remarkable that they simply handed me a microphone and knew full well that I would know what to do with it.

Certainly, it was a letdown not playing for Peachtree, but with all of our varied pursuits, I stayed extremely busy. Besides, I was a charter member of a comparable brand of basketball every week at the elementary school outdoor courts across from my house. Chesnut Saturday pickup games became an institution. Along with my mentor and round ball cohort Craig Smith, we forged a legendary weekly gathering place for local ballers.

Clearly, in many areas, I was doing some good things. Academically, well, not so much. Let's just say that my heart wasn't really in my "studies." Early on in my high school career, I had found that the challenge was not in learning the material but in working to beat the system. The school was overcrowded and disorganized. And that provided an outstanding opportunity to try and maneuver my way to a diploma without doing very much. As the demands of our extracurricular lives dramatically increased in our sophomore year, time to devote to such mundane tasks as reading material and studying just was not available. I had a knack for being rather charming, and my personality was such the teachers seemed to respond to me. I also became mindful that schedules could easily be finagled and open periods were certainly times to relax and enjoy life. In that sophomore year, I was mistakenly assigned to football physical education. The thing was, I didn't play football that year. I never went to the class. At the end of all three quarters that school year, my report card featured an A in football PE.

I also had the aforementioned Fred Franks for typing. However, just a couple of weeks into the opening quarter, for some reason that I can't recall, I was asked to transfer to a different typing class. It was being conducted by a short blue-haired lady who had put shoe polish over all of the keys. Hunting and pecking were not going to work in there. I never darkened the doors of my new class assignment after the first day. Couple those new holes in my schedule with the fact that I had an assigned study hall in the library that I never attended, and my schedule was ideal and fixed. Out of the six daily class periods, I had class in three of those hours, and the other three were wide open. With one of them coming on the back end of lunch, I was free to basically beeline down the street to my house for an extended period of midday R and R virtually every day.

I had also infiltrated the inner sanctums of the Peachtree counseling office and befriended one of the coolest ladies ever, Mary Frazier. Originally, she had tried to put me back on the right path, but quickly to her credit, realized that I was far more suited to charting my own course and determined to do so. She helped work my schedule in my junior and senior years and assured me that if I stuck to the formula, I would be receiving my diploma on time despite my lack of earlier diligence. One of the provisions was during the winter quarter of my senior year, two nights a week, I was required to attend a class at Clarkston night school. The place was a dump, and my fellow students weren't exactly shining examples of youthful achievement. Somehow, one of my more colorful Peachtree classmates, JP Perryman, found himself in the position of having to also attend this lower rung institution of learning. He dubbed the school, Clarkston Bite! We quickly found a way to make the best of it and managed to turn it into somewhat of a fun activity. Especially on nights when we decided to hell with this, the Flames are in town, let's blow off class and head to the Omni.

The plan worked well until the final quarter of my senior year. I needed one more English credit and after looking at alternatives, Janice Shackleton's senior English class looked to me to be the best fit. People warned me against that decision, citing this teacher's reputation for not tolerating nonsense and not being forgiving in terms of her approach. I however, did not shy away from that challenge. Besides, Jim was in that class and was very enthusiastic about me coming aboard. My charm and charisma were effective on the allegedly hard-core English teacher. I stepped up my game to be more entertaining than ever and was determined to make her loosen up and laugh. And I did, but unfortunately, she had the last laugh. On the Friday of the prom, she had scheduled a test that afternoon. My friends and I had no intention of being bothered with school on that day and were prominently absent. Despite the fact that it was obvious that we had cut the class, several of my friends, including Jim, presented notes on Monday that explained their absences due to various contrived excuses. Jim's cited a visit to the dentist, yeah right? Now I was scheming and nonconforming, but I was never blatantly dishonest. When asked for my excuse, my creative and comic instincts could not be repressed ... I asked did she not see the major disturbance out in front of the school Friday afternoon? I told her, as I returned from my house intently studying my notes for the test that I had wandered into the path of an oncoming farm vehicle hauling hundreds of chickens to market. I explained that thankfully the swerving truck had merely clipped me. Unfortunately, it overturned leaving scores of squawking chickens running in frenzied circles up and down N. Peachtree Rd. I explained I was so disoriented by the mishap, that I had not been able to collect myself and make it to class on time. Everyone laughed and was thoroughly entertained, including Ms. Shackleton. But as she was chuckling, she wrote a big red zero under that test column in her grade book.

Upon learning of my latest transgression, Ms. Frazier tried to intercede on my behalf and find out if it was still possible for me to slide by with a passing grade. Shackleton dug in and stood her ground. There would be no make up test or nonsensical extra credit, a vehicle utilized in past classes to slide by, or any other opportunity to make a grade except the final exam. She indicated that I would have to come very close to making a perfect score in order to pass. For one of the only times in my high school career, I actually read, studied and prepared for that now critically important test. My score was only in the mid-80s range. There was no compromise, no reprieve from the governor; in my final quarter of Peachtree High School in Spring quarter senior English, I was given an F. Allegedly negotiations took place, but the principal John Snodderly supposedly made the decision himself that I would not be able to march with my classmates

Undeniably, my behavior was silly and stupid throughout those years, and it culminated with me getting what I deserved. However, the senseless, punitive gesture of not allowing me to collect my diploma with everyone else was equally silly and stupid as my tomfoolery. The fact that for my final three years at that school, I had been allowed to get away with an appalling lack of effort and missed as many classes as I attended, was a pretty serious indictment of the woeful, inexcusable administrative performance of the staff. I was forced to attend three weeks of a summer school program and retake senior English. The class was so comically easy and non-demanding that once again I barely had to expend any effort or energy at all. Before July, I received my coveted sheepskin via US mail from a half block up the street. To this day, Jim Heavern maintains that I almost certainly only collected half of the credits that should've been required for me to graduate.

My school days were behind me, and sadly so too my childhood years. New adventures were on the horizon, higher academics and career paths waiting to be forged. With my newly acquired scholastic knowledge from my outstanding educational experience and my highly developed work ethic from those years of toil, I was uniquely positioned to rocket into the next stratosphere of challenges. Or, perhaps not.

KEEFER STORY

Lights Out ... Glory On the Gridiron

Following my magnificent experience as a high school football player in the eighth grade, I never really had any serious intention of suiting up for the red white and blue Patriots ever again. After all, with the maturity of a well-developed fifth grader, playing with and against what appeared to be to be grown men, was not an enriching, remotely successful, or satisfying experience.

That attitude changed as my junior year at Peachtree wound to a close. Suddenly, I was socially active for the first time. Status became an important consideration. Physically, I had finally started to develop some muscle and had undergone a fairly significant growth spurt. Athletically, seemingly overnight I had become a respectable baseball talent. Of course, every Saturday at Chesnut, I was playing basketball with many of the best players in the area and certainly holding my own. Never one to not want to be relevant and relegated to obscurity, I made the decision. I announced early in the summer of 74 that I would indeed strap on the pads, don the headgear and reappear between the white lines of the football field.

Football practice starts in July, and to say that conditions are brutal for those activities would be a spot on description. Mercifully, our brilliant coaching staff, headed by Park Turner, devised the schedule that included the traditional two-a-day practices but placed them wisely, early in the morning and extreme late afternoon. Never a fan of early rising, the 7:30 AM practices were certainly not my favorites. However, I had made up my mind I was going to do this and persevered.

Playing high school football in the mid-70s was a time when old school practices and beliefs were still very much in effect. The earliest of innovation on equipment was in its infancy stage. Compared to today's gear, the armor we were issued was woefully deficient. There were also fervent opinions on how to do things that are opposites compared to modern day routine procedure. The most moronic of these was a long-standing belief that too much water in the course of the heat, humidity and extreme exertion was somehow detrimental. The nonsensical slogan that was always associated with the unthinkable intake of water during practice was it makes you weak. Of course that did not mean diminishment of physical strength, but indicated forfeiture of character and toughness. So instead of water, we did have a cutting-edge product to keep us hydrated that summer. It was called Quick Kick. It came in these large packets of powder and was supposed to be mixed meticulously with just the right amount of water. On some of those close to 100° days, we would've been happy to drink out of the vats used by Jim Jones and his cult in Guyana. I don't recall who was in charge of that particular function of mixology at our practices, but I do remember the concoction being a little substandard. Basically, during practice, a big mixture would be prepared in giant orange plastic dispensers. Then small Dixie cups were dipped and filled. Never mind that there were frequently blades of grass or other foreign objects floating along with the 4 ounces of the refreshing beverage. I'm sure it was a very germ-free process.

As the endless practice days started to dwindle, excitement built for the start of the new season. Our first game was to be against the new school that had formed and robbed us of half of our classmates in our sophomore year. Dunwoody, the upstart new high school playing their first varsity game. There was much anticipation, even press coverage leading up to the grand event. Of course, all of us knew just about everybody who played for them, and vice versa. What we didn't know, was how haphazard and inept our preparation from our genius group of coaches truly was.

I was delighted to be receiving a lot of mentions in various articles. Of course, that was somewhat prompted by my constant yakking at Coach Turner that I certainly felt deserving of some press. The night before the game, in an article in the Dunwoody Neighbor newspaper, Turner singled me out as "a player we expect a huge contribution from this year." The final part of the quote was, "Keefer has worked really hard and is a tremendous spirit." Man, I was pumped up and ready to go. On game night, we played like a train wreck. We were totally out schemed and beaten soundly. My amazing work ethic and tremendous spirit earned me not a single play on the field. I did, however, have a great vantage point to watch the only real highlight for our team in the game. It was a tremendous diving catch by my boy Mark Random. And, of course, I kept a close eye on all of the moves of the awe-inspiring Peachtree cheerleaders. Without question, they were by far the best team on the field.

The next week, we traveled to Adams Stadium to play Briarcliff. And if it sounds like a school named Briarcliff should probably be lousy at football, well, they certainly were. Basically, we ran them out of the stadium by halftime. Two more scores in the third quarter made it 35 to nothing. The coaches finally decided it was time to unleash their highly spirited, hard-working secret weapon. On our next offensive possession, number 29 in your program, but number one in your heart, raced onto the field for his first varsity football action.

With a 35 point lead, there is not going to be very much razzle-dazzle displayed by a high school offense. Regardless of the score, we ran a very vanilla, dull, unimaginative offense. With the five touchdown cushion late in the third quarter, our milquetoast approach would become even more conservative. In other words, as I split out to my wide receiver position, far from the hitting and contact of the interior lineman, my assignment was to simply run out and perhaps block the cornerback in my area. The exhilaration of the green grass, bright lights, and modest crowd fueled great enthusiasm and adrenaline. On the snap, I rocketed off the line, sprinted eight or 10 steps and heard whistles indicating the end of our one-yard gain running play up the middle. In all the hoopla and excitement, I had not even noticed the defensive player assigned to keep all of my dangerous arsenal of weapons in check. I first became aware of his presence, just as I had slowed down and prepared to sprint back to the huddle to receive the exact same assignment as the play before, to do nothing. It was then, after the whistle, that by far the most notable aspect of my first-ever play would occur. As the striped side judge official waddled in to help spot the football, the combatant in the blue jersey grasped my facemask. Somewhat shocked, I stood there dumbfounded for a second or two. Suddenly, inching up right to my face, he harshly delivered a stern warning. "Don't be thinking you can be running around out here; I own this area, you're not shit." He then proceeded to attempt to emphasize his words by jamming his hand up under my mask and using a couple of fingers in an effort to poke me in the eye. Now a macho self-respecting football player has to take exception to this kind of physical and verbal abuse. And I certainly did. Incredulously, I pushed away from him, but my predominant feeling was bemusement, not anger. So mustering a tone of great indignation, I loudly said to him, "Are you insane? It's 35-0, you guys suck. We're not going to throw the ball." Then I trotted back to the huddle. On the next play, this great defender of wide-open turf that will never be contested came up after the snap and slammed into me with all of his might. Indicative of the athletic prowess of his team, it was not a very powerful blow, so I laughed out loud. On third down, he finally seemed to understand the situation and this time actually angled in seeking to jump on the pile or something in the play. He paid no attention to me after that. So much for my first varsity football game. I was running around on the field uncovered and by myself. What a spectacular debut.

As the season progressed, I saw some sporadic action. In the Lakeside game, one of the best teams in the state,

Random had executed consecutive sneaky blocks known as crack backs on their all state, all everything middle linebacker Rusty Moore. Mark totally wiped him out twice in a row and both times stood over him chastising and trash talking. Pointing to the ground and telling him you might as well stay down there, that's where you're going to be all night long. Needless to say that Random's actions and especially his words did not sit particularly well with Mr. Moore or his teammates. Late in the first quarter, Random caught a pass and was angling for the sidelines being hotly pursued by seemingly all 11 members of the Lakeside defense. It looked like the Indiana Jones scene from Raiders of the Lost Ark, the one where he's running full speed with hundreds of tribesmen just behind in hot pursuit. The mass of purple-clad bodies and gold helmets engulfed him just as he was going out of bounds. Their frenzied anger and full speed momentum carried the group of bodies beyond the bench and onto the adjacent concrete pole vault area. He was literally implanted in the ground with tremendous force by three or four tacklers. His facemask literally shattered into pieces as it made contact with the hard surface. There would be no more crack back blocks on that night. Random's helmet and assuredness of his personal safety were both casualties of the play. I checked in the lineup as a result and had extensive playing time the rest of the way. And the ball was actually thrown to me twice. I wish I could tell you I snagged one of the aerials and charged in for a triumphant touchdown, but telling the truth compels me to admit that I did not haul in either throw. One was knocked away just before it arrived in my waiting arms, and the other, on a play where I was actually wide-open right down the middle, sailed harmlessly and hopelessly over my head.

Several weeks later, it was our major road trip to Athens, to play Cedar Shoals, a team that featured several future Georgia Bulldog stars. In a morning pep rally, the highlight had been the dramatic, choreographed entry of two of our players after the spirited gathering had already started. Since this was a big out of town trip (which is hilarious now with Athens basically now considered a suburb of Atlanta metro), everyone on the team was dressed up. However, none of us were dressed as flamboyantly as my two receiving corps mates Random and Ralph Kinnemore. Ralph, the only African-American player on the team, was wearing an all white outfit. Random was wearing basically the same leisure suit, but his was completely black. Yes, and I did say leisure suit! Embarrassingly, those outfits were all the rage for a brief period in the mid-70s. To see a picture of someone adorned in one now is absolutely laughable. They were both wearing outrageously high platform style shoes. The band cranked up some sort of R&B music as Mark and Ralph made their entrance and methodically strutted together stride for stride, in a slow-moving shuffle that began at the far doors and ended at the stage. We loaded up in buses on game day afternoon and headed northeast. We stopped on the way for our pregame meal. You can tell our booster club fund was overflowing with money as we pulled in to dine at Bonanza. It was a low-level steak chain. The beef still had whip marks where the jockey had been hitting it (my apologies to the late great Rodney Dangerfield for stealing one of his jokes). We arrived in Athens well before game time. I guess they had built-in plenty of time, we certainly would not want to be late for this appointment. There really were no suitable locker room facilities, so we basically congregated in the gym near the stadium. The game was being played at the historic venue in Athens where Hall of Fame quarterback Fran Tarkenton had once piloted the Athens High offense. As we huddled in small groups for pregame meetings, all of a sudden the back doors to the gym burst open and these huge human beings wearing football pants and T-shirts charged onto the floor. There was an array of gymnastics equipment set up, which the invaders immediately started jumping, swinging and catapulting from. These were our opponents, obviously extremely uptight for the game that was just a couple of hours in the future. It was an intimidating sight. Their coaches soon entered and shooed their players out of the gym. But the damage was done, we knew we had no chance.

A half-hour later, our special teams group headed down the hill to the field for the first phase of our warm-up. What an honor it was for me to be on that prestigious unit that first took the field each week. I had very important responsibilities. My job was to stand in the end zone and shag the footballs from warm up kicks. Just as we began that week's ritual, all the lights in the stadium came on as darkness had set in. Everything was routine with me chasing footballs around launched by the kicker and punter. Once retrieved, I had the important responsibility of throwing the ball back so it could be kicked again. Our session would end when the backs and receivers joined us on the field for the next phase of preparation. Those guys were just appearing on the field when one of the last kicks sailed past me and rolled a good distance away up against the fence behind the back of the end zone.

To properly set the scene, the stadium had been built many years before. To say that the set up was a little outdated would be understating the case. As was usually the case, there was a running track circling the entire perimeter of the field. On the edge of the grass and up against the concrete track, approximately every 50 yards or so, there were giant utility poles. At the very top of each was a set of lights. All the poles were connected by these large, fairly low hanging wide wires. As I picked up the errant football, I was suddenly struck with the impulse not to walk it back to the field of play and throw it back to the practice area, but instead, punt it back and challenge myself to reach the area where the other guys were starting the new drills. I assumed the stance, strode forward confidently and boomed a beauty off of my explosive right foot. I had not stopped to consider the aforementioned wires in my path. Predictably, my kick sailed skyward but was almost immediately knocked to the ground due to a solid collision with the obstruction above. As the ball thudded to earth, I took a step in that direction to retrieve it. That is when I noticed that the wire I had contacted was swinging wildly back and forth. It was swaying rapidly enough that I had a brief thought that it may even come loose. I cautiously advanced and then it happened … KABOOM! It sounded like a cannon had been fired. My first thought was that the Cedar Shoals Jaguars were taking the field. But quickly I deduced that my handiwork had been responsible for the explosion. At that very instant, every one of the lights on the poles above the field went dark. There is a great scene in the movie Caddyshack when assistant green keeper Carl, played by Bill Murray, in an attempt to rid the golf course of a pesky gopher, basically blows up the entire place. As the course lays smoldering in ruin, Carl looks around, and then slowly and methodically, slinks away. That is exactly what I did that night from the far end zone. As I innocently arrived in the group of the other players, it did not appear that anyone had witnessed my activities or suspected me as the perpetrator.

It turned out that my pregame play was the best thing anyone in a Peachtree uniform did all night long. I should've been awarded the game ball. After a 45-minute delay, the slaughter began. By the end of the game, the majority of our team was physically injured, and all of us were emotionally scarred with embarrassment. We did not come close to scoring and lost about 30-0. My favorite moment was in the fourth quarter when yet another of our defensive lineman came limping off the field. Defense Coordinator coach, Jimmy Parham, realizing that someone needed to enter the game, turned and looked desperately at our sidelines in hopes of instantly locking on to the right man for the job. Everyone kind of shuffled and looked away, no one was anxious to enter the fray at this stage. Suddenly, the coach bellowed, "Autry, get in there at nose tackle." Lee Autry was a fine athlete. His specialty was baseball where he excelled. In football, he was a little-used running back, now he was being sent in on the defense of line right over the center against these man-children who were destroying us. Lee's response was something I'll never forget. To answer the coach's call, he exasperatingly replied, "Nose tackle? What the hell do I do?" To which Coach Parham encouragingly and famously answered, "Just stay low and play football." That was probably the most brilliant insight and strategy our team had been armed with the entire year.

So now you know the real story. The Night the Lights Went Out In Georgia, it was not the little sister, the one who doesn't miss when she aims her gun. (Who puzzlingly never stepped up and admitted guilt while her brother hanged for the murders she committed.)It was none other than yours truly. Yes, it was I, putting the signature touch on yet another classic Keefer Story.

KEEFER STORY

Dynamic Duo

In all the world's history, it is doubtful that there has ever been a more immediate or seamless friendship fit then Jim Heavern and Kip Keefer. In the first days of our high school careers, fate facilitated the inevitable intersection of our paths. From our very first conversation and recognition that we had countless things in common, we were fast friends right away. This story is about that cohesion and how it served us extremely well in a couple of competitions. But really it extends to much greater territory than that.

We meshed together perfectly in terms of things we enjoyed doing and the way our thought processes complemented one another. Jim is brilliant, analytical and has an imaginative sense of humor. I share many of those qualities. Jim is more guarded and meticulous, whereas my style is to be off-the-cuff and rambunctious. In our school years and beyond, many lines that I blurted out that were well received originated from a quiet comment that Jim privately related to me.

We quickly established certain procedures and rituals that we adhered to without fail. One of the best was our snow day protocols. When there was a chance that school would be called off, for whatever reason, we both closely monitored from our respective stations (our houses) any source that could give us information as to our fate for the status of the impending day of education. There certainly was no Internet, and unlike this era when officials err on the side of caution to the point of absolute absurdity, television was seldom helpful. Local stations were the only broadcast outlets. They all went off the air around 1 AM and did not resume until about six the next morning. As difficult as this is to believe for millennials, most of our information had to come from AM radio. If one of us was able to obtain confirmation that the news was positive, there was a requirement to call the other immediately. There was no preface conversation. The caller conveyed the news by singing the following words:

"No school tomorrow, no school at last. No school tomorrow, it's a pain in the ass!"

As levelheaded and sensible as Jimmy is, when the spirit moved him, he always had the capacity to do something to shock you. His great resolve and personal code of behavior always led him to follow through once he made the decision to go forward. Another word for that would be his stubbornness. Once Jim makes up his mind or takes a stand, he is unwavering.

Sometimes it was something simple. One day in our sophomore year, Jim and I were accosted while wandering the halls by the assistant principal Dewey Holbrook. No really, I did not make that up, he was not an animated character, it was really the man's name. He insisted we accompany him to a nearby classroom presided over by a teacher named Tony Anderson. It was an eighth-grade Georgia history class in session. Holbrook instructed

Anderson to stringently require that Jim and I show up during this period every day for a study hall in the back of his class. Anderson told us he would tolerate no nonsense. Upon entering the classroom he dispatched us to sit in the back of the seating formation completely on opposite sides of the room. We had no books or writing material on our person, so the next 30 or so minutes idly having to sit there seemed like an eternity. After a couple of minutes of this slow torture, I stole a glimpse across the room towards Jim's position. As if he was anticipating my glance, he had already assumed the posture of having a contrived befuddled look on his face and having his hands up in the air in a shrugging gesture simulating incredulity. I immediately cracked up at his antics. I had to quickly look away to keep from busting out emphatically. Some of the eighth graders in the class were already sneaking looks at us wondering what these disruptive goofballs were doing in the back of their class. Undaunted, the teacher Anderson continued to lecture whatever magnificent aspect of Georgia history was being covered that day. Another minute or two passed before I summoned up the courage to look back at Jim. This time, he was not looking at me but had struck a pose to definitely elicit a reaction. He was sitting impassively, looking straight ahead. However, he had his hands crossed but very slowly and methodically was executing the well-known gesture to hasten the passage of time, rotating his thumbs. I laughed out loud. Then, he unclasped his hands, and with clenched fists, slowly started a rotary motion with his hands and wrists, like an official calling an illegal procedure penalty in football, or a basketball referee signaling traveling. I was supposed to be the outrageous funny one, but Jim was killing me. Anderson's authoritarian tone had pushed Heav's buttons and prompted a senseless and stupid response that matched the absurdity of the situation . He had made the decision to push the limits and the repercussions be damned. Bravely, I dared one more peek. Now he was looking right at me again, varying the speed of his arm rotations. It range from super slow motion, to hyper speed. I busted out laughing uncontrollably. He then shifted gears and started doing the motion in reverse. Some of the young class members were also enjoying the spectacle. To try to contain my laughter, I put my head down on the desk. When I looked up a few seconds later, Anderson was coming right towards me. He said something to the effect of how dare I disrupt his class. He told me I had to stand outside the door in the hall for the remaining few minutes. Looking at Heavern on my way out, now he had his head down on the desk trying to suppress laughter for his defiant antics leading to my ejection. Anderson chastised us at the end of the period. He emphatically told us that we would show up every day on time and would conduct ourselves properly. After that day, we never showed up there again.

One Friday night, we were visiting our favorite teacher Trudi and her husband at the time at their sporting goods store they owned. It should be noted that Trudi, then McCullough, now Black, my English teacher, was my all-time favorite educator, and all these years later, someone I think the world of. Jim and I were messing around in the store when we came upon a shelf with boxing gloves. Naturally, we put them on and started playfully jabbing around, mimicking big-time fighters in a ring. After a minute or so the novelty began to wear off, and I sort of stepped back and barely had begun to lower my guard from my face. All of a sudden, I was rocked as Jim delivered a straight right-hand haymaker and busted me right in the mouth. At this point in time, I was wearing a mouthful of metal braces. Orthodontic braces in the 70s were still rather prehistoric. I suppose they were effective, but they felt more like a medieval torture tactic than beneficial, corrective devices. Needless to say, I staggered back and was stunned. I looked at Jim incredulously as I began to taste blood in my mouth. I said something to the effect of, "What the hell?" With an expression which combined a mixture of contrition and bemusement; he replied with a tone befitting for a defense attorney, "I couldn't help it, you left yourself wide-open." Always the fierce competitor, when an edge appeared, he had to seize the advantage. It was just his way.

On two different occasions when he was in one of these moods, I made the poor decision to get in the car with him. The first time was just after a tornado roared through our area, and there was extensive damage particularly to the woods behind our high school. Jim always the inquisitor, wanted to go and assess the damage. As we drove the road that ran behind the high school, still extremely wet from the downpour of the massive storm, we approached a severe curve that we were well familiar with. It was so abrupt, it was almost a 90° angle. Jim was traveling at a decent rate of speed when he suddenly declared, "Not braking." I only had a second or two to absorb the implications of that proclamation. We had already entered the curve and the legendary red gremlin, and its likely well-worn tires, were desperately clinging to the wet roadway. Blessedly Jim had let off the accelerator but steadfastly was sticking to his guns and not using his brakes. About halfway into the curve, the back tires relinquished their grip, and we suddenly felt the odd sensation of going sideways. This only went on for seconds, but it felt much longer than that. It was pretty obvious at that instant that we had entered into a full-fledged spin. By this time speed had diminished greatly, and thankfully the car was losing momentum. Mercifully, after a few more torturous seconds, the realization struck me that we had come to a stop. The car was still upright but was now facing back in the direction we had just come from about three-quarters of the way through the curve. I looked at Jim, who sat there with a silly grin on his face. No question was necessary, he just reiterated, "I told you, I wasn't braking."

On another occasion, Jim dropped by late night after taking his future wife Craige home for our late-night catch-up session. On many of these evenings, others would already be present, but on this particular midnight hour, it was just me. Jim and I chatted for a while, and then it was decided that I would ride back over to his house and spend the night. As we pulled out of the driveway out onto N. Peachtree Rd., Jim did not make a right turn, which was the route to his house. Instead, he went straight across into the elementary school parking lot across the street. It was there that he declared there was something he'd been wanting to do, and this seemed to be a good time to give it a shot. He declared his intention to drive to his house, which was three or four miles away, totally in reverse. Momentarily forgetting his unwavering, unassailable will, I basically left off the notion. Seconds later as we backed onto North Peachtree I was no longer chuckling. Incredibly, we proceeded at a decent speed, in the correct lane, but going backward. When North Peachtree hit Peeler Road, he accomplished the necessary maneuver to the right and we continued to proceed. Only a handful of cars passed us going the other direction, all of them moving forward. It was not until the last half-mile or so that a car heading in our direction came up behind us. If there were any thoughts of aborting the mission because of this complication, they were quickly dispelled for two reasons. One, we were now within a quarter-mile of the destination, his house. And two, at the fork of Peeler and Tilly Mill roads, the intruder who had the audacity to try and interrupt this spectacular attempted greatness, opted to bear right why we veered left. We were in the homestretch, and it was wide-open spaces. As Jim backed down the hill on his street, he must have felt like Charles Lindbergh, landing the Spirit of St. Louis in Paris culminating the first transatlantic flight. In that ten- minute endeavor, he had made the transformation, from merely a man to a legend.

The individual and collective attributes that the team of Jim and Kip featured are best defined by two of our finest competitive hours. In the summer of 1978, our pal Steve Hardy was home for the summer from college. He was attending Coastal Carolina, in Myrtle Beach, South Carolina, on a basketball scholarship. For fun, and to stay in shape, Steve, and Random, began playing tennis regularly. For some reason, one weeknight evening, Jim and I agreed to go with them and perhaps play some doubles. It needs to be said here, that as tennis players, Jim and I were not very skilled. Both of us were good athletes, but the game of nets and racquets was not something we spent any time pursuing.

After much discussion on how we would configure teams, somehow it was decided that Mark and Steve would team up and play us. If Las Vegas was making a betting line, suffice to say, Heavern and I would have been a monumental underdog.

The match began, and our stylish opponents clearly had the edge. At some point in the match, Jim and I decided that we were just going to play super aggressively, particularly at the net. Somehow after eight games, the set was tied 4-4. The favorites were showing some cracks in their foundation as they squabbled with one another as to who had caused points to be lost. Jim's steely competitiveness and a good sequence for me as far is being lucky enough to be properly positioned at the net on numerous occasions started to pay off. Up 5-4, somehow we were serving to win the set. I don't remember the specifics, but I know there were endless deuce situations in the deciding game. And I remember the instant of our winning point as being one of those shots that hits the tape at the top of the net and grudgingly falls like dead weight just to the other side of the opponent's court. The giants had been vanquished. Like David and his slingshot, American revolutionaries against the British, Harry Truman, Joe Willie Namath, and the '69 Jets, the miracle on ice 1980 US Olympic hockey team and Buster Douglas, Heavern and I had shocked the world.

Mark and Steve argued for a moment as Jim and I wildly celebrated by indulging in the time-honored tradition of leaping over the net in victory. We were immediately assailed with what a fluke our victory was, how lucky we had gotten and bitter taunts that we both sucked. That all may have been true, but we had the scoreboard on our side. After a water break, I walked back on the court and Mark was urging us to get in position for the second set. I looked over at Jim, who was sitting contentedly up against the fence, elbows on his knees. We all were looking at him for a moment, wondering what he was waiting for. In an agitated tone, Random implored him to come on. What Jim did next is still one of his most classic of moments.

Jim said matter-of-factly, "I don't see any reason for us to play again." Random and Hardy immediately went ballistic. They protested and vehemently reminded him that tennis was a two out of three set proposition. But Heavern had made up his mind, declaring that we had won, and he wasn't going to play again. True to form, I was anxious for another set, thinking that if we could beat them again, there would be no doubt who ruled the world, well, at least, the Doraville tennis courts. However, Jim had reasoned, and almost certainly accurately so, that the chances of us duplicating the perfect storm of circumstances that led to our stunning victory were highly unlikely to materialize again. He concluded that getting stomped in the second set, or coming up on the losing side at all, would greatly take away from our glorious triumph. He was not going to play, and no matter how much Mark and Steve tried to appeal, cajole and browbeat him into changing his mind, it was not going to happen.

Random became furious, and he and Hardy stormed off the court. They walked directly to Mark's car, hopped in and noisily pulled away, slinging gravel as they left the parking lot. In a defiant huff, Mark had left us to emphasize his disgust and anger. After it had become apparent that they had really left us, Jim and I looked at one another and immediately busted out in uncontrollable laughter. We recounted every detail as we began the two-mile walk to his house. To this day, I'm not sure what was more satisfying, especially for Jim, our stunning upset or Random's post game actions.

Many years later, in 2006, I had driven over on an October Friday to Jim's house from Birmingham. We were going on Saturday to a Georgia/Tennessee game in Athens. I arrived early afternoon and Jim told me that we were going to play golf in an hour or so with our friends Rod and Dave. Jim lived in the same neighborhood, and they frequently played golf together. I had been there a number of times and participated in playing in the past. I also knew both those guys well from many years of annual golf trips that all of us were included in.

Jim and I would be playing Rod and Dave in a golf game called a Nassau. That basically means the outcome is based on three factors. Which team wins the first nine holes, which team wins the second nine holes, and the team that wins the overall 18-hole total. However, rules imposed by Rod allowed for unlimited presses. Each press is an additional bet that can be declared and must be accepted at the beginning of each hole. It was not unusual in these games for there to be nine or 10 bets working by the end of the match.

As we warmed up, Jim gave me a pep talk and told me that he had played with a variety of partners in recent months against these two and was on a terrible losing skid. Even playing with outstanding partners, Rod and Dave somehow always found a way to come out on top in the betting game. This was particularly annoying for Jim since he was clearly the best golfer of the bunch. However, Rod and Dave were incredibly formidable and very difficult to beat. Dave was a former star athlete and could best be described as a ferocious competitor. That trait became particularly apparent in clutch times when he had to come through the most. Meanwhile, Jim told me that Rod had improved considerably from playing so often, and during this hot streak, he had settled into a groove where for stretches during the matches, he came up with some incredible, timely shots.

Jim had partnered with players superior to me and had been recently frustratingly unsuccessful. Golf for me was always a game where I was capable of playing well but was subject to being highly erratic. In other words, I was a good teammate with a steady partner like Jim. In the course of 18 holes, there would definitely be times where I would contribute heavily and other times where I would be a serious liability.

The greatest example of that fact goes all the way back to 1989. Playing with my brother-in-law Rusty Blair, my friends Bobby Henry and Mike Fynmore, we had played amazingly well and won the Oldsmobile Scramble tournament at our club. We qualified for the regional event held in Memphis at the classic Colonial Country Club. We competed against 35 or 40 other teams from three different states. In that round your four-man team also picked up your club pro. In our case that was a very good thing as a young outstanding player, Dick Henken was now in the fold.

I didn't really play very well that day; however, in that one round, I hit perhaps the two greatest golf shots of my life, which also turned out to be two of my most significant. On the same famous par five, where PGA golfer and later extremely popular, colorful TV analyst Gary McCord, once hit five consecutive shots in the lake in front of the green guarding the long par five, I blasted a massive 3-wood shot that carried the water and rolled up onto the green. I was the only one of our five players to clear the hazard. That shot set up an eagle opportunity, which we converted. On the very last hole, we knew we were having a very good scoring round, but were not sure if it was going to be good enough. We figured that we really needed to make a birdie on the narrow, hilly par four. Perhaps feeling the pressure, or just by coincidence, all five of us uncorked really bad drives. Three of the players in our group, including myself, had to hit shots into the woods. Of the two balls still basically in play, neither was in a good position. We faced a 190-yard, blind shot to the green. It was pretty much a hit and hope situation. We did ride up to see the target, but standing over the ball it's a strange feeling to be hitting it to a spot that you really can't see. Everyone hit and the hope was that at least one of the shots had found the green. I had swung hard and hit a laser-like, low to the ground shot that I knew was the right direction. My ever-optimistic brother-in-law, Rusty, immediately declared, "That's no fucking good." Actually, this time, he was wrong, very wrong. Arriving at the green, we were all flabbergasted to see a golf ball proudly perched five or six inches from the hole. It was my no fucking good shot. We tapped it in for a birdie and went to turn in our card in hopes that our score was good enough. We soon learned that we would be involved in a three-team playoff. The unlikely, miraculous birdie we had made on the final hole had tied for first place with two other teams. Suddenly, my shot looked better than ever. Whichever team prevailed would be moving on to the national Oldsmobile Scramble PGA tournament at Disney in Orlando.

Two of our guys hit great shots to set up a five or six-foot birdie putt. We learned as we arrived at the green that the other two teams had made par. If we made this birdie, we were going to Florida. Putting second in our rotation, I actually was the player that knocked in the fairly easy putt. Our triumph was so unlikely against many large, upscale, hoity-toity clubs. Meadowbrook Country Club, from West Memphis, Arkansas, was going to the big dance.

Jim had actually brought his family down to Disney and walked with us for one of our rounds in the tournament. It was one of the great experiences you could ever describe to be in that tournament. All the participants were treated like professional golfers. Our families had a wonderful time as we had the run of the Magic Kingdom as well. The tournament was contested over three days, and the top 20 teams out of the 90 in the event were allowed to advance to the final round. Those teams would then be paired with the PGA Tour player. Unfortunately, we didn't play very well there, but just being in the event was an unbelievable experience and once in a lifetime accomplishment.

Back to the historic clash at Château Elan, 17 years later. In the early parts of the match, Team Kip/Jim was rolling. We seized an early lead and took advantage of the fact that our opponents were not playing well, certainly not up to their capability. Several new bets were started from the aforementioned press policy. As we reached the conclusion of the first nine holes, Jim and I were ahead on each of the four bets that were active. Through the first 15 holes, we had won our share, tied on most, but lost outright on not a single one. Heavern was solid and steady as usual. I also was playing fairly well, satisfyingly stepping in once or twice at important moments when Jim actually needed some help. In golf, the term is "brother-in-lawing" meaning partners are alternating in picking one another up. It felt like we were totally dominating the match.

Rod had continued to lob a flurry of presses. The stretch leading up to the last three holes, as darkness started to descend, had come out even. On the 16th hole, a Rod miracle, similar to what Jim had described on the driving range, seemingly came out of nowhere. From a difficult spot in the trees, he had a miraculous shot just a foot or two from the hole and recorded a birdie. It was the first hole that their team had won all day, but with the unique betting situation, that one winning hole had dramatically tightened the game.

After a tie on the 17th, resulting from Jim rolling in a testy pressure putt, we teed off on the last hole. Jim had furiously calculated all of the scenarios posed by the outcome of the last hole. If we won it or even tied, we would win the match. But, I was shocked to hear, if they beat us on 18, they would come out one bet ahead. It seemed ridiculous to me that we could theoretically only drop two holes out of 18 and still be declared the loser.

They had the honors and hit first. Rod sliced his shot into the trees to the right. Dave had a usable shot in the left rough. For the only time in the entire match, Jim mishit his tee shot. He uncorked a big hook into the deeper trees on the left. Now with pressure on, on a rare occasion with Jim in trouble, I needed to deliver. I busted one right down the middle. I was feeling a little bit of righteous indignation that we could play so well and be threatened with "losing." Basically, it came down to Dave and myself with our respective playing partners in trouble. Dave was able to advance his ball from the deeper grass but came up short of the green. I had a short iron in and hit it solidly but pushed it slightly right and received an unkind bounce from a small hill surrounding the green. It fed the ball down about 15 yards off the green parallel to the flagstick. Dave's third shot wound up just off the back of the green but a good 60 or 70 feet from the hole. I had a short pitch shot that I had to get far enough to clear the hill to make sure I got on the putting surface. I could not afford to be short. I hit a really nice shot, but on the fast green it slid past the hole, stopping about 30 feet away. Needing only to tie the hole, it appeared I had a complete advantage.

To his credit, Jim had battled back and actually had a long putt for par. He knocked it up close and recorded a five. That removed all pressure for me, since the only way we could possibly lose, was if Dave was able to make his putt from another area code. He walked around and studied it, went to his golf ball, took his position and sent the sphere on its way through what was now total darkness. I have memories of watching that putt roll seemingly forever. Incredibly, in what felt totally surreal and almost bad dream-like, the putt gently settled into the cup. The overjoyed reaction from Dave and Rod was quickly drowned out by the wounded wails of my lifelong best buddy, Jim. Heavern had literally keeled over and was lying flat on his back on the ground declaring over and over, this is what always happens. He also threw in a couple of shouts of "I can't believe it." The feat of Dave making that putt was one of the most remarkable things I have ever witnessed in any level of sports, whether it be fandom or participatory. Their team had made an impossible, and miraculous, four. After soaking in what had just happened for 10 or 12 seconds, it occurred to me that I still had a putt to hang up that same score.

It's hard to describe what was going through my mind at the time. I didn't feel trepidation or pressure, and I really didn't spend a lot of time grinding over my assignment or even carefully analyzing it. Jim had recovered enough to ask me if I thought it was going to break any particular direction, and I replied it looked like straight in. Seconds later, I stood over it, stroked it and sent it on its way. I had made sure to hit it hard enough to get it to the hole. With the game on the line, leaving it short would, of course, give it no chance to go in. It felt like I had whacked it too hard. The ball barreled toward the hole, and much like a rabbit trying to elude a predator when it reached the entry point to safety, it simply dove right in. Standing in place, I raised my arms triumphantly, and in the next instant absorbed the blunt force of my leaping partner jumping into my arms in celebration! Truth, justice, and the American way had indeed prevailed. Ding Dong the wicked witches were dead, their streak of otherworldly dominance ended. Their latest miracle finish, while indisputably spectacular, had been defused and rendered meaningless in the final results. Of course, I was extremely happy to come through, but to this day, my satisfaction over that second in time was seeing Jim's reaction and knowing I had done something meaningful for him.

I had felt similarly a few years before but in circumstances that were far more significant. It was on the heartbreaking occasion of his dad's funeral. Being very close to Jim Sr. myself, I was tremendously honored when Jim and his family asked if I would speak at the service. I stepped up on that day and delivered a heartfelt, personalized eulogy, which is always a highly emotional and difficult task. I felt when it was concluded that I had emphatically contributed something impactful at an incalculably important time.

Sometimes, I think about how different my life would have been had I not crossed paths with James Neville Heavern Jr. I think it's safe to say that neither of us would be the same person that we turned out to be without the influence of one another. I can't help but feel that I was the greater beneficiary, that's a tribute to what an extraordinary person this guy is. Even though the demands of career, family, and geographic distance have severely limited our own personal interaction since adulthood, there is one absolutely undeniable fact that is always a source of tremendous reassurance and comfort.

Jim and I are kindred spirits and a duo that will always be a force to be reckoned with. On that September day in 1970, I not only became friends with Jim Heavern, I signed on with a fellow who has been since that day, and always will be, the best friend a guy could ever have.

Post 5

Industrious Lads

"I'm proud of the fact that from an early age, I did not automatically buy into "conventional wisdom." When I was told that something was not possible or achievable, my inclination was to try and find a way to prove that conclusion wrong. I soon found others inclined to the same kind of thinking. The first rule of being a hustler is to try and make something happen while rejecting the notion that it can't be done. Even though success is not always assured, one critical tenant is vital ... There is no need to fear failure because it is not an option."

As teenagers, my friends and I were extraordinarily enterprising young men. Through a combination of ignorance, swagger, and really not caring what anybody thought about us, we formed our alliance. One of the greatest things about my collection of best friends and myself was that we all had unique gifts to contribute individually that made us a formidable force collectively. Jim was a classic thinker, planner, and analyzer, Mark, audacious, fearless, and cocky. Joe, thoughtful, trustworthy and game for anything. Hardy, confident, inquisitive and ambitious. I was the organizer, the extrovert, always determined not to acquiesce to conventional wisdom. Together, five suburban kids enjoyed a magnificent, constantly active run through their teenage years.

Perhaps our greatest achievement was to carve out an amazing system to be able to attend countless Atlanta events that generated lots of fun, often times even making profit while doing it. Not a single one of us came from homes of significant means, but we consistently lived the high life nonetheless.

The National Hockey League Atlanta Flames began playing at the now defunct Omni in Atlanta in 1972. During the second half of that initial season, Jim and I started attending games. It was problematic because neither of us was old enough to drive so we had to scramble for various means of transportation. It was always a challenge to find rides to get downtown for games. During the course of that eight or 10 games we attended, we were hooked. The sport was exciting, brand-new to the south and wide open. We couldn't wait until the beginning of the 1973 season.

Of course, the big game changer that fall involved the fact that we were turning 16, and some of our friends had already arrived at that threshold. That meant drivers' licenses that equated to mobility. Mark, with a late February birthday, had been driving us around all summer. He did take advantage of his position as our primary driver by constantly demanding gas money and or mandatory treating at our various food stops. When that season began in October, I had received my license and was now able to transport groups of our friends down to the games. We began a string of attendance that stretched across the next three seasons that basically involved hardly ever missing any home games. Flames games became our primary social function. Everything was centered around those exciting nights at the arena. The crowd was hip and always excited, the team was young, dynamic, and feisty. It was largely comprised of a ragtag bunch of expansion players and some heralded young rookies. In just their second year of existence, the Flames made big progress and shockingly advanced toward a playoff berth. They played hard, were extremely scrappy, and when I say that I also mean they were perfectly willing at all times to drop the gloves and commence fighting the opposition.

Our small group began to expand as other people tagged along and got hooked like we were. It wasn't unusual for three or four carloads of our friends to eventually make it down to the games. My 1975 or third full season in action, it was certainly not unusual to have up to 30 or 40 people we knew from our school and immediate social circle on hand. We could account for their presence in two ways. Number one, we arrived early for every game so we could set up shop at various points around the arena. We had gotten extremely experienced as to the right places to work the crowd as we wheeled and dealed looking for tickets. We would belt out things like "Flames can't win till we get in." And, of course, the tried-and-true, "Who's got extras!" During the frenzied approach to our pregame process of acquiring tickets, selling tickets, and working for just the right single ticket to get each of us in, we would pretty much run in to everybody we knew either working the same angle or coming to attend the game on tickets 1 acquired elsewhere. At the end of the first and then again second periods, we had a gathering spot in the Omni. These gatherings in the corridor at Portal 44 became legendary. There was enthusiastic discussion, game analysis, planning for the next several days social activities, and of course, the acquisition of refreshments. Tuborg Beer and Omni Pizza were the prized items.

The ritual of acquiring tickets to each game was both uniquely challenging and extremely gratifying. In all of the years that I was dispatched to go to games, only once was I ever denied and unable to come up with a ticket. It was April 1974, the last regular-season home game of the year. The Flames were hosting the hated New York Rangers and had to win on that Friday night in order to stay alive in the playoff race. The team's unexpected success had really set Atlanta on fire. For the first and only time ever, tickets were gobbled up faster than I could acquire them. The other problem was it was truly a sellers' market, which was unusual for hockey games in Atlanta. As devoted as we were as fans, our economics and ethics prevented us from spending a lot of money for seats. That of course, was also coupled with the fact that, typically, we didn't have hardly any money, especially in 1974. Many others were successful that night in getting in and witnessed a fantastic game. Late in the first period, I found a door toward the back of the building that one of the curtains at the portal was open. Incredibly, I could see the net minder and the goal at the far side of the arena from that doorway and the scoreboard. Talk about a big-time fan, I laid on my stomach for almost half an hour watching only when the action shifted that far in, but I knew the time left and the score by assuming that position. Of course, we were a long way from cell phones and communication devices at that point, it was the only way to keep up with what was going on. Unfortunately, shortly after the second began, and overzealous usher emerged and closed the curtain. It was infuriating. Mercifully with 10 minutes left in the game, the doors of the Omni were opened up. I was able to witness the final 10 minutes of the season as the Flames, despite a constant barrage of offensive of effort in the final moments, fell short in a 3-2 heartbreaker, eliminating them from the playoffs.

But every other night, it did work. As mentioned, we would arrive two hours early, assume various positions around the parking decks and the main arteries of where people came to the games. Some of the folks who were regular attendees started actually looking for us, and if they had an extra ticket would oftentimes just give us one or charge us a very nominal amount. We would also solicit offers from others that had tickets to sell, and managed to buy tickets at greatly reduced prices. We deduced that a lot of these were corporate tickets or Ducketts that had been given to these people for free. If they could score 15 or $20 for two tickets, they were happy. The good news was, so were we, because we could turn those into cash money. Acquiring a valuable pair of tickets gave you something that you could really do some business with. A pair of tickets you bought for $15 could frequently be sold for closer to their face value to someone else looking for a pair of seats. So it wasn't unusual for us to get 25 or $30 for those tickets and make a nice tidy profit. Again, the trick was simply acquiring a single ticket to get into the game, and then working toward either improving that seat in terms of its position or hoping that economics worked out to allow for a profitable and fun evening at the game.

Our proficiency increased with every game and every season. We became far more immersed in the culture of Atlanta hockey. By that time, we had finished high school and were all young adults. The drinking age then was 18 and that was a whole new world to explore. The Flames acquired a player from Toronto named Tim Ecclestone. In his second season in Atlanta, Ecclestone opened a terrific sports bar and after the game hangout in Marietta that he named Timothy Johns.

The social fabric of game nights had never been better. We would arrive as per usual and ply our trade out front, wheeling and dealing for tickets. We'd attend the games, continue to congregate at portal 44, and after hopefully securing an Atlanta victory, stop by next door at the Omni International/CNN Center to a small bar called The Hatchery. It was the first stop post game for us and many of the hockey players. We were able to get to know several of the guys on our own, but meantime one of the girls in our group, Debi, had begun dating a Flames defenseman named David Shand. By mid-season, we knew quite a few guys on the team. We were in a small group talking to our Flames pal Harold Phillipoff. He was a hardnosed, tough enforcer who played and partied all out. He was our guy. Hanging out with him one post game, he introduced me to a veteran forward, Gene Carr. He had just been acquired by the team and was talking to me, Harold, and several of our inner circle including Jim, and Mark. Who knew, that moments later we would be engaged in the largest indoor peanut throwing battle in modern American history? The Hatchery featured giant buckets of peanuts on every table. From across the room, another Flame's player, Bobby Simpson, started lobbing peanuts from the opposite side of the bar, trying to hit Harold on the head. Of course, he eventually returned fire. Next thing we knew, everyone on our side of the bar was squaring off with everyone on the other side. The air suddenly became thick with flying goobers. Running low on ammunition, I made a bold decision. Grabbing a half-filled bucket and putting an empty bucket on my head like a helmet, I charged toward the enemy and poured upon them massive fire as I advanced.   With my head lowered to deflect incoming shots that they were firing, I was able to invade their side, grab two full buckets, and return successfully to my allies. The battle raged for several more minutes and became a legendary chapter in Atlanta sports history lore. I never received a decoration or award for my heroism, but I did win the undying respect from my comrades.

On most nights after the Hatchery, the next stop was usually the world famous Varsity Drive-In. After all, no matter how socially relevant a guy is, a chili dog is still hard to turn down. Weekend games usually meant a fairly immediate transition to Timothy John's, Ecclestone's establishment. We were part of a young Atlanta in-crowd.

We also became more brazen with age. Hanging around later and exploring the back halls, nooks, and crannies of the arena, we found passages that led to promised lands, such as sometimes unlocked doors to dressing and locker rooms. Security was sparse, and we knew how to stay out of sight until most of the activity died down.

One Friday night, after a hockey game, we somehow found ourselves in the dark and quiet Atlanta Hawks basketball locker room. They were out of town, and lockers were secured. We rummaged around and found some wristbands, tape rolls, nothing special. We scattered out the back when we thought we heard someone unlocking the main door. We scrambled out of there and returned to our respective vehicles, parked in various locations and headed for my house, the designated meeting spot. Four or five of us had been there for quite some time, and Random had not yet shown up. We began to speculate and expressed concern that perhaps Mark had been accosted or even detained in trying to escape from the Omni. Those fears were allayed just moments later as the indestructible Dodge Dart wheeled into the driveway. We pressed him with questions as to where he had been, and also sought to find out if he had any difficulty in getting out. He explained that he had tried to go out a back way through what looked like some sort of laundry room. Then he added, "But I did find something while I was back there." He took a step back, lifted his sweatshirt up over his head and revealed the prize he had collected. It was an authentic Atlanta Hawks game jersey, number 44 with "Pistol" in the name area. Ole Smilin' Jack, our boy Marky Doodle Dandy, was wearing a Pete Maravich game jersey. He immediately broke into an invigorated version of the Random Jig, the bizarre Happy Dance only unleashed to display unbridled joy and exuberance for the most noteworthy occasions. His odd little two-step, arms thrusting motion was appropriate for several reasons. It was an amazing treasure, and little did he realize at the time, it was an item that proved to be of tremendous value. Approximately 30 years from that moment, he would sell that jersey to a collector for an astonishing sum of money.

Our collective expertise was not limited to only sporting events. Utilizing similar techniques and at times stumbling upon unexpected opportunities and capitalizing upon them, we were able to attend an astounding array of top-flight concerts. Knowledge of the Omni played a part in three of our most interesting stories involving accessing events.

When the band Aerosmith first stormed on the scene in the mid-70s, their popularity was an incredible phenomenon. Our group like them okay, but to say we were even fans would've been a stretch. But when they came to the Omni in the winter of 1977, we felt compelled to go down and see we could do on the old ticket market. Shockingly to us, the answer to that question was, absolutely nothing. The average age of the crowd was 18 to 21 and those people were clutching their tickets like the greatest trophies they could possibly ever earn and had no interest in any kind of negotiation. And the worst case scenario for ticket hustlers is a sellers' market. The professional scalpers that always littered the area were in all their glory on these rare locations. They could demand and receive absurd markups on even the worst of tickets. It became obvious that we were not going to wedge any tickets loose in this most undesirable environment. Remember there were no Internet sales, just telephone and showing up at ticket outlet locations. This tour had sold out in literally moments.

Undeterred, we decided to take a shot at walking around the entire arena to consider our options. Our knowledge of the building from all of the hours we spent there was always a very strong resource and hold card for our efforts. We found ourselves in the area of the double doors that led to the entry hallway for sports teams and personnel. The area was deserted, no one insight, no activity taking place. We tried the door, of course, it was locked. But instead of stepping away and moving along, Mark suddenly stepped up and knocked on the door like he was an Amway salesman or Girl Scout peddling cookies. When Jim, Joe and I heard the distinctive noise of the door being opened, we stepped to the side leaving Random alone in the doorway. The guard who opened the door, a young African-American neatly dressed in his uniform, eyeballed Random warily. The question that emanated from Mark's lips had to have shocked him because it's directness and simplicity was completely unexpected.

"Will you let me in?"

The guard, of course, responded, "No, I can't do that. I'll lose my job." Mark countered, pointing out that no one was around and nobody would ever know. Listening to all this, I can't tell you how surprising it was to hear the next thing uttered by the guard.

"Okay then, come on in."

Random stepped in, and we stepped out into the open. Mark asked his new reluctant partner in crime if his friends could come in too. He grudgingly relented, and the four of us broke into a dead sprint down the deserted hallway. We went to a corridor we were familiar with which led out to the far corner of what usually served as an entrance to the hockey rink. Floor access was being controlled from the bottom steps of the seating areas. As we worked along the floor seats we soon were in view of the stage. There were lots of people we knew who had paid top dollars to sit up in the nosebleed sections of the Omni and watch Steven Tyler and the boys do their thing. We watched the entire show from a tremendous vantage point on the floor absolutely for free. The only cost was audacity, invaluable nerve, and the cockiness of our friend Random.

Incredibly, just a few months later in the summer, we actually outdid ourselves and, this time, had even a better vantage point for a show that all of us desperately wanted to attend. The Eagles were riding perhaps at their highest point. Their string of hits was unbelievable, and their tour was highly anticipated. The band they had signed as their opening act, shortly before the tour, in the interim, hit it big. All these years later, it seems almost inconceivable that the Eagles and Fleetwood Mac appeared on the same concert bill.

As was the case with Aerosmith, the ticket market was tighter than tight. Prices were outlandish and seats were scarce, to say the least. After our miraculous admission to that previous show, we unrealistically thought that maybe it would work again. Confidently, we returned to the scene of the previous crime. This time, the knock on the door was answered immediately by an older, Caucasian gentleman. Upon receiving our request to be let in, the guard basically scoffed, laughed, snarled and told us to get the hell out of there. He then quickly closed the door.

Seemingly defeated, we trudged further into the back areas of the huge arena. The opposite far back side of the building served as a loading dock area but also had an inclined walkway that facilitated an entry for performers and VIPs. It was heavily secured, and we stood around for a while watching how things operated. It was nearly show time for Fleetwood Mac, and the activity in that area was fairly benign since anyone who was on hand as part of the show was already inside. We followed Random to the loading dock area where an African-American guard with a walkie-talkie and nice sports coat, shirt and tie attire minded the entrance to the ramp. His demeanor and body language reminded me of how the troll must've looked in fairytales when unfortunate souls tried to cross his bridge. Random, still engaged the gentleman in a conversation and pulled the million-dollar question once again.

"Is there any way that you let us in?"

The man responded professionally, "Only if you have credentials." He only became agitated when Random followed up with his appeal that no one would even know. The man's tone changed abruptly.

"Why in the hell would I risk my job to do anything for you? You have been oppressing my people for 200 years."

Seeing an opportunity to unleash our smart ass selves, we began to question the man as to his opinions. Amazingly, the guy sort of lightened up. At one point, I expressed that it would've been difficult for me to oppress people for the past 200 years since I was only 20 and my voice had only changed a couple of years before. He finally got sick of us and shooed us away. Seemingly out of luck, we had just stepped back behind the first line of cars to consider our options when fate once again smiled brightly upon us. A gigantic white stretch limousine pulled into the area and pulled up just between our position and the ramp. Doors started opening and three or four scruffy looking characters started to climb out. The exiting figure from the door closest to us was a slender, long-haired guy adorned in his sunshades, despite the fact that it was nearing evening. He looked at us quizzically and we nodded our acknowledgment. He took a couple steps toward the front of the car and then stopped abruptly, turning to us. What he said next was one for the record books.

"Hey, do you guys want some passes for the show?" Of course, you know our enthusiastic reply. He went back to the door that he had emerged from, shuffled around inside for just a bit and produced stage passes for the Eagles/Fleetwood Mac show. These were the lanyard kind that had strings around them that you threw over your head and wore around your neck. As we approached the antagonist on the ramp, Random insisted on going first and with an evil grin said, watch this! He broke into this silly strut that would've made James Brown proud. As he reached his friend the security guard, with his thumb and forefinger he lifted his pass up to face level to make sure the fellow got a good look at it. The astonished guard was not even capable of comment, and Mark continued his blatant sashay as he climbed the ramp successfully. Moments later, just at the very front edge of the stage, we witnessed the opening song from Fleetwood Mac.

We were literally just yards away from Stevie, Christine, John, Mick and Lindsey. I felt very certain that I made a telepathic connection with Stevie that evening and we sealed a solemn bond that she would come to find me at some point in the future. Oh well, 38 years later, I'm still waiting. Their show and the Eagles that followed were indescribably great. We had the same access to Glenn Frey, Don Henley, Joe Walsh and others. That event sealed the deal, we were the Masters at gaining access to anything and everything in the sports and entertainment world. In other words, truly legends in our own minds.

KEEFER STORY

Holiday Hijinks

A couple of weeks before Christmas 1978, Random and I, after an evening of Flames hockey and I'm sure quite a few cocktails at some local establishments, headed back toward our shared apartment in the wee hours. We were living in the Northwest area of Atlanta at the time in an apartment. Our third roommate, of course, was none other than my dad, Dollar Bill. During our year or so there, dull moments were few and far between. We always had people over or some kind of competition being staged. It wasn't unusual for me to come home from work to find my dad and Random engaged in a high-stakes dart showdown, or some other manly challenge matching their skills. It seems these battles typically would be organized after both had enjoyed, and continued to imbibe in some powerful adult refreshments. The usual result was, Random would find some sort of way to win and be excused from making the rent payment at the first of the month as the spoils.

On this night, we were speeding along in Mark's Scirocco up West Paces Ferry. It is the exclusive, old money section of Atlanta. There are a number of spectacular homes along that stretch of road, many that have been there for a number of years. Included in that group is the Georgia governor's mansion. It's a big impressive estate sitting majestically behind beautifully maintained grounds and a giant iron fence all around the perimeter. Cutting over to Marietta from downtown, it was not unusual for us to be on this route. But on this particular late evening, early morning, for whatever reason, Mark did something completely unexpected as we passed the mansion. He slowed down and suddenly pulled over against the curb. Confused as to what was going on, I looked at him quizzically, and he simply said, "Let's go look at those." I had no idea what he was talking about.

We hopped out of the car, which was still running and were greeted by the sight of a festive, lavishly decorated scene. Bright, colorful, twinkling lights hung from the massive house, in the trees and along the fence line. However, what had caught Random's attention were six or eight gigantic Christmas wreaths, spaced evenly all along the front fence. We walked up to closely inspect one of them. In circumference, they were as big around as a 19th-century wagon wheel. To our amazement, we discovered that everything that was part of this wreath was natural. These perfectly circular decorations were actually very sophisticated hanging shrubberies. It was made out of Pine, Holly and other decorative to shrub material perfectly weaved together. Incredibly, it was then decorated with an array of actual fruits and nuts of seemingly any and all varieties. The highlight was in the top center, which featured a full-scale, large pineapple. I really can't explain why, but to two slightly inebriated 21-year-olds, riding around at 2 o'clock in the morning, this item was mesmerizing.

Random studied the ornate item and started walking around it, even hoisting himself up on his toes to get a look at the top. I did not suspect at that moment what he was looking at, but it became clear when he said simply, "This will lift right off of here; we're taking this." Any thoughts that he may have been simply testing the waters to gauge my reaction, or actually joking, was quickly clarified when he lifted up the bottom of the wreath and told me to reach up to the top and lift the cord attached to the back of the spike at the top of the fence. Upon my completing that mission, Random still raising the base up in the air, stumbled back from the weight of the colossal shrub. I quickly secured the top half and we carried our prize the few short steps to the car.

This thing was so big, there was no way it was going to fit into the car. It was quickly decided that the only way to transport it back to our apartment was to lay it on the roof. Since we had not preplanned any larceny, theft or possible offense, we could do three to five years in the state prison for that night; we had not brought anything to secure a payload on top of the car. No, this was going to require basic old-fashioned strategy. Despite the December chill, I would pretty much have to lean out the passenger window and clamp down the right side of our prize while Mark, steering with his right hand, would need to hoist himself up enough on the driver side to secure the holiday decoration with his left arm. The plan was quickly deployed and away we went. If the sight of a German sports car, rolling down the street in the early Atlanta Saturday morning hours captured anyone's interest, we were oblivious. Fifteen minutes later, we pulled up in front of our bachelor pad at the Cumberland Club Apartments and triumphantly brought our new acquisition to our front door. Using the same attachment on the back we had dislodged, we strung the monstrosity over the top of our door. It was a sight to behold.

The wreath in all its glory hung down from the very top of the door, three-quarters of the way down to the bottom of the door. It was so wide that on either side of the doorframe, the sides protruded two feet on each side beyond its width. To enter the apartment, one was required to reach through the opening in the middle of the wreath, maneuver a key to the lock, step to the right and pull back that side of the shrub far enough sideways to limbo yourself inside. Random and I had further cemented our infamous legend. People came from miles around to see it and appreciate its magnificence. Governor George Busby may have been angry that one of his decorations had been stolen, but arguably more citizens of Georgia were able to enjoy it up close and personal with that hanging on our apartment door.

Of course, it never occurred to us that we could've potentially faced big trouble had our caper gone awry in any way. Someone could easily have ratted us out. But the miracle of the 1978 holiday season featured no such Grinch or Scrooge interventions. Sadly, just after New Year's, we grudgingly conceded that our glorious Christmas treasure, with some of its decorative fruit features visibly starting to rot, had to be permanently retired. In a sad ending to a magnificent saga, we unceremoniously discarded the wreath in the dumpster.

We never attempted another heist from the governor's mansion. Perhaps instinctively we knew that any follow up would be tempting fate after the clockwork success of the original, spur of the moment adventure. Sometimes, I think about how dumb we were not to take a picture to chronicle and archive this event. The site of that monstrous wreath, hanging on our door, it would still be hilarious to look at all these years later. Of course, had social media existed, surely someone would've posted that spectacle which probably would've led to big time trouble for Smiling Jack and myself.

In summary, that Christmas unquestionably when we decided to "Deck the Halls," we did it in spectacular fashion. Those pictures in my mind are still vivid, and the memories everlasting. The great holiday hijinks of the late 70s, it was quite the madcap caper that produced not only immense holiday cheer but memories that will last forever.

Post 6

Stage Setter

"I find myself asking an impossible question frequently these days, What if? Is wondering if you would have zigged instead of zagged, stayed put as opposed to leaving or spoken up and not remained silent, would things have turned out differently? If the answer to that question is yes, what about the things that unfurled perfectly as a result of the choices and circumstances that actually did transpire? The answer to all of these questions, it is what it is, there are no answers."

Billy Joel's song, Scenes from an Italian Restaurant, describes that Brenda and Eddie were still going steady in the summer of 75. For me, the summer of 75 involved planning what I would do later that fall. My three-week summer school stand had pretty much eliminated any opportunity to celebrate the conclusion of high school with a trip or other noteworthy event. However, after several years of basically being estranged from my father, contact was renewed and discussions about college plans took place. Dad lived in Memphis and was regional manager for Johnson there. He asked that I travel there to discuss our options.

In late July, Joe Lipham and I set out for our big drive out to visit Dollar Bill Keefer in Memphis. On the night before we were to depart, my dad called and adjusted the plan. Instead of us meeting up with him and staying at his apartment, he now had made arrangements for us to stay at a hotel just off the expressway near his place. Joe and I arrived on the appointed evening and checked in. We heard from my dad early the next morning. It turned out, like Ricky Ricardo, he had some "splaining to do." He revealed that in the just 10 or 12 days prior to our visit, he had decided to remarry. The blushing bride was a woman a few years older than him and by all indications was of considerable means following a lucrative divorce with a local high-profile lawyer. Apparently, Bill had moved a few things over to her stately manor in East Memphis. He went on to explain that the honeymoon went sour pretty much right away. He detected a degree of insanity in her, and she picked up quickly on the fact that his commitment was a little less than airtight. After just four or five days of wedded bliss, Bill retreated to his apartment to sort things out. That afternoon when he returned to the apartment from work, he was greeted with quite an unexpected debacle. Every item in his entire place that was made of glass, his scorned lady had shattered on the ground. Included were ashtrays, drinking glasses, television screens, large liquor bottles, and several mirrors. Hurricane Wanda had visited his abode and the damage was devastating. Of course, that was the day prior to Joe and me embarking on our trip to the river delta city. Needless to say that issues with his now wife were a bit contentious and far from being resolved. After breakfast, we rode over to the apartment where he showed us the carnage. It did fill two rather unworldly inexperienced fellows from the peaceful village of Dunwoody with a little bit of trepidation. Well, that was my reaction. It scared Joe shitless. Particularly when he had added that

Wanda had threatened him. She had told him she had access to the services of two hardcore, African-American enforcers who sometimes handled indelicate matters for her ex-husband. This threat of danger was a little difficult to digest for two dazzling suburbanites visiting this unknown city for the first time. To my indomitable dad's credit, he had a plan to calm our nerves and help us focus on other far more interesting distractions.

When my folks split up and divorced, one of the principal causes was another woman in his life. She was a bartender that he had met downtown at a place he frequented. A couple of years later when he was transferred to Memphis for his promotion, she went with him. Their relationship had soured once she got established in her new home area. Let's just say she attempted to introduce my dad to an active, sexually progressive lifestyle that was even beyond what he could comprehend. The premise of many of these new approaches apparently involved group dynamics. It was clear that she believed that monogamy was a kind of wood. Bill had taken an exploratory walk on the wild side while she pitched a tent and decided to become a permanent resident there. Her fast lane circles had led to meeting some wealthy, mostly Italian, prominent individuals in Memphis involved in a variety of, let's call them, fringe businesses. Some of those investors set her up in her own business. Over by the airport, she was now the proprietor of GIGi's Angels. It was not a religious themed store selling heavenly artifacts, it was exactly what it sounds like, a full-fledged strip club. When we arrived there that afternoon just in time for happy hour, I was 17 years old, Joe was a worldly 18. To say it was a little odd to be introduced to the woman who was co-

conspirator in the home wrecking of my family would be an accurate description of the event. However, at that time, I was not remotely aware of all of the sordid details. She did make a very nice first visual impression, bleach blonde, curvaceous and very friendly. We settled in at a table near the stage where a girl was performing. In just a matter of moments, two large draft beers were placed in front of each of us. The business owner sat with us at our table and we chatted amicably. To characterize it as surreal does not even begin to lend proper credence to that scene. Discussing my plans for the future with my father's sordid former mistress in her club filled with naked women is a plot line that could only be penned by the most bizarre, incredibly imaginative scriptwriter. Suddenly, Bill asked Gigi to entertain Joe, who had been sitting there with kind of a shell-shocked, wide-eyed, bewildered glazed expression as he gazed around this darkened, debauched puzzling alternate universe. Gigi motioned for two"performers" to come on over. Standing between Lipham and me, we experienced the rite of passage and time-honored ritual known as the table dance for the first time. It was quite the eye-opening experience! When the song they jiggled to began, Joe's twin 24-ounce beers were completely full. By the time the song ended, both glasses sat on the table drained and empty. All the color in Joe's face was totally absent. For quite a while, he sat there with a bemused, shell-shocked expression. After several moments of silence, he slowly turned to me and in a quiet, monotone voice said, "Well, that was fun."

An hour or so quickly elapsed, and I mean quickly. Had we stayed for much longer, I'm not so sure that Joe and I would've ever willingly left. But it was time for our next stop on this historic day. Time to head to Southland Greyhound Park, over the bridge in West Memphis, Arkansas for the nightly races. Little did I compute at that time what a stepping stone for the future that would reveal clues to. That night, I was not only introduced to the eventual starting point for my career but also met my future father-in-law, employer and namesake and grandfather of my future children. All in all, a very fateful evening, particularly for someone who was not even legally of age to be there at the ripe old age of 17.

The next day, when my dad made the sales pitch for me to come live in Memphis and go to college at Memphis State, I folded like an accordion when he threw in the deal sweetener that he would provide for me my own vehicle. Up until that point, I had shared a car with my mother. The lure of having my own ride was too powerful. I agreed to come back in a couple of weeks to take the ACT exam and enroll at MSU.

From late August to May that next spring, I attended two semesters at Memphis State University. My dad had moved to a bigger apartment in the same complex as the great glass catastrophe to accommodate our new arrangement. He had managed to annul the marriage with Wanda but still saw her occasionally as unfortunately did I. Sticking to the theme of a bizarre B-movie, we would notice her in a trench coat and dark glasses in the back of a bar or restaurant where we were patronizing. On one occasion, she shuffled up to the table, dropped an envelope and scurried away. Incredibly, the note was addressed to me. Its contents talked about how my presence had taken away Bill's time, attention and affection from her. That was laughable even for my young mind because I was already aware of two new involvements the big fella had going on. I was hardly the distracting factor that monopolized his time. In fact, most of the time in Memphis I was by myself. That fall hockey season was going on in Atlanta and I was exiled to Memphis. The car I had received was a former salesman's big green station wagon purchased from his company. It was wheels, so I didn't really mind, but I was not exactly tooling around in my new community with a babe magnet, prestige ride at my disposal. Not to mention the fact, as a newly turned 18-year-old, where women were concerned, I had no game whatsoever. More on that later.

In the bicentennial year of 1976, at the end of the spring semester, my time in Memphis was done. It was back to my house on N. Peachtree Rd. to resume my rightful spot as one of the leaders of our social organization. I returned like a mafia boss paroled from prison and sought to reclaim my former turf.

That fall, I enrolled at West Georgia College and shared a small house with Joe in Carrollton. However, as close to home as that was and as much fun as it should have been, my lack of finances made it difficult to partake in virtually any activity. My father had provided tuition money and nothing more. After the second semester at West Georgia, I walked away from higher education forever. My path to enlightenment was going to be completely unique and classrooms were not ever again to be involved in the equation.

Certainly there has been much reflection over the years wondering how my life would've turned out differently if I had been supported properly by my parents through their wisdom, experience, guidance and financing. And I certainly do not hang the blame squarely on their shoulders for not providing enough assistance. I was immature, not inspired or driven, and actively pursued the loopholes and shortcuts to beat the system and skate my way through. Outsmarting everyone was the goal, but sadly I really only cheated myself. Bottom line, I was not only lacking support, I was missing something else just as important ... I did not have a clue!

KEEFER STORY

Green Enough

Summer 1976. I returned home from my two semesters of college in Memphis and the veritable exile of living at my dad's. It was an exciting summer shaping up. The Fourth of July that year was going to be America's 200th birthday, the bicentennial. And it was special for the city of Atlanta. In late June, the USGA was bringing the national championship of golf to the Atlanta Athletic Club. The U.S. Open in our fair city! It was a really big deal for obvious reasons, but primarily because it had never been contested in the south before. It was just another emphatic sign of how Atlanta had grown to a full-fledged major sports city in a very short period of time.

I was already intrigued with the idea of somehow being part of this historic occasion. But reality certainly revealed that was a long shot due to the fact that I had limited funding and no connections. My mother was harping on me to find gainful employment, so one Sunday, stretched out on the couch, I read the Sunday Want Ads. In that era, that section of classifieds was absolutely gigantic. The employment ads themselves probably spanned 15 to 20 crammed full pages. Companies and entities who had sprung for a few extra bucks bought display ads, and that's always where I started if I was seeking employment. I figured if they were serious enough to spend a few bucks promoting their opportunities, they were almost assuredly far more legit. And what to my wondering eyes did appear? It was a display ad placed by Burns Security seeking personnel for the 1976 United States Open Golf Championship.

On Monday, I hopped in my station wagon and drove downtown to the instructed address. I filled out an application, and they said they'd let me know. Two days later, I received a call and was asked to come back for an interview. Now if there is one thing that Kip Keefer has absolutely excelled throughout his entire existence, it is sitting down across from any human being and making a great impression. After a short discussion and a handshake, I was shuffled into a nearby room to pick up my credentials and be issued my official uniform. It consisted of a pair of lightweight blue slacks with a red stripe down the side and a blazer of light material that was fire engine red with a snazzy Burns Security patch emblazoned on the breast pocket area. I was instructed to report that Saturday for orientation and familiarization with the grounds. Despite the fact that the hourly wage was bordering on what Lords of Middle Ages Manors paid feudal serfs, it really did not matter. I was excited about this gig because in my interview the man had answered the only question I posed. Would my credential allow me access to the grounds at all times? His answer was yes. Regardless of what they asked me to do or the minuscule wages, I felt like I had just gotten the best job I'd ever had.

The tournament was still a couple of weeks away, but I immediately started being assigned shifts. There were some early events associated with the tournament going on already. Included in that were some practice rounds where people were allowed to access the course. There was also a tremendous amount of activity with ABC television as far as stretching cables everywhere around the course, erecting and outfitting towers, etc. I was placed to keep unauthorized personnel out of these areas. Two straight Sundays, I was assigned to stand in front of the operations center checking credentials and only allowing certain individuals from the tournament staff or ABC to enter. I met some incredibly nice people who would bring me soft drinks from inside and one time even a sandwich.

When the week of the actual tournaments arrived, I reported for my shift on Monday and was informed I was being shipped out to a parking lot where shuttles would bring people back and forth to the course. After being directly on the grounds for the first couple of weeks, to get this crap assignment was very disheartening. We're talking several miles away literally in a field with a makeshift rock driveway and a couple of crude signs. My task was basically to stand at the edge of the driveway where all the dust was being kicked up and wave cars in, ideally keeping them moving so things did not back up. Georgia can be a little on the sultry side in the latter parts of June and that week was certainly shaping up as a scorcher. Initially, word came down that we had to stay attired in our fabulous blazers, but thankfully, wiser heads somewhere up the ladder deduced that was not a good idea. The unfortunate hired hands broiling out in the hot sun surely was not a winning formula for performance or morale. We were allowed to peel off the jackets and strictly work in our white dress shirts and snazzy blue slacks. It was still a ridiculous uniform for that particular task. After eight tedious hours, which now included a sunburn and a sour attitude, mercifully my endless day of employment discontent finally came to a close.

Tuesday and Wednesday were more of the same. At the very least, they had changed course and issued us some sort of crude looking polo shirt to wear, which was slightly more tolerable. I also caught a break toward the end of the second day when one of the supervisors, who had been assigning me previously, happened to drive out to that site on some sort of mission. He recognized me and asked how it was going? I expressed a less than exuberant reaction to this not so desirable assignment. That turned out to be a fortuitous conversation. About an hour later, a supervisor informed me that for the final couple hours of my shift they wanted me to do something different. I was moved to the area where patrons boarded the buses and was told that I was to answer their questions and welcome them to the event, etc. It was much better than the parking lot driveway gig as I actually got to interact with golf fans and talk about the event and generally utilize some of my communicative skills.

The Open teed off on Thursday morning early. My shift was scheduled to begin at noon, or 1 o'clock as I recall. And when I arrived, I learned with great delight that my annex parking lot duties were not in the cards. I was being assigned to dutifully watch over the ABC communication center and tower. The location was just 60 or 70 yards from the edge of the fairway, and although the view was not very good through some trees, I still was able to see golfers walking by and listen to the sounds, buzz, and excitement of the tournament. And at the end of my shift, now being allowed to stand in the shade, I felt far more energetic to spend some spectator time. My Saturday and Sunday hours would be quite desirable for that purpose as I was scheduled with one of the early shifts both of the concluding two days. The most exciting parts of the tournament, watching the leaders finish up on Saturday late afternoon and then the conclusion of the tournament on Sunday were going to be available for me.

Saturday in front of the tower passed uneventfully, and I did go to the locker room area, change clothes and enjoy this mega event on a golf course so majestic that I had to pinch myself that I was actually in the midst of it. For an 18-year-old kid, it was pretty heady stuff. My friends and I had relied on our wits and creativity to get into all kinds of great sporting events, but this time my own resourcefulness allowed me to witness the US Open, I felt elated.

And then It was Sunday, the final round. As I arrived for my shift at 8 AM, the skies were ominous and threatening. I clocked in and headed over to my spot which once again was designated to be my domain for that last day. I stood there in a light rain for just an hour or so before a golf cart pulled up and a well-dressed official hopped out. He let me know that I was going to have a different assignment that day. He tried to pump me up by telling me that he had been assured that I was one of the best men on duty and was really needed for an important job. I hopped in the cart, and we headed off to my new mission. He explained on the way that there was a parking area directly adjacent to the course that was reserved strictly for ABC television personnel. The man assigned to that area earlier in the day had apparently allowed some unauthorized people to park there, which led to his dismissal. It was emphasized to me that it was imperative that I painstakingly maintain order in that lot and not allow anyone without the official green ABC sticker access. I assured him I was the man for the job.

Unfortunately, the ABC lot had an extremely limited view of the golf course. To make matters worse, just moments after I had been dispatched to that location, the heavens opened up. It was a fully authentic Peach State thunder boomer, and the rain came down in sheets. A couple of cars pulled in with the proper credentials and I waved them on by. The second car in line was a large tan Lincoln Continental. As it pulled in, suddenly it stopped. The back window rolled down, which caught my attention because it was electric, which was new and rare in those days. A cheerful voice said, "You're getting drenched out there, want to climb in here for a minute?" I scurried to the door on the opposite side, opened it and asked if getting in was all right since I was soaked. He said in a very familiar voice, "Sure climb in, sit here for a minute, maybe this thing will let up." It required only about a second and a half for me to realize that I was sitting in the back of a car with ABC's sports anchor, the legendary Jim McKay. He asked me my name and shook my hand. I was probably the biggest sports fan on the planet and knew everything about him and his remarkable career. Needless to say, the few minutes we were able to converse, there was certainly no shortage of topics.

I quickly acquainted him with the fact that like himself, I was a native of the great state of Maryland. I also was well aware of his love of horse racing and even that he owned some racing thoroughbreds. Immediately realizing that I was well-informed, he seemed to quickly reach a comfort zone and enjoy our discussion. Now, we were just two guys waiting out the conclusion of the downpour; we were having a substantive, enjoyable few moments of interaction. He was a huge star but a tremendously down-to-earth, world-class man. He asked me to tell him about myself.

I told him about my sports acumen and aspirations to be a broadcaster. He gave me words of encouragement and urged me to doggedly pursue my dreams. This was the man who four short years before while anchoring Olympic coverage in Munich had been on the air for endless hours during the horrendous Israeli athlete hostage crisis. When the attempted rescue debacle that night at the airport had been revealed and the information tragically confirmed that all of the hostages had been killed, McKay uttered the words that would become legendary in television history, " They're all gone."

The shower was letting up, and I knew he had to go. I remember thanking him profusely for being so thoughtful and letting him know how appreciative I was to have had the unbelievable privilege of visiting with him for a few moments. His response was something I will never forget because it exhibited class and was a very meaningful demonstration to a young person of how someone should conduct themselves and treat others. He said, "You are an impressive young man, the pleasure has been all mine." We shook hands, and my brush with a legend was concluded. His driver pulled the car forward, and I returned to my sentry spot.

There was sporadic action over the next couple of hours. A few more ABC cars trickled in. Most of my activity was shooing away people who were trying to park in the lot that were not authorized. By early afternoon, my speech to the offenders was pretty standard.

"I'm sorry sir, this lot is restricted to only ABC television personnel. You have to have a green sticker to enter."

Then at around 1:00 pm, the game changed. A gigantic Cadillac pulled into the driveway and once again electric windows were lowered. The driver looked like a Texas oil man outfitted by central casting. He was a big robust character with a booming voice and 10-gallon hat. There were several other associates, similarly attired, in the car. He even called me "Podnah!" And asked if it was all right to pull in and park there. Which, of course, I informed him that this was the ABC parking lot and that a green sticker was required for entrance. He fumbled around for a moment and then held up something that I had seldom seen before. It was currency, a $50 bill with the portrait of Ulysses S Grant staring up at me. As I stunningly eyeballed the loot with my head spinning in multiple directions, he delivered the classic line ... "Is this green enough for you?" Now stop for a moment and consider this: it was 1976, I was not yet 19 years old. I was working for just above minimum-wage. That astounding figure was probably about $4.50 an hour. No, really, I'm not kidding! So think about that, for my eight-hour shift,

I would be grossing $36. So there was little suspense; without hesitation, I barked out my enthusiastic answer ..."Yes, sir, that is green enough!" I snatched the bill as the electric window returned to its upright position and the massive Caddy lurched forward. It rolled down the hill to claim a course-side parking spot.

I had done some speedy, made to order, rationalization in contemplating that transaction. It led me to take a major step to becoming a skilled capitalist. I reasoned that the tournament telecast was underway. With that being the case, it was certainly reasonable to assume that all of the ABC personnel were present, accounted for, and parked in my lot. Yet, there was still ample room for more vehicles. And then the clincher, I had three hours left in my shift on my last day of employment. I had nothing to lose. If I got fired, that would be a shame, but at this point, not a terribly impactful action. I weighed the dilemma of compromised integrity and decided it really was not applicable. It was clear cut, cold hard cash took precedent in this case. After all, I was not selling state secrets to the Russians. But I did decide at that moment if comrades named Boris or Vladimir pulled up, I would happily sell them a parking spot.

At that very instant, another car pulled in. My subconscious had reprogrammed my internal mechanisms, and I was shocked when I heard my voice deliver a now altered response to the request to park in my lot. "Well, this lot is reserved for authorized personnel, I'm not supposed to let you pull in here without a green sticker." That driver held up a $10 note. Well, OK ... Pull on in. Over the next two hours, I encountered 10 or 12 more cars and virtually every one paid an honorarium to me and I let them park in the lot. The standard was a 10 or 20, but if the person was nice enough, I even accepted a couple of fives. Right on schedule at 4 PM, a golf cart appeared and my relief man hopped out. I was shuttled back to the employee area. My work for Burns Security at the United States Open golf championship had come to an end. My shift was over, but my time here was not done. I donned my civilian clothes, reported to the uniform return area and relinquished my official snazzy garments. They informed me that my check for the previous week would be mailed promptly and that was it. My employment was concluded, but my credentials to access the golf course were as good as gold.

A couple of hours later, I was on the opposite side of the 18th fairway and watched Jerry Pate's audacious, memorable 5-iron shot, over water, to the final green. It set up a birdie which clinched the title. Later that week, Sports Illustrated came out with a picture of the new national champion on its cover with the caption, "You Were Great Jerry Pate." It was ultra satisfying to see and appreciate the incredible fact that I had witnessed it. It was also gratifying to pat my pocket and realize that the $180 I had collected in the final hours of my employment, was one of the greatest windfalls of my young life to that date. Amazingly, I had accumulated an additional week of wages in just over three hours. And it all had been made possible through my effort to hustle up the opportunity to work at the tournament. It was a good lesson about the value of making things happen and simply showing up. I felt like the king of the world.

After all these years, those words continue to resound in all things, back then as they do today ... "This Green Enough?"... "Yes, Sir, That's Green Enough!"

Post 7

Not So Gainful Employment

"I had too much fun growing up and was far too busy to plan what I was going to do with my future. However, once you're responsible for taking care of yourself, you find out the hard way that winging it is not necessarily an effective, and certainly, not a foolproof, strategy. The road to your destination, particularly when you don't know where, or even what, it is, becomes more difficult to navigate when you have little or no direction or guidance. The good news, at least for me, was eventually, somehow I found my way."

My early adulthood was a complex, twisted pathway that took me a number of different directions. Basically, I settled into a pattern of taking on various jobs, but after relatively short periods of time turning to something else. Initially upon coming home from school, I was right back in my house on North Peachtree. But like Bob Dylan saying, those times were a Changing. My mother had worked her way up from administrative support to sales and was offered a position in the Norfolk/Virginia Beach area. The house went on the market, and shortly thereafter sold.

But fate intervened as the now omnipresent Bill Keefer was back on the scene. Johnson Wax had assigned his employment to a subsidiary company they had bought called Northern Laboratories. Amazingly, he was sent back to Atlanta where travel was much more manageable. He, myself and Mark Random teamed up to share a townhouse apartment out in Marietta.

I had accepted the job offer by Jim's dad to be the mail room/office guy at Reynolds Metals. I wore a tie every day and worked a regular business Monday through Friday schedule. I quickly parted with some of my newfound cash and purchased a brand-new, beautiful silver Monte Carlo. When the big boss in the office decided that I was too big for my britches and not humble enough in his majestic presence for the position, I was transferred to the building products division. It was hard work but a good job. At first, I pulled the windows and doors from hundreds of racks in a massive warehouse for construction sites and loaded them on trucks. But after a short period of time, it was me not only loading, but driving the truck myself to job sites all over the southeast. It was a huge responsibility, backbreaking, hard work. Also, incredibly long hours, sometimes even including Saturdays. I worked so much that I had a pile of three or four paychecks on my dresser that I didn't even have time to cash. After just six months, it became too much, I burned out and quit.

Besides, my dad once again through a contact had me on a different path. His friend, a regional manager for a restaurant chain, met me and was convinced I was a strong candidate for their management program. He sent me to Jacksonville, Florida where I was supposed to begin undergoing training. When I arrived, with little experience of living on my own, I settled into a cheap apartment and reported for duty. The manager of the restaurant had no knowledge of my impending arrival. He did share that he had an opening in his lunch waiter corps that I could fill to get my feet wet. And so it was, I had relocated to wear a bright red pirate vest and giant black belt and wait on tables at lunchtime at the Jacksonville Baymeadows Smugglers Inn. On my first day, approaching a table of four elderly ladies, one looked up and was on a level staring into my gigantic, square belt buckle. She craned her neck bent down to be able to look all the way up my torso, finally making eye contact, and declared ... "Oh my, aren't you a big pirate!"

I worked for several weeks and eventually even made my way onto the dinner schedule. This was all allegedly part of my training. I wasn't a particularly good waiter technically, but I hustled and was personable. I was making decent tips. Of course, being that it was a restaurant, you also were fed, a nice bonus for a fellow raking in less than $200 a week.

I may have stuck with it for a while if not for the intercession of fate once again. I had met some people from the restaurant, and they invited me out to a popular nightspot. I actually was starting to make some friends. But late that night coming out of the bar, I discovered that parking across the street in a strip mall lot might have been a mistake. The old green Dodge I was driving had been towed. With no vehicle, I had little choice but to hike the two miles to my apartment on foot. And so it was for the next week or so. I either walked or hitched rides to work.

What was to be my final weekend in Jacksonville started off with a classic Keefer Story that will follow this section. On that Friday, I was not aware that my time on the northeast Florida coast was quickly coming to a close. It would be greatly influenced by the arrival of, you guessed it, Mark Random, who was coming down for a visit.

It occurs to me that I have no idea how in the world we used to communicate in those days. Obviously, it was strictly by phone, but I know when I lived in Jacksonville, I didn't have a telephone. All I can figure is I must've been keeping in touch with the Atlanta boys on the restaurant's phone. In any event, Mark arrived on a Sunday morning around 9:00 AM. He had attended Hardy's wedding on Saturday night, and after the reception hopped in his Volkswagen Scirocco in the dead of night and headed south. He drove till he was absolutely exhausted and had to pull over to sleep. His early arrival time the next morning was explained by the fact that the rest stop where he shut it down was unknowingly to him less than 10 more miles to my apartment.

The first night he was there, we went on a mission to find where my car had been hijacked to and stored. At this stage of his life, Random was always up for the major caper. He was always ready to right the wrongs perpetrated on innocent citizens by the dreaded "Establishment." We found the car in a large impound lot that was not secured. I had an extra key, but trying it, the engine would not start. Obviously, it had been tinkered with, or something had been removed to prevent it from cranking. Our bright idea was to put it in neutral and push it out of the lot, get it rolling down a nearby hill and discreetly park it at a nearby shopping plaza. We would then return the next day, with sunlight as our ally, and figure out what they had done to the engine. This brilliant Master Plan went off without a hitch. Unfortunately, the next day, the disreputable slime masquerading as a towing company, had executed their own counter move and re-impounded the vehicle. Naturally we needed to regroup. We fell back to a bar on Atlantic Beach where strategizing soon gave way to numerous malted beverages and a night of shooting pool with friendly young ladies and local beach bums. Sometime during that evening, it was determined that the best course of action would be to abandon the car, blow off Jacksonville for a while and head back to Atlanta the following evening. It seemed like a good idea at the time. Fully intending to return in the coming days to retrieve the rest of my things, I was on my way back to the ATL. As things tend to work out, especially for me, I never saw many of my possessions again and would not return to Jacksonville for a number of years. Unknowingly, and with no planning or forethought, It was time for a brand-new chapter.

Arriving back in Atlanta after the impromptu withdrawal from Jacksonville with Random, once again, I had no place to live. I was like the family's great-grandmother, one of my friends would take me for several days. Then my meager belongings would be packed up and I would ship to someone else's spot. Frequently, I wound up at my old stomping grounds, the Heavern house on Cherry Hill Ln. Mark had started a new job with his old boss from Florsheim shoes. He had launched several stores in local malls retailing women's shoes and accessories. Incredibly, I found myself interviewing for a position. A $200 loan from my mother was used to purchase some dress shirts, slacks, and a sports coat or two from JCPenney. Voila, Kip Keefer, women's shoe salesman was born. I was Al Bundy from the future hit comedy series Married With Children, many years before it even came out. Amazingly, I was instantly good at the craft. I was a high heel, with matching purse, selling machine. I was originally assigned to Perimeter Mall for my training. The manager of the store was an elegant, stunningly attractive, sexy, sultry ... woman. Really, the first one of them, grown women that is, that I had ever directly interacted with. Incredibly, there was an immediate spark and controversy loomed on the horizon. You see this sultry, sexy temptress was wearing a ring and was someone else's fiancé. (Details on that to come later in the train wreck, err, cautionary tale romantic section.)

In less than a month, I was elevated to an assistant manager position and transferred away from my burgeoning new love interest. That probably was a good thing because just after we had discovered that the storeroom was an ideal spot for some retail relief, I was assigned to Northlake Mall under the direction of the manager of that store, yes indeed, the man of the hour, Mark Random.

That year was characterized by serious social activity and constant quest for entertainment. It was reckless, outrageous and no holds barred. I slept on the couch many nights at Mark's apartment in Marietta. It was a good place to be, not just for his delightful company, but his two delectable, knockout roommates, Debi, and Margo certainly made spending evenings there immensely attractive.

The year of fun and frivolity took its toll when suddenly virtually all of us were fired from the shoe stores. For some reason, the owner did not take kindly to our practice of putting IOU's in the cash register. We were not stealing, per se, just advancing ourselves in lieu of the next check. Apparently, that was frowned upon, and we were all out on our collective backsides.

I had hustled up one really good thing that fall. I had managed to secure an internship at WGST radio in Atlanta. They were experimenting with a new concept that I was greatly intrigued with, sports talk radio. The bulk of their programming was news and information, but they were doing some cutting-edge programming in areas like game previews and result shows. It was a natural for me. I displayed great aptitude and promise in that environment and became a popular addition to the station. Unfortunately, it was an unpaid position and despite the invaluable experience, if I wanted to get into that line of work, I had to have some sort of income and stability. At that time, I had neither.

It was clearly time for a change, and a sudden desire to finally settle into a more structured situation and acquire some money was a powerful urge. The best place to pursue that course of action at that time was obviously in Memphis. My dad had been transferred back there and had a good set up, with numerous friends and associates there. And, I had my eye on the racing industry. I was a Keefer, it was in my blood. Once again, it was time to hit the road, but this time not just to seek fun and leisure; instead, the time had come to seek my fame and fortune.

KEEFER STORY

Couldn't Miss

So I'm working in Jacksonville, Florida at the Smuggler's Inn restaurant in my management training program. (Ha) The first six weeks of my rigorous instruction consisted of waiting on tables. I had actually settled in and was just starting to feel comfortable in the environment there. I had even ventured to the greyhound races a couple of times for some quality entertainment.

Some of the guys I worked with at the restaurant had been talking about coming to the races with me sometime. I assured them I had all of the tools and expertise to guide them to a winning evening. We made plans during the Friday lunch shift that week to meet at the track that evening. I could not ride down with them because they were going right after work that afternoon for late afternoon classes. That activity was not scheduled to wrap up until around 8 o'clock, and then they would proceed to Bayard to meet me. At that time, I was enduring the annoyance of having my car towed after allegedly illegally parking it during an evening outing a week or so before, thus, at that time, no wheels. I decided that I could take a taxi to go to the track and would later catch a ride back with those guys after the races. Around 6 o'clock, I called for the cab and went to the track.

The program began around seven, so I watched the first couple of races and made a few wagers. I was supposed to meet my coworkers at a bar on the track level at around 8:30. At first check, there was no sign of them. I paced around that particular bar expecting their arrival at any time. I made a couple of small bets, unfortunately enjoying no success in the first few races.

As my guests still had not made an appearance, I turned the page in the program and discovered that next up was a top rated Grade A race. Two of the track's best dogs were in the field. The memory is as vivid as if it had only happened yesterday. In the outside box post number eight, was Jams Uncle Jake. I had watched him a week before annihilate a field from an outside post. In the number two box was a lightning fast early speedster, named Visa. Her performance pattern was always the same, she broke quickly every time and ran to the turn faster than all of her foes. To my young, but somewhat experienced racing analyst eyes, this lineup presented all of the elements of what we call in the business, a Cold Number. Two dogs, clearly superior to their opponents, with complementary running styles, and posted in spots where they could perform at their best. The quinella, which is the combination of the two runners featured odds of 4-1. That meant for every dollar wager on that combination, 2/8, if they ran first and second, you'd receive four dollars in return, plus the dollar you wagered. Remember, these were not days where I had very much cash on hand. I probably brought about $50 to the track that night and by this, the seventh or eighth race, I was down to around $30. I quickly calculated that if I bet $20 of that stake, I would have the quinella 10 times when it came in 2-8. That would create a return of $100. I stepped to the plate and made the bet boldly and with no trepidation.

The race broke beautifully just like I expected. Visa sped to a good lead early and to my delight, the powerful #8 cleared second, on the outside in perfect position. It was like clockwork. But a funny thing happened on my way to the cashier's window. I learned a valuable lesson about greyhound racing in the most difficult way possible. Jams Uncle Jake was so powerful and had such clear sailing, that approaching the far turn, he caught up with the speedy front runner. He powered on past and set sail to a dominant win. Visa, now overtaken and totally vanquished without the lead, began to weaken. A front runner excels when they're in the lead. When that front-running status is taken away, many of these speedballs lose valuable incentive. It still looked like an easy payday with just 30 or 40 yards to go. But a horrifying sight suddenly emerged, the number one greyhound, Manilow, had saved ground right against the rail and was gaining with every stride on the tiring Visa. The two racers arrived at the finish line at the exact same instant. Had the race been a single foot shorter, I'm in the money. The photo finish sign was illuminated and an agonizing wait for me began. Then the numbers were emblazoned on the results section of the odds board. Official result 8-1-2. My sure thing, two best dogs, who had run first and second every step of the race except the last two feet, was a loser. I now had only nine dollars and some change left in my pocket. Over the next half hour, I anxiously looked for the arrival of my cohorts. They had adamantly insisted that they were "definitely coming." Then around

10 o'clock, with only two races left, it dawned on me, they were officially, a no-show. My cab ride to get to the track had cost $13. I didn't have that much but was confident in my abilities. I still thought I could grind out a few more dollars despite being shaken by my gut-wrenching loss. I decided I would invest the remaining cash I had and simply make the money necessary to summon a taxi for the return trip to my apartment. Obviously, I was young, clearly, I was also stupid.

Sadly, the wagering overlords did not smile upon me, and soon I was flat broke. I considered all of my options and decided that I would begin trudging up US-1 and hitchhike home. Surely someone leaving the track would recognize me as a fellow enthusiast who had fallen on hard luck, and mercifully give me a ride. I set out briskly on my journey, my thumb extended as a steady line of cars poured out of the now completed racing program. It was pitch black, that stretch of road was not very well lit at all. I walked backward with my thumb extended for a good while, but every motorist blew past me indifferently. In about half an hour's time, the steady line of autos dwindled to a trickle.

Suddenly a somber thought dawned upon me. If I was driving on a dark Florida highway at 11 o'clock at night, would I pick me up? The answer was, certainly not! I computed the amount of distance to reach the destination of my apartment to be just over 20 miles. I can remember thinking that I am young and in good shape and people run 26 miles in marathons. Surely I could walk 20 miles without any problem. So onward I hiked through the pitch black late evening. With my determined stride, I felt I was making some headway. Then I saw a very disturbing sign on the left-hand side of the road. A small Sunoco gas station, now closed, was directly across the street. When driving to the track, this particular landmark was the one that let you know that you were almost there. The full impact of what I was attempting to do, suddenly was fully realized. I had a very long way to go.

How could it get worse? It certainly found a way in the next half hour. The air gradually began to feel much cooler and shifting and blowing in from my right. That meant airflow coming from the ocean. I detected some slight rumbling in the atmosphere and suddenly feared the worst. The winds quickened and the first raindrops began falling. Yes, a full-blown thunderstorm had arrived and was open for business. Within moments, it was pouring. The wind was swirling, causing the relentless raindrops to attack from all sides. Within moments, I was absolutely soaked, a miserable wet rat staggering along. I was wearing a pair of jeans which seemingly quadrupled in weight within moments. Every step was met with resistance. Still, I relentlessly moved forward. Blessedly within a few moments the rain ceased. For the next couple of miles, even the breeze settled down.

The next plague unleashed in this modern day retelling of the Odyssey was the uncomfortable and then painful effect of the soaking wet denim rubbing down on my tender inner thighs. After a time, every step became agonizing. It was my first experience with the heartbreak of chafing. I resorted to grabbing a fistful of material and pulling it away from my beleaguered upper legs to avoid the assaulting friction. The irony did not fail to register that as I staggered along, I felt a kinship to those who had been somehow stranded in the desert, despite the fact that the desolate wasteland I was wandering aimlessly along in, was pretty much the opposite, a barren coastal highway.

In the calm of the early morning hours, I must've transitioned into some sort of out of body mode. With no idea what time it was, and extreme fatigue setting in, somehow I found that special reserve, fueled by desperation and adrenaline, that can only be summoned when the circumstances are most dire. Incredibly, I found myself on my street of residence and staggered through the finish line with absolutely nothing left that could've propelled me even 10 yards further.

Entering my sparsely furnished apartment, I noticed the small clock atop my television, which revealed that it was 4:30 AM. I was suffering from severe dehydration and extreme hunger. I remembered that miraculously there was one edible item in my freezer. The week before at the grocery store, there was a special, buy two Chef Boyardee frozen pizzas and get one free. Now, that extra bonus source of enrichment and revival was poised to save my life.

Literally crawling on the floor, I fished the frozen disc out of the freezer and extricated it from the box. I reached up and managed to spin the dial to activate the oven and slid the cheese pizza into its place on the rack. With all my might, I pulled myself up to the sink, filled up a sizable cup of water and drained it in a single gulp. I laid on the kitchen floor waiting for the endless 10 minutes necessary to complete the cooking process. When I realized it was time, with great anticipation, I hoisted myself upward and found a plate. Salvation was just seconds away, but fate had one more devilish card to deal me. Deftly I began to slide the pizza slowly off the rack and onto the plate. Somehow my calculations malfunctioned and the under section of my wrist contacted the red hot oven rack edge on the same hand holding the plate receiving the hot offerings. Reflexively, I pulled the plate back, which caused the pizza riding half of its surface to hurtle in the same direction. The discomfort on my wrist paled in comparison to the sickening sight of my pizza sliding off the front of the plate, deflecting slightly off the front open oven door and landing with a splat face down on the tile floor. The cruelty and unfairness of the universe were incomprehensible. I ran cold water on my burn, all the while staring at my fallen food casualty lying sickeningly on the floor. The next thing that happened was pure instinct. On my knees, I commenced an excavation process. Salvaging critical sauce and cheese and placing it back on the circular crust methodically. With the precision of the finest surgeon, I salvaged all of the vital ingredients that I possibly could. A night of total humiliation, great hardship and incredible stupidity ended with the indignity of my having to consume a pizza that I had dropped upside down on the floor. Quite fitting don't you think?

If memory serves, I slept until five or 6 o'clock the next afternoon. I had learned countless valuable lessons from this one catastrophic experience. Besides never trusting people to do what they say they're going to do, I also had a far better understanding of the danger of creative rationalization, particularly justifying actions resulting in the overestimation of your physical capabilities. The most important nugget of knowledge was clear. Never ever put yourself in a position where you do not have a backup exit strategy and cab fare. This particularly when patronizing businesses or activities where cash can quickly dissipate. It is a concept I've embraced and practiced every day since that fateful late night Florida stroll. Oh, and I almost failed to mention, without exception, don't ever forget, wear an oven mitt!

What A Nightmare

It was a chilly winter evening in Memphis, and finally, I had concluded my long day of work-related assignments. Arriving back at the house where I was living at the time with my father and his new wife, spouse number three if you're keeping score, Barbara, it was nearly 11 PM. There was also one other resident living there at the time, the ever-present Mark Random. In Atlanta several years before, Bill, Mark, and I had teamed up to room together at Cumberland Club Apartments. After the heart breaking and unexpected passing of both Mark's parents if anyone week of each other, he chose to come spend some recovery time in Memphis and return to our previous living situation.

He had found a job working as a front desk clerk at the Hilton Hotel in town. On this particular evening, he had returned from work at approximately the same time as I did. We visited a few minutes and then retreated to our respective rooms. I was pretty worn out. At the time, I was working two jobs. I was working for a liquor company as a bar salesman, a rather fascinating occupation. And to give myself a solid in, I took a job as a doorman/bouncer at the hottest new country western bar which was just opening. Working there would be very good for successfully placing product lines I represented on their bar liquor shelves.

In a very short period of time after laying down, I was out. Soundly sleeping, it is apparent that I immediately went into an REM state of slumber. I experienced a vivid dream in which a monster tornado was bearing down on my location. It was one of those dreams where every detail was incredibly distinct. There were others with me in the nightmare, and I quickly scrambled to try to usher them and myself to whatever degree of safety we could find. In a highly agitated and alarmed state, I had leapt to my feet and frantically began shouting to my companions, "Get on the floor, and stay down." Then, in the ultimate move to illustrate that I was summoned to drastic action, I had actually flung myself on the floor and attempted to crawl into the closet. Obviously with the shouting and the banging around, I had made some unusual racket. The impact on the rug and hitting my head on the edge of the closet door had limited any somnambular condition I may had been in. I remember laying there on the floor, retracing what in the world just happened, and realizing that I had just concluded a nasty dream. I felt the bump on my head and the stinging pain of a now skinned up knee. I clearly remember thinking, God, I am an idiot!

I staggered back to bed, and in no time drifted back to sleep. That session of slumber was not going to last for very long. I was awakened this time by strange noises coming from just outside my window. This was a single level house with a length of the hallway which contained all four bedrooms. Mine was the very first one, and the view from my window was into the backyard just past the back of the carport. As I lay there in the dark, I was almost positive that I had heard a voice coming from just outside my window. As I contemplated that possibility, I distinctly heard another voice. There was also that kind of static noise that accompanies use of some form of transmission device, such as a walkie-talkie. And then, shining through my window, I clearly saw a bright beam of light. I rose and lifted one of the blinds to peer outside. I was stunned to see the clear image of two police officers, appearing to be in full gear of some kind. One was crouched down, shining his light across the backyard while the other officer stupid, several feet behind him, grasped a radio device in one hand and a drawn handgun in the other. Naturally, I was startled, to say the least, and immediately ran hundreds of scenarios through my head as to what in the hell could possibly be happening. My best guess was, they had been pursuing some sort of suspect and were searching the neighborhood hoping to find said desperado in hiding. My dad was out of town, but his wife was home and, of course, Mark. I was attired in a pair of gym shorts and a T-shirt, so I went to my door and out into the hallway to investigate further.

The house was dark and quiet; there was no sign of the others. I wandered around for a moment, entering the kitchen and flipped on the light. At some point, I walked into the adjacent dining room, which was on the front part of the house with the window that looked out into the front yard and driveway coming off the neighborhood street. I gazed out the window and was greeted by a sight that was almost too bizarre to comprehend. In the street and front yard, there was a full-scale police crisis set up firmly in place. One of the big SWAT style trucks, a number of police cruisers and at least 10 to 12 officers visible. And, standing front and center, wearing a forest green, logoed Christian Dior robe and fur-lined slippers, holding a Wilson T2000 tennis racket was none other than my close compadre and housemate Random. As I stood there absolutely befuddled, I noticed that my image in the window had been spotted. A policeman standing next to Mark pointed at me and exchanged some words. I still had absolutely no clue what was happening.

Any confusion about what I should do next was erased almost instantly by a loud rapping on the front door. The previous owners of this house, obviously very security conscious, had installed these large iron security doors in front of the standard wood door. I slowly pulled back the standard door and was greeted by the sight of an officer standing on the ledge outside behind the glass and iron security door. He asked me who I was, and I quickly replied that my name was Kip Keefer and I lived here. He then asked, "Tell me who's in there with you." I answered no one. I had seen Mark standing out in the yard, and there had been no evidence of Barbara's presence, even since the time we had returned from work. He asked me to open the security door, and I explained that it required a key and I would have to go look for it. Usage of the front door by all of us in the short time we lived there was extremely rare. He seemed confused that I had to unlock the door from the inside and asked me again was I sure that no one was in the house. This time, I remembered Barbara and said my stepmother may be asleep in the back. It seems everything I said confused and even irritated the policeman more.

Just then, I heard noises and sensed movement behind me. I turned to discover that there were four or five officers, a couple with weapons drawn now right behind me in the entry hallway. It was a rather unnerving moment.

Thankfully, the officers quickly seemed to summon a posture of at ease and appeared satisfied that there was no hostage crisis or shoot out scenario posed here. Suddenly, more officers appeared from down the bedroom hallway. And the first view of the evening of the illustrious, new Mrs. Bill Keefer, still appearing to be half-asleep and absolutely baffled. Even the resplendent Mr. Random, still carrying his tennis racket was now in the suddenly crowded vestibule. I had a close look at the officers and realized they were wearing full tactical gear. Except for one, obviously the commander of this operation. He stepped to the front of the group, looked at me and asked this probing question, "Have you been drinking this evening?" I assured him I most certainly had not been. His next question was a rather snarling request for somebody to explain what in the hell was going on here?

I simply shrugged; I still had no idea myself. So Mark picked up the ball and said that he had heard strange voices down the hall from his back corner bedroom. He had heard the order shouted, by a voice he did not recognize, for me to get on the floor and stay down. He then heard sounds of what sounded like a scuffle. He quickly reached the conclusion that intruders had entered our home, and I was unfortunately immediately accosted. He had no intention of suffering the same fate, so he grabbed his tennis racket for protection, raised his window, kicked out his screen and shimmied out over the bushes. In his robe and slippers he went dashing down the street into the winter midnight darkness desperately seeking help. A kind soul in a van had seen him running on the street, pulled over and offered assistance. Ironically, that put him in full defense mode, as the only person on this evening that was potentially going to be put into a tenuous situation. However, the van driver did deliver him a block or two down the road to a pay phone. Mark called the police and told them that intruders had come in the house and apparently his friend, me, was in a grave predicament.

This certainly explained the police presence and the point of entry they had used to access the house. They had crawled in through the same window in Mark's room from which he had exited. Now, I had to step in and fill in the missing links to how this colossal misunderstanding and debacle had begun. So, I described the nightmare to the ever-increasing incredulous officers. The head honcho looked at both of us with disgust and lectured us on wasting valuable police time and resources. It was hardly a premeditated scheme. He then asked if we could possibly get the front door open so they could leave. Barbara quickly responded and found the key, and the army of dedicated public servants headed out the door to break down operations.

The immediate aftermath of all the excitement, everyone went back to their rooms and went back to bed. The days that followed offered opportunities to hear the stories again from both of our perspectives as we told our friends what had happened. Despite the high tension and uniquely bizarre circumstances, in the end, all that the drama really produced was a classic, often repeated, invaluable, beloved Keefer story

KEEFER STORY

Diddler On The Roof

It was early October 1981. I was finishing out my final weeks working for the first time at Southland Greyhound Park in West Memphis, Arkansas. Earlier that summer, I had given up my job in the bar supply business as a salesman and began working full-time at the track. I was serving as backup announcer and the critically important task of assistant chart writer. If memory serves, I believe I was earning the astounding amount of $28 per racing performance. With five shows a week, that was an astounding gross of $140 a week. But soon I would be returning to Atlanta for fall, and all would be right with the world. I had already accepted an offer from my bud, Steve Hardy. He was bell captain at the Marriott at Perimeter Center and signed me on to join his staff that winter.

The previous two years I had been in the Memphis area, I had lived at my dad's. He had remarried just months before, wife number three if anyone's counting. We had settled into a house about 25 minutes from the race track on the east side of Memphis. A combination of events had led to a change as far as my living arrangements and finishing out the season. First, the fantastic Dodge Omni that my father had negotiated for and got me such a great deal on basically had its engine completely malfunction. The car was a pile of garbage and not worth what was being asked to fix it. Combine that with some friction that had started to develop between myself and my father's new bride. In order to be able to work, hopefully setting the stage for an opportunity the next year, and to keep the peace in the new arrangements, it was agreed that I would finish out the last four weeks by living somewhere over in West Memphis.

Since my father had engineered some of the events that had transpired, you would think that perhaps he would feel a sense of responsibility to get his son into some sort of temporary living arrangement. And further, it would be a logical, much-appreciated gesture on his part, to actually pay for it. That would've made sense for most fathers, apparently it never occurred to mine. After all, I was a grown man of 23, I was out on my own. Another topic for another day!

I had ridden with my paltry possessions over to work on a Friday night and was going to be staying from that point forward for the next 30 days. My friend, the full-time announcer, a most interesting case study, had earlier invited me to stay on the couch in his apartment until the end of the season But that plan went sour when unexpectedly he was ejected from his apartment the very week that I was slated to occupy some of that space. He was involved at that time with a big, friendly girl, one of the employees at the track. His end of season living plan changed abruptly, and he suddenly moved into her trailer.

Since my backup arrangements had gone awry, I stepped up and rented a room across the expressway from the track at a luxurious establishment known as the Mari

Jes Motel. If Zagat's had rated this magnificent lodging establishment, it likely would've earned about 1/8 of a star. Not exactly in the same class as a Ritz Carlton. I had a couple of hundred bucks, and for the princely sum of just $119, I was able to secure an entire week. The prospect of crossing on foot both east and westbound lanes of I-40 to be able to go to work was quite a daily challenge. Probably not the brightest idea on those late nights returning to my room after the races. Somehow, my impeccable judgments of when to break into a scurrying sprint paid off and I avoided catastrophe. That would prove ironic just a few yards away in the not so distant future, but that's a different Keefer story.

There were a convenience store and a popular breakfast oriented diner on either side of the fleabag motel. And, of course, the scrumptious concession items were available at the track. At the conclusion of that first week, the announcer had invited me to occupy the couch at his new abode at his girlfriend's trailer. My week at the motel had run out that Friday morning and with my funds running low, I decided to give that a shot.

I rode back to the dingy trailer park and entered the dwelling. It could best be described as something out of a very low-budget B-movie. The couch was ancient, completely worn out and one of those four to five footers. It was hardly going to be a very accommodating or desirable place for a night's rest. What was worse, the entire layout was so tiny that I would literally be just a few feet away behind the paper thin wall from the resident couple. The bed they slept on was astoundingly small. And as I mentioned, this particular lady, who was extremely nice and good natured, was a very large person. It was difficult to imagine, and frankly rather disturbing to think about, how the dynamics of both of them occupying this tiny space worked. Curled in the fetal position and wondering how things could've gone so horribly wrong, I somehow endured that first night.

One night, around the middle of that week, my worst fears were realized. Apparently, desire and temptation in those close quarters of the master chamber became too much to resist. So despite my presence, raging passion and desire won out. In what can only be described through my recollections as horrifying, suddenly the structure began to shake and move, A sickening creaking sound filled the airwaves, and moans and groans were heard as if they were being directly transmitted to my ears. Hearing and directly experiencing the reverberations of their dirty deed just a few feet away was simply too much for me. Despite being spared from seeing the unfathomable abhorrent experience visually, I was still way too close for comfort.

The 2 1/2 weeks that remained suddenly seemed like a period of months. Like an inmate at Alcatraz, I had to devise a brilliant strategy to escape. Finally, when Friday rolled around, I concocted a story for them that I was going to be going back to my dad's during that weekend after the races. He never missed a weekend night at the track, so the story was feasible. It was payday on that Thursday, so I had a little bit of money. The daily rate at the hotel was $23. By the time we arrived at work on that Friday afternoon, I wouldn't be able to check into the hotel until well past midnight. It just seemed like a lousy value. Therefore, I devised an alternate strategy.

My plan was to linger after the races, outlast all of my colleagues on the rooftop judges stand, and stay in there until late night/early morning watching television. I procured a couple of beverages and snacks and settled in. By around 5 AM, I had grown extremely tired. I was already on a schedule where being up most of the night was common and sleeping until late afternoon was standard procedure. It was a Saturday, a matinee day, and I knew a cleaning crew would be coming upstairs at some point. I didn't think it wise to allow myself to curl up on the sofa and sleep there. So I departed from the judges stand, locking up behind me. I crossed the long covered walkway to the exit door that led back down the stairs to the main facility. I exited the tunnel and as first light barely flickered, made my way next door to our adjoining property, the Ramada Inn. Once there, I went to the pool area, stretched out on a chaise lounge, and dozed off. No one bothered me the hour or so that I napped, but I was awakened by the combination of sunlight and the activity of people scurrying about preparing to leave. Within my view, in one hallway were several people who must've been traveling together, leaving several rooms at the same time. I watched them drag their luggage down the stairs, casually walk to the front of the property and witnessed them loading up and leaving in a large van. I went up the steps toward the outdoor corridor where their vacated rooms were. Just on a whim, I tried their doors to see if they were locked. Amazingly, the middle door had the latch security extended, and I was able to access the room. Knowing check out time was 11 AM, I quickly put a do not disturb sign on the door. I stripped one of the beds, found an extra sheet that had not been used at the top of the closet and settled in for a blissful four hours of rest. I then enjoyed what I suddenly appreciated for the first time as a luxury, an actual bathtub/shower. The trailer options in the bathing department were far from ideal.

After working the matinee and evening programs, day two of my plan went into effect. Knowing that the cleaning crew did not work on Sundays when the track was closed, I smuggled a pillow and sheet from the hotel in a large garbage bag that I had found in an unused trash container and stealthily brought it into the track and stashed it upstairs on top of a seldom used storage space. My intention for that night was to spend the entire time upstairs until late morning. The plan came off without a hitch, and around 11:30 the next day I stowed my gear and happily set off intending to check in for a glorious day at the Mari Jes Motel. A day of relaxation, good food and watching NFL football. I locked the judges' stand door behind me and set off down the walkway. Reaching the far end, suddenly everything went wrong.

Reaching the door at the end of the walkway that led into the main building, I was absolutely shocked to find it securely locked. In six months of working there, I had never encountered this door being locked. I was trapped on the roof of a giant facility on a day where it was completely closed down.

I considered my options, and none was very good. I knew that the security office on the main floor two levels away would be manned by an officer. There was no way to contact him, but perhaps I could periodically bang on the door and make a lot of noise hoping that I would be heard if he was making rounds. I rejected that notion because I didn't really want to be discovered as I had no real explanation for my presence there. I also talked myself into option number two, which took that out of play.

On the far right side of the building, there were several descending smaller patches of roof that looked potentially negotiable for climbing/jumping. From the very top of the roof where I was dropping down to a smaller section that overlooked the roof to the Greyhound Paddock and racing offices. After one more lap around the entire gigantic roof area, I decided that was my best option.

The drop from the upper level was about 10 feet down to the next smaller section. I originally was just going to jump it and try to land softly but then thought better of that idea because I didn't know if the roof would hold as I thudded to the surface. I decided the more judicious way to do it would be to slowly crawl over the roof edge, clinging to the ledge portion of the upper roof, dangling my legs as far as possible and then only having to drop about four feet landing upright. Almost on impulse, I began to lower my legs down over the edge trying to hang on with my hands as I lowered my torso slowly down to hopefully assume a hanging position. As my chest became level with the edge of the roof, my leverage and hold began to slip away. All of a sudden, I felt myself dropping in kind of a sickening position where I realized that my shoulders were angled out further than my feet. I had watched enough Olympic gymnastics to know that there was no way I was going to stick the landing. I furiously tried to have my feet absorb the impact, which they did fairly well, but predictably as soon as I made contact with the lower surface, I hurtled backward landing on my rear end (obviously the spot my brains were occupying at the time) and the small of my back. Thinking about it now, it was probably miraculous that I didn't smash the back of my head. It did not exactly go according to plan. And my tailbone was to be sore for several days. Other than that, I was no worse for wear. I had made it to the next level.

After a few minutes to regroup, I started looking at the next phase of the process. It immediately became evident that I had not looked at it closely enough from the higher level where I started. The next rooftop was about 15 feet down, and the landing area was not the tar-based surface above. It appeared to be filled with small rocks, and I didn't know how solid it was underneath that. The structure covered by that roof was a build on the area not part of the main building where all the greyhound racing activity for weigh-ins and holding kennels, etc. occurred. And if that wasn't enough, that landing area immediately below the level I was now on was rather narrow, only about eight feet across. It widened after 15 or 20 feet, but that was little consolation. It would not be practical to make a 12-foot drop and lean forward to try to land in the wider area. I was faced with the same ominous dilemma as before. I did not feel comfortable in jumping to the next level due to worries about the lack of solidity of that roof and the most unpleasant prospect of perhaps losing my balance and falling over the edge some 15 additional feet to the ground below. The vision of me being found the next morning stuck with my legs dangling into an office below from the waist down in the roof, or curled up on the ground in a crumpled mass with a broken neck suddenly seemed rather unappealing. By this time it was about 2 PM. Of course, I had no idea exactly of the time, because I did not wear a watch, and we were years away from the introduction of cell phones. I stood contemplating and calculating my dilemma for quite some time before deciding that I would go and try and seek a little bit of shade from the adjoining upper level back against the far wall where I originally dropped down. As the sun crept west that afternoon, the shade dissipated. Luckily it was October and probably in the area of 65 to 70°, so it was not uncomfortably warm. Actually, it was blessedly in light of the circumstances, a delightful weather day.

Now to say that Southland Greyhound Park in 1981 was a very quiet, deserted location on a Sunday would be a tremendous understatement. There was no traffic out front, no activity whatsoever in the parking lot from what I could see. There didn't even seem to be any birds in the area.

Over the next couple of hours, I attempted several times to muster up the stones to just go for it and either jump or try and ease myself down again. I was already a little banged up from the earlier building rappelling mishap. I was pretty unsure about the next phase of the operation. As darkness started to descend, I made a fateful decision … It was a no go! The hopes I had harbored to wiggle out of this mess without any fanfare or notice were suddenly out the window. I would simply have to tough it out the next 12 to 13 hours and humiliatingly wave someone down for help when activity resumed on Monday morning.

To entertain myself, I sang probably 100 songs and thought long and hard about every aspect of my interesting life up to that time. It was a dazzling clear star-filled night, which provided some entertainment. I channeled ancient inhabitants of this planet and looked for constellations and anomalies in the sky. Mostly, I just sat there, bored shitless. I asked myself repeatedly how in the hell did I get into these messes? I reminded myself that the ones that go wrong are the ones that stay prominent in mind. The maneuvers and capers that come off without a hitch are oftentimes quickly forgotten. In some ways, the endless time on the roof was a chance to achieve acceptance that I was not exactly cut from a conventional cloth. The one blessing to my plan had been that I had slept probably for only four or five hours in the judges' stand. There had been intentions to occupy much of my time at the hotel in a state of slumber. Blessedly, I had been carrying a bag with a change of clothes that now served as a makeshift pillow. Some time in the early morning hours of that new Monday, on a tar roof, I stretched out and actually managed to get to sleep.

Several hours later, discomfort roused me and I sat up and realized that the sunrise was just commencing. Greyhound trucks were rolling by on their way to the kennel facilities at the back of the complex. There was also a small parking lot for racing department employees as I stood perched above their building. As I waited for someone that I could flag down, it occurred to me for the first time since the ordeal began that hunger and thirst were becoming a factor. The wait was not much longer before I saw the familiar pickup driven by the track's director of racing Gene Rhodes pulling up into the parking lot. Standing on the ledge about 35 feet above him, I observed his steady progress toward me up the sidewalk. When he was close enough that I knew he would be able to hear me, I shouted his name. He stopped and predictably looked around before I repeated it and said something brilliantly original such as "Up here!"

Without going into all the dreary details, I simply informed him that I was stuck and needed some help. Gene was a good guy and spared me the indignity of interrogating me at the"height" of my predicament. Shaking his head and snickering as he unlocked his office, he immediately summoned maintenance who quickly showed up with a ladder. In just a short minute or two, the survival test on the roof uneventfully ended. It was just past 7 AM. I had officially been marooned on the roof for the period of approximately 20 hours.

Of course, I was forced to stand there and admit to the nonsensical sequence of events to the gathering horde of curious onlookers from racing, the kennels, housekeeping, security and maintenance. For a half hour, I was peppered with questions like a man who had just been rescued from the rapids of a raging flooding river. Always a fan of having center stage, this one circumstance was not highly enjoyable. Some kind soul brought me a cup of water. Soon thereafter, I excused myself with the explanation that I needed to go and grab some food and catch some proper sleep. I was scheduled to be back at work at 5:00 PM.

I enjoyed a hearty breakfast and was allowed to check into the hotel and slept right up to the time I needed to get up for work. Walking into the track that day, it was immediately apparent that everybody throughout the entire facility knew of the great Kip Keefer roof saga already. I was an overnight sensation, a rock star. But my sense of celebrity was short-lived when informed that I was being summoned to the general manager's office. Lou Dereen was a tough, no-nonsense kind of administrator. I was directed into his impressive office and sat down in a large chair across from his humongous desk. His opening comment was something to the effect of, "I understand you owe me a little bit of a lodging fee?" I explained to him the circumstances, and he suggested that the next time I decided to check into the judges' stand/roof accommodations would be the last time that I would be allowed access to any area within the confines of the facility. I didn't get the sense he was really angry, however; actually, more bemused. I should've told the tight wad that it was my incredibly meager wages that forced me into ridiculous decisions. All journeys have to start with the initial steps, and that is what that season of working for next to nothing was. A beginning, the building of a foundation.

Who would've believed on that October night that just 11 short years later I would be occupying a similar general manager's chair at a major race track? That's right, the same guy that had spent the last two nights at a hotel pool and someone else's room and a judges' box and rooftop, making $28 a performance, broken down about $5.20 an hour, would rise meteorically and make tremendous strides as well as waves in this industry.

The ribbing and harassment of everyone, coupled with the constant questioning was very annoying. Thankfully, the end of the season was just one week away. My dad, of course, heard about my misadventures as soon as he walked into the track that night. Perhaps out of a twinge of guilt or in a rare noble gesture on his part, he actually gave me $100, money for the final week of lodging across the street. Those final days came to an end quickly. And closing night, the regular announcer Michael and I packed up his gigantic ancient Cadillac and whisked out of West Memphis. He was going to drop me off in Atlanta on his way back home to Miami. The book was closed on that tumultuous year in Memphis. It was the ATL's turn once again to provide the next contribution of Keefer Stories.

I suppose in retrospect, the roof debacle can be classified as some sort of primitive camping outing or what the Native Americans used to call a Vision Quest. Unfortunately, I did not see any great revelation or experience anything resembling an epiphany. So let's call it kinship with my ancient descendants who probably spent many nights lying in the past year looking at the night sky for enlightenment. Or let's just call it what it really was, a prototypical Keefer screw up. One only I was capable of fashioning. My buffoonery resulted in being stuck on a roof for almost an entire calendar day. As I continue to state and repeat, you can't make this stuff up.

Post 8

Question– "It must be great to believe that you know best? To always think that you are the smartest person in the room?"

Answer– "No ... it's Awful."

Career Launch, We Have Liftoff

I returned to live in Memphis in the spring of 1980. I worked in various jobs, mostly by following up on contacts of my very socially active father. I worked as a salesman for a wholesale liquor company, a disc jockey and contest host at a popular nightclub, a doorman/bouncer at a wild country-western bar, and for a bar and restaurant supply company. Of course, any and all open evenings were spent at the greyhound races. Saturdays were particularly enjoyable. I would go with my dad around noon and we would drink, socialize, handicap and bet the matinee performance. During the break, prior to the evening races, we always went somewhere outstanding for dinner, then, it was back for more racing action till late at night. Those were typically 12 or 13 hour days, exhausting, but I loved every minute of it.

I was constantly working, but I was determined that I would be enjoying my leisure time and be constantly loaded up with activities. I took out a classified ad in the local newspaper seeking a softball team to play for. Phone calls rolled in from gravely serious softballers soliciting my services. Most of them involved weekend travel for elaborate tournaments, which was not what I was looking for. When I fielded a call from a fellow by the name of Joel Neel, I knew I had found my team. Joel described that they played once a week in a recreational league and that their team, The Panama Reds, had never enjoyed very much success. He kept telling me throughout the conversation that I surely didn't want to play for them. After all that, he added, "Cold beers after the game are most important to us." For next four summers, I suited up and played shortstop for the Panama Reds. The team improved, and I was at the peak of my softball skills; it was a blast!

As fortuitous fate would have it, I was joined during that period in Memphis by two of my best friends. Joe had accepted a graduate school opportunity at Mississippi State and spent a number of his weekends in Memphis. And the ever-present Mark Random, soon also arrived on the scene. Tragically, Mark had suffered the loss of both of his parents within a week of each other earlier in that year. Coming to Memphis was a chance to get away after that incalculably tragic heartbreak. Mark, my dad and myself were once again housemates.

One of the most memorable days of that year occurred in late October. It was a Saturday, and Mark, Joe, and I settled in to watch the Georgia/Florida game. It was Herschel Walker's freshman year and Georgia came in undefeated. It looked throughout the day like the despised Gators were going to ruin George's chances at a perfect season and possible run for the national championship. On fourth down with just a minute or so to go in the game, and trailing 16 to 14, from their own 9-yard line, the Dawgs pulled off a Houdini-type escape. Slumped in our chairs, downtrodden at the prospect of what we're watching, and in a malaise where we had basically given up, 92 yards Belue to Scott miraculously occurred. The visual of the three of us jumping around the room like orangutans who had just received a shipment of bananas, yelling and screaming at the top of our lungs, is a moment in time I will never forget. And the day was just beginning.

That very same evening was closing night at Southland Greyhound Park for the season. We had dinner and made some bets. The last race of the year, what was it called— the au revoir stakes. The boys and I had boldly bet against a favorite and backed a speedster by the name of Dark Rumor. Despite his long shot status, he won convincingly, and we were rewarded big time. Probably just a couple of hundred dollars, but it seemed like we were kings of the world. We attended several post racing, closing night gatherings and somehow hooked up with some local girls who invited us to a big party. By this time, it was probably 3 o'clock in the morning, and we followed a procession of cars literally to the middle of nowhere. The venue for the big party? It was a double-wide trailer in the midst of a rural area that none of us were vaguely familiar with. Drinking continued, and then the highlight of the proceedings was introduced. On a turntable, a record was playing, and in the narrow living room, dancing actually commenced. Lipham sidled over to the stereo and held up the album jacket that had produced the record blaring from the stereo. It was actually a K-Tel Monster Hits of 1978 album. For years, we had laughed and made fun of the cheesy commercials peddling the abhorrently bad K-Tel compilation records. Now, in a country trailer, at 5 o'clock in the morning, with a variety of East Arkansas' finest plus-size girls, we were dancing in a new day. What a social highlight on all of our resumes for which we will always be eternally proud. As the sun rose, the hostess had for some unknown reason closed in on me, luring me outside for some extracurricular activities. I was just mind numbed and stupid enough to willingly acquiesce. Blessedly, Mark and Joe decided it was time to go, saving me from putting an unwise exclamation point on what had been a crazy 24 hours. To this day, I do not know how we found our way back to Memphis. What a memorable day/night/morning!

A few months later, I began working at Southland. They created a position for me where I served as a backup in various spots of the racing department. One of those, of course, was in the announcing booth. At the completion of the season, I caught a ride to Atlanta and began a wintertime ritual that would last the next three years. Hardy was bell captain at the Marriott at Perimeter, and his staff was made up of the motley crew of our friends. I became one of the bag carrying, customer service specialists. The record for my best tip was $50 which resulted from another celebrity encounter. Singer Luther Vandross checked in on a Friday, minutes after Hardy had gone home. Amongst his baggage was a crate of iced down stone crabs that he needed to store in the hotel freezer. I assured him I would handle it, and was rewarded with the generous gratuity. The job as a bellman was always subject to surprises, good and bad. But overall it's a tremendous job, particularly for young guys willing to hustle.

By the start of the next greyhound season in West Memphis, I was the full-time announcer, the voice of Southland Greyhound Park. It was also my first full-time access to radio handling promotional updates, previews, and a nightly results show. In that era, the track was immensely successful. Huge crowds every performance, considerable attention and immense wagering handle were the orders of the day.

Almost immediately, voluntarily I inherited the assignment of writing the daily column in the official racing program. Instead of highlighting just the races, some days I branched out and wrote features on a variety of topics and personals related directly to the track. The stories quickly grew to a much-anticipated read for everyone who worked there or patronized the establishment. Just by exhibiting some time, talent, innovative approach, and enthusiasm, within just the first two seasons, I made myself invaluable. On top of that, my race calls were also highly creative and entertaining. The local NBC affiliate ran the stretch calls of the first two races every night, which constituted the daily double. I made certain that those calls always had a high degree of flair and excitement. At the conclusion of the 1983 season, I was offered a year-round, salaried position. I was now working in my own office even during the non-racing winter months. I didn't have a lot to do, but I was being paid for it. It definitely was my kind of gig.

The next significant bend in my career path was the opportunity to go to St. Petersburg and work as a trainer in the winter of 1986. Working on the greyhound side of the business was tremendously valuable and enjoyable. The drawback, of course, was the seven days a week round-the-clock schedule.

I worked for a wonderful lady there, Mrs. Marriott. She had inherited running the kennel business at Southwind and St. Petersburg after the untimely traffic accident death of her husband Robert. At that time at the Derby Lane track, there was an unbelievable collection of prominent personalities from the greyhound business. I found myself spending a great deal of time with a legendary Irish trainer named Don Cuddy. His stories and incredible wisdom about greyhounds and racing in America and Ireland were lessons and tales I could listen to endlessly. The collection of characters, including my future brother-in-law Rusty Blair and others, introduced me to a highly entertaining, never stopping, for lack of a better word, wild lifestyle. We ran a lot, and boy did we run hard. Many nights after the races, we would load up in several vehicles and generally a crew of 6 to 10 of us would hit across the bridge into Tampa. Typically on the agenda was a stop at the jai alai Fronton to catch the last couple of games of that most exciting betting sport. When that ended around midnight, usually the next destination was one of the clubs that catered to male customers. The most popular of those stops was an establishment called Mons Venus. In the wee hours of the late night/morning, things were known to get out of hand in that environment. I had never been a major party animal/hell raiser and had never particularly indulged heavily in the consumption of alcoholic beverages. However, keeping up with the Joneses, or more specifically, in this case, Blair, Henry, and others, I had to step up my game. It probably was good that my assignment to St. Petersburg was only for a couple of months. I may not have survived, otherwise.

The other incredible aspect of being at Derby Lane that winter was watching the greyhound that had been named after me, Keefer, dominate the racing season at the world's most prestigious track. His owner, Hall of Fame, lifelong greyhound racing icon, Keith Dillon, had told me a couple of years prior that he was going to name one of the first male pups sired by his great champion Perceive, after me. Perceive was a tremendous racing star who was indisputably the greatest dog on the Southland/St. Pete circuit when I first became involved in the business. As a fledgling racing writer, he became my obsession and I chronicled every accomplishment he achieved. In essence, I became his personal press agent, and my work appeared in the form of epic articles in a variety of racing publications. He won 98 races in his career, including several major stakes. He was also named in the prestigious greyhound All-American team an unprecedented three consecutive years. On the night he retired at Southland, we staged a huge celebration tribute/sendoff. At a reception following the races, Dillon, in appreciation for all of my efforts, made the naming promise.

Less than a year later, I received a letter from Mr. Dillon in Kansas. Inside were these few words, Kip meet Keefer. A Polaroid of a red greyhound pup posing with his granddaughter was enclosed. Just over a year later, a massive, 84 pound, red male pup appeared for the first time in West Memphis. He quickly succeeded, winning several races before sustaining a minor injury, which precipitated him being sent to Florida to prepare for the winter season. Before ever increasing, hugely appreciative, massive crowds, he electrified the bay area track. His come from behind, dramatic winning style, created a sensation. As did his antics when being paraded on the track and playing to the cheering crowd as if he sensed that they were there just to see him perform. And perform he did! He ripped off an incredible 14-race winning streak, including the $100,000 Derby Lane Distance Classic. T-shirts with his image and the slogan "I saw Keefer run at Derby Lane" sold like hotcakes. He, and trainer Jim Shulthess, appeared on several local television morning shows. And incredibly, a reporter for the Wall Street Journal, who happened to be visiting the area working on another story, picked up on the Keefer exploits. A front page feature story in that prestigious business publication appeared with a charcoal drawing of my remarkable namesake. In the midst of the lengthy piece, were three different quotes from yours truly. To this day, I find it unbelievable that I have actually been quoted in the Wall Street Journal. Keefer continued his great season, and his legend was cemented. He did return the following season and once again won the $100,000 race. Unfortunately, nagging injuries and setbacks shortened his career. His accomplishments were still astounding, and for me the ride and recognition were incredible. I will never forget that winter in St. Petersburg.

When I returned to Southland that spring, many things in my life suddenly changed. By November that same year, amazingly, I would become a married man. Just a month later, I learned I was soon to be a father. Needless to say, the bar had been raised and the stakes were considerably higher.

During the 1987 season, the announcement was made that for the first time ever, the track was going to race year round. The timing seemed ideal. Cathie and I were building a house and preparing for our new addition. Life had seemingly fallen nicely into place. Case arrived in August 1987.

There was much anticipation during the winter of 1988. It was time to negotiate salaries and benefits for all the now year-round employees. Being a family man now, I had great expectations for a sizable increase. After all, I was now handling five additional months of announcing duties and media responsibilities. I had been a year-round salaried employee for a number of years, but the compensation was pretty much based on the job I performed during what used to be the racing season. When I was told of the nominal, and by that I mean almost nonexistent, amount of increase, I was stunned and outraged. My meeting with the general manager, to say the least, did not go well. I demanded a 20% increase, and he basically told me not a chance. I told him I would not continue at the current rate, and he basically said, "There's the door." Much to my surprise and dismay, I discovered at that moment, that I was not invaluable.

I was not totally reliant on my salary from the racetrack at that point. Several years before, I had come up with the idea to share my extensive knowledge of the skills of the racing participants and wagering at Southland and created a daily tip sheet with my picks and betting recommendations. I typed it up each day and ran copies on the race track's copy machine. I ordered specially printed envelopes to give it a high-class quality. The two existing sheets that were sold on track, were crude in comparison. They charged one dollar for their rags while my price was three dollars per issue. My distribution outlets were surrounding businesses, convenience and liquor stores and a popular breakfast diner near the track. My product, The Insider, was scoffed at by the old bums, who had held an exclusive on that type of product for many years. They thought I was insane to think that people would pay three dollars for a tip sheet. What they didn't factor in was that mine was three times better than theirs. When I enjoyed initial success, they sought to block me in a different way. Using their connections, suddenly the city of West Memphis added a new item to the list of business types, which required a privilege license. Amongst a variety of different enterprises requiring licenses costing an average of $20, race track tip sheets suddenly appeared. The rate for a license to conduct that type of business, was now set at $500. Now that, was low down, unfounded, indefensible stinky cheese. Furious, but undaunted, I paid the larcenous fee. By the end of the second year, my profits from the tip sheet exceeded my salary for working at the racetrack. During that year, Jim had come for a visit from Atlanta. He rode with me on my route putting out the new days sheet and picking up the returns and proceeds from the day before. As he watched me collect nearly $300 in cash that morning, he was amazed. He dubbed the tip sheet route, " The Gravy Train" and forever more that was its title.

Over the next two years, I worked on the greyhound side of the business and ran my tip sheet empire. In 1989, I had the incredible opportunity to train the Southland-based kennel of perhaps the most decorated, celebrated man in the history of the sport. Keith Dillon, the great gentleman who had named a future champion greyhound Keefer in my honor several years before, provided me with the honor of working for him. The kennel was no longer loaded with stars, but we still enjoyed a solid year of success. It was culminated on closing night by a stunning victory in the prestigious season-ending stakes event, the Southland Derby. I had managed to successfully train a raw, big, powerful young racer named Jamaican Episode successfully through qualifying races and into a spot in the finals of the Derby. Set off by the crowd as a huge long shot at 28-1, the 85-pound-beast stormed to the lead and never looked back. Dillon retired as a kennel operator that winter. That Derby win was his final major title in his illustrious career. Being the winning trainer, especially for that hallmark achievement, is a career highlight for which I am immensely proud.

During this time, I was also retained by two different groups to work on race track startups and applications in Kansas and Wisconsin. My contribution to those projects and talents while working at Southland had not gone unnoticed by executives in Southland's ownership company, Delaware North Inc. At the beginning of 1990, they contacted me with an enticing offer. The company was involved in acquisition and expansion in the racing business. I was asked to join them as a consultant.

My first assignment was to report to Buffalo, New York, DNC corporate headquarters. Licenses for tracks in Texas were open for bid. Extensive applications had to be completed and submitted. Soon thereafter, I was dispatched to Green Bay, Wisconsin. The new DNC track in nearby Kaukauna was scheduled to open soon and frankly, it was an disorganized mess. I reported it, and within a month of basically around-the-clock effort had salvaged the marketing and advertising efforts necessary to make it work. I also produced and anchored a two-hour television special highlighting the opening and a weekly program thereafter. I was given the choice to stay there but found the alternative option far more enticing. In January 1991, I was assigned to be the assistant to the general manager and marketing start-up specialist for the conversion of the Melbourne Jai Alai Fronton into a greyhound track. It was an innovative, even audacious project. I loved being back in Florida, and Cathie and Case soon joined me. After five or six months, the track was up and running. I waited for my next assignment with Delaware North, and it turned out to be a return to West Memphis to assist in the transition to a new general manager. It was great to be back at our house and surrounded by family, but the assignment was unsatisfactory. My primary duties centered around a return to the announcer's booth. I had not taken a forward step despite a long list of accomplishments. As new year 1992 dawned, I was 34 years old and anxious for my next opportunity.

In the early parts of the summer that year, fate smiled upon me once again. The failed horse track in Birmingham was under new ownership. A dynamic, Montgomery-based businessman, Milton McGregor had acquired the license for Birmingham. His first accomplishment was spearheading the passing of a local ordinance allowing greyhound racing to be added to the track. Birmingham was poised to be the first pure dual racing operation in the world. I quickly applied to join their team and after a visit that summer, it was obvious that I was an ideal fit for what they needed to be done.

I served as director of marketing and incredibly we were open for business by October of that year. The effort to make that happen is hard to describe. It involved days and weeks of constant motion, the most intense business experience of my life, and by far the most satisfying. I was a key member of the team that pretty much changed the way the racing industry operated. The slogan that I conceptualized for our operation was, "Redefining American Racing." The greyhound track was built just inside the massive horse racing oval. The opening performance drew over 14,000 fans. The scene was indescribable. Since I was marketing director and responsible for crafting the messages and spreading the word, it was a most satisfying evening.

The assignment over the next year was difficult. Cathie had given birth to Clayt our second son in April. She was not excited about moving again and elected to stay in West Memphis while the Birmingham employment situation defined itself. She and the boys spent significant periods of time visiting, particularly in the summer. Every other Saturday night after the races, I hopped in the car and made the four and a half hour drive back to Arkansas and stayed until Tuesday before heading back each time. Many of those late-night drives were ultra-challenging and harrowing. I definitely had the presence of a guardian angel seeing me safely back-and-forth. The employment dynamic evolved rather quickly. Early in 1993, I was added to the upper management team as director of greyhound operations. I was still marketing director for the entire facility. In 1994, the general manager resigned, and I was elevated to that post. Four months shy of my 37th birthday, I was now general manager of the world's only dual horse and greyhound racing track and its 900 employees.

My family moved down immediately, and we purchased a house. Life was idyllic. The job proved to be extremely difficult. Not only were the duties challenging and mentally exhausting, the constant scrutiny, criticism, and interference of the three corporate officials was unbearable. Many times I felt I was manager in title only.

One of my greatest career highlights did occur during this era. An informal discussion I had at an industry conference with a colleague from Florida, Tony Fasulo, led to the formation of an extremely innovative idea. Annually horseracing stages its huge event, the Breeders' Cup. There is so much money involved in that event, it attracts the greatest horses from around the world for a series of lucrative races at one location. Without the money to entice movement of star greyhounds, I posed the scenario of producing a national broadcast, starting in the northeast, swinging down south, progressing out to the midwest and finishing up in the desert. The best greyhounds showcased in a race from each participating track on one national program presentation. I called the concept, The Night Of Stars. To make it a standalone event, we convinced tracks to donate one premier race to the national card. All of the tracks were already uploading their signals, and what would be required would be a download and redistribution for our broadcast. Betting would be facilitated through a national totalizator hub. To tie it all together properly and create a big event feel, we needed a professional broadcast with dynamic, entertaining, knowledgeable hosts at a central anchor position. The first Night of Stars was presented in November 1997.

I served as the on-air anchor of that first broadcast from a studio in New York City near Times Square. This ambitious, innovative broadcast was my brainchild, but I also was supported by a terrific group of co-founders. The contributions of Tony Fasulo, Ron Wholen and Tim Leuschner were critical to the success of the endeavor. My coworker here in Birmingham, Stan Flint and I secured Hooters as our primary sponsor. Tony worked with the satellite folks on the complicated challenges presented by this idea from a technical standpoint. Ron is a master organizer and made sure that everyone and their various parts were working in conjunction. Tim handled the wagering details and brought aboard an incredibly important element. He negotiated it with a company and reached an agreement for an insurance policy guaranteeing a $1 million payoff on a Pick-8 wager. Needless to say, that attracted a lot of attention to our initial offering. Amazingly, the morning of the event, The Daily Racing Form, the newspaper that serves as the central source of information for horse racing, ran a front page story on the Night of Stars. The piece praised the originality and audacity of the program. The horse racing industry typically regards the greyhound racing business as a rag muffin stepchild. This article suggested that horse people would be wise to adopt a pattern of thinking similar to what we had instituted. If you want to talk about a satisfying career moment, that one was pretty good.

The night of the broadcast, a snowstorm threatened the northeast corridor. Despite some early satellite difficulties, we got those races in and the show was off and running. It was a four and a half hour broadcast with 15 races from coast-to-coast and it was a phenomenal success. National total wagering handle was well over $1 million dollars. The dissenters that said it wouldn't work, it was too complicated, people would be confused, had to eat their words. And incredibly, a group of bettors did indeed pick eight winners and won a million dollars.

Over the next seven years, I would host 12 more Night of Stars. To this day, people ask me, "Why it can't be revived?" It had a tremendous run, but like any initiative, it needed to be refreshed and updated. By the time it was discontinued, I was no longer affiliated in a management capacity with a racetrack and was no longer invited to participate in the final broadcasts of the event that I had conceptualized and founded. Sadly, it was allowed to simply die out.

With so much seemingly going my way at this point, I was called on twice in three years to be a participant in the most important gathering of industry officials each year, the University of Arizona Racing Symposium. It was held annually at one of my favorite places in the country, in Tucson at the Lowe's Ventana Canyon Resort.

People still tell me all these years later how much they enjoyed my 1996 speech at that meeting. I was on a panel discussing what the racing industry could do to better position itself in the face of increasing competition in the entertainment industry. For many years, tracks had charged for parking, admission to the facility, upgrade to levels with more amenities and even seating. That approach was fine when the local track was pretty much the only game in town. With the approach of the new century closing fast, that landscape totally changed. I decided not to stand up there and make a straight-laced presentation; it's just not my style. So as I began talking, I casually reached under the podium, picked up the white doctor's lab coat I had stashed there, and slipped it on. Without missing a beat in my speech, I announced that my name was Dr. Keefer, a leading specialist in Raceology. I reached into my pocket and pulled out a full-fledged stethoscope and placed it around my neck. At that point, I articulated that I was here to give a diagnosis and specifically designed treatment specifications for the patient, the parimutuel racing industry. I covered the number of topics, including my rant about the absurdity of continuing to charge people to pay to park and enter the building. My argument was, the more money you allow them to enter the building with, the better chance they have to succeed, allowing that money to stay in circulation. The concept is called churn. The track gets a percentage of every dollar wagered. The more the dollar stays in circulation, the more churn is created.

It was the conclusion of my speech though that became so fondly remembered. Perhaps it was because it was an unusual choice of device to emphasize the main point. I like to think that it was the fact that it struck a nostalgic cord with the audience of that time since it referenced a popular, cultural phenomenon from many of the people in that room's childhood. Here was the conclusion of what I said in the speech that day.

I lifted the microphone off the stand and walked from behind the podium to the front of the stage. I was so very much in my element and had never felt more empowered and in control. I gazed out of the audience and began my conclusion.

"I know you all remember the great television series of the mid to late 60s, Batman. It starred Adam West as the Caped Crusader. It was campy, tongue-in-cheek and fun. My favorite thing about the show used to be the anticipation to see who the bad guy was going to be for each week's show. The episode that comes to mind today was Batman and Robin matching wits with the beautiful, alluring but diabolical Catwoman played in the series by the lovely, sexy Julie Newmar. It was the very end of the episode, and Catwoman had made a huge score by stealing from a museum exhibit a huge stash of rare crown jewels worth millions. Of course, Batman had arrived just in time to foil her getaway. As he and Robin easily dispatched of her motley crew of henchmen, she slipped out and made a run for it. Batman chased her into a nearby cave. Catwoman then came to a large crevice and was momentarily stifled as Batman closed the gap between them. Her only chance for escape was to try to jump across. Swinging the heavy bag of jewels over her shoulder, she backed up a couple of steps and attempted the treacherous leap. She came up short but did manage to grab on to a precarious hold with her free arm and attempted to pull herself up. Meanwhile, Batman arrived on the scene on the other side. He implored her to drop the bag and pull herself up. He desperately continued to encourage her to do so.

"'Catwoman, the weight of the bag is pulling you down. If you don't let it go, you're going to fall into that bottomless pit.'

"The feline criminal mastermind babe in her skin-tight black leather outfit, which was too much to comprehend and really appreciate at my tender young age, responded, 'I can't let it go, you know what's in here.'

"Batman responded desperately, 'it's dragging you down, you have to let it go so you can pull yourself up and go on. Let it go, and live for other days.' However, Catwoman refused as the weight of the bag had almost completely pulled her away from her weakening hold with the other hand. 'I just can't let it go; you know what's in here and how valuable it is. It's parking and admissions revenue.'

"At that very instant, dramatically, Catwoman fell into the dark opening, screaming in terror as she plunged downward and out of sight."

Slumping my shoulders, I lowered the microphone with my arms hanging down at my sides and sadly looked at the crowd, shaking my head. Then I delivered my finishing comment ... "Today, I am Batman and our industry is the Catwoman, which is a pretty good deal because I'm Adam West, and you are all Julie Newmar.

Anyway, in our respective roles, I implore you, It's time to think about moving forward. You have to let it go!"

Riding tall in the saddle off of this bountiful, high-profile period, I was contacted and asked if I would be interested in discussing a job opportunity in Wichita, Kansas, managing the racetrack there. Any doubt that it was a serious inquiry was erased by the fact that the owners' private jet was dispatched to Birmingham to pick me up. That same evening, I was picked up by a longtime friend and associate from the Greyhound business and driven to the home of Phil Ruffin in Wichita. Ruffin was a self-made multimillionaire who had started out in retail as a young man but quickly became prominent through his dogged determination and relentless approach to any and all things business. Long before the trend became popular, he became involved in the conversion of gas stations to dual facilities also offering convenience stores. One by one, he acquired a group of stores and the real estate they occupied. Some of them were made 24 hour operations, an unheard of practice of in the 60s. He later leased the stores but retained the ownership of the properties. He also made a savvy investment in a warehouse equipment company specializing in hand trucks and turned it into a gold mine. His success is characterized by one central factor, you never stand still. Once money is made, it is put to work to make more. He acquired real estate, hotels, and casinos and watched over personally every morning how all of his businesses were operating and performing. He currently owns the Treasure Island Hotel and Casino on the Las Vegas Strip. He previously owned, the now demolished, iconic Frontier Hotel, which once belonged to Howard Hughes. He purchased it for roughly $170 million and sold it in a matter of years for over one billion. No matter how you add it up, that is astounding ROI! One of the buyers of part of the property was none other than his good friend Donald Trump.

Mr. Ruffin is not one for chitchat or wasting time, but our initial meeting went very well. He told me he had become disgusted with the operation at the racetrack in his hometown, so he decided to buy it. That investment was also predicated on his belief that he had the political components in place to secure casino gaming for the state of Kansas's racetracks. I was sitting across from one of the most accomplished negotiators imaginable. This guy made million dollar deals on a routine basis. But I had a surge of confidence when I realize that I was the one dealing from a position of strength. The initial candidate that Ruffin and had proposed to be general manager had not been approved by the Kansas Racing and Gaming Commission. He needed someone qualified to step in and had received a number of recommendations telling him that I was the guy he wanted. I certainly wanted to take the job as the situation in Birmingham was continuing to deteriorate, but my young family had settled in nicely and operating man was a major concern. We talked about some initial numbers. I threw what I thought was a high figure when he insisted I throw out an initial number. He certainly didn't flinch, but he did counter down. I later found out in getting to know him, that he always made who he was negotiating with reveal their figure first. He told me that he never had consummated a deal that was not lower than the other party's starting point. We left it with me promising to get back to them first thing in the morning with my decision. Overnight, I spoke to my wife, and we agreed it was too enticing to pass up. That came as a bit of a surprise since change had never been something that she readily embraced. The comfort zone to making a move for her may have been the fact that both her parents had been born and predominately raised in Kansas. We were heading for the Sunflower State.

The next 4 1/2 years was an amazing ride in my career and family life. Unlike Birmingham, where basically I was a figurehead, in Wichita, I literally was tossed the keys and told to make it work. As far as innovation, introduction of new ways of presenting the racing product and incredibly creative marketing concepts, The Kip Keefer idea factory at Wichita Greyhound Park was undeniably cutting-edge.

For the first couple of years, I assumed the role of being a valued lieutenant in the Ruffin regime. This was a remarkable era of transportation via private jets and high-powered meetings on a regular basis involving possible acquisitions and high-level political strategies. Frequent trips to Las Vegas were required, and I certainly never tired of that assignment. In fact, on a number of occasions, I was accompanied by my very best friend and constant sidekick, my son Case. Our adventures in Vegas, from the time he was a very small boy, developed for him a love affair with the city. Little did either one of us know that in adulthood, the city would become his home and career base.

For the first couple of years, the track in Wichita performed very well. However, profits were not considerable because operating costs were outrageous. Much of that could be blamed on the ill-conceived legislation that authorizes racing that was loaded down with costly, unnecessary requirements and a state racing commission which was decidedly anything but pro-business. In fact, during my time there, that organization basically made my life a continual misery. If not for their interference and relentless efforts to complicate anything and everything, the Kansas experience would've been so much greater. Of course, unbeknown to me at that time, I would someday be in the role of director of a regulatory agency. My experiences in Wisconsin and Kansas proved to be monumentally educational, predominantly by observing what not to do in the execution of that role.

During the first year in Wichita, Mr. Ruffin and visited the offices one day and noticed a copy of the industry magazine, The Greyhound Review, on my desk. There was a picture of the industries top racing star at that time on the cover. He asked me simply, "How can we get dogs like that to run here?" I quickly answered, if you put up $100,000 for a big stakes race, I will create a phenomenal event and draw every luminary greyhound and prominent person in the industry here. To that he simply replied, "Do It." Three months later, The Invitational Greyhound Race of Champions became a reality on Labor Day 2000. The event was a spectacular success creating records for attendance and betting totals.

Sadly, Kansas is a very conservative state by nature. Despite repeated innovative concepts, business levels started to decline. I had actually engineered something truly revolutionary in being the first race track to ever televise locally the actual races live every racing performance. I had worked a deal with the local cable provider to buy a package of annual advertising on their system in exchange for an unused channel. Simulcasting to other tracks and casinos had become a common practice after my Birmingham cohorts and I had pioneered that approach years earlier. Now by sending a simple decoder to the cable company, Voila, The races were now in your living room. To accompany that, a nominal investment in a television studio set was made and the daily program was born. Typically, I anchored and was joined by a variety of co-hosts and guests. It was the ideal promotional and advertising vehicle. It was tremendous for fan education and instruction on what to look for, how to handicap and how to bet. It also became popular and infamous at the same time because of the presence of a stunningly attractive, but extraordinarily ditzy, airheaded blonde named Christie. She didn't really add much to the show in terms of her verbal contribution but became quite a conversation piece because of her revealing outfits and wondrous frontal assets. On local television and around the country at wagering outlets, men of all ages, sizes and persuasions tuned in to watch her on the show. In one episode, and this is absolutely a true story, I was highlighting one of our tracks that took our signal in Bridgeport, Connecticut. That turned the conversation to New York City, and I asked Christie if she had ever been there. She said no and followed up by asking me if it was cold there? After explaining the concept of the four seasons, which I'm not so sure she grasped, a mischievous thought entered my head just to demonstrate the capacity of her gray matter. I asked her, "Here's a New York trivia question, who is the George Washington Bridge named after?" Her answer, "You know I don't know things like that." To this day, as I travel to other tracks or receive correspondence from industry associates, people ask about her. I have not seen or heard from her since 2001. With the races now on television, more innovation was required, and after a protracted fight with the racing commission, I was finally granted permission to install drive-thru wagering. Like I said before, cutting-edge, out-of-the-box thinking was standard operating procedure during my stint at Wichita.

Despite all that, all good things have to come to an end. Mr. Ruffin purchased a defunct race track near Pittsburg, Kansas, in the extreme south-east part of the state. I was put in charge of getting the dormant facility up and running. It was a Herculean task. The major problem was as far as operations, there was not very much population in the area, and those who lived there, for the most part, did not have considerable wealth. And as far as being extremely thrifty and conservative, this area probably has few challengers. We had an overflow crowd for our tiny track on opening night of almost 2000 people.

My father-in-law, Carroll Blair, had traveled up from West Memphis to be on hand with his best friend Joe Scott in tow. Joe was a former Negro baseball league star in the 40s and 50s and in his advancing years was a huge racetrack enthusiast. More than anything else, he was a terrific guy. Always ready with a story or great embellishment regarding his career. He was definitely an all-star in the sense of being a world-class self-promoter. He carried around copies of his baseball card. He was always ready to hand one out to whoever would accept it. He would autograph it, "Yours in sports, Joe Scott." My favorite story he featured was one about him playing on a barnstorming softball team in the 1940s. In those days, uniforms typically did not have numbers. On the southern swing of their tour somewhere in North Carolina, Joe strolled up to bat to lead off the game. As he dug in the batters box, the catcher, with a distinct southern drawl said to him, "I don't know how we're going to tell all you boys apart, you all look alike." Joe always mentioned at this point of the story, that he was by far the team's best player. He claims to have doubled and come around later to score. When returning to the dugout, he reported to the manager what the catcher had said. The manager's response, "Well, that's real good news, Joe, because now you're going to bat every inning."

My father-in-law was never short on stories either. He had an inventory a mile long from all of the years he had been involved in racing. But it was a fairly recent incident that everyone who hears it finds particularly hilarious. After many years, management at Southland had changed. The new head man was not very popular and looked to Carroll to be a liaison for him in dealing with the greyhound guys. At one of their meetings, the manager mentioned that the West Memphis police were conducting a drug selling investigation and suspected a member of the kennel community was involved. He had agreed to allow them to install a hidden camera in the area referred to as the cool out. This is where trainers took dogs after their races. It was also a major congregation area throughout every racing performance. The manager went on to explain there was no evidence found from their surveillance of any drug related transactions. But he did inform Carroll that the footage revealed that one of the trainers had consumed 21 beers in the course of one matinee racing performance in that area. Carroll quickly responded, "He must not have been very thirsty that day."

That night at Camptown Racetrack, yes that is really its name, once again you can't make this stuff up, as I stood with Joe Scott at the bar, we looked around the gathered crowd. At some point, Joe looked at me, and what he said was extremely profound and prophetically ominous. He said thoughtfully, "You know, I believe I am the only black fella here." At that very instant, I knew the track was doomed. Every gaming operation I had ever been involved with featured a very diverse audience. This crowd was all local, mostly rural-based folks. There was an undeniable absence of expertise and, with all due respect, sophistication. Despite the sizable crowd, the total of dollars wagered was low and telltale. These attendees did not bring much money to spend, and they only spent a little of what they brought.

The second track was nothing but headaches, and just months after opening, Ruffin ordered it to be shut down. I had to travel there and deliver the bad news to all involved. I was not subsequently blamed for the track's failure, but the stench of being associated with it from a leadership position was impossible to shake off. At Wichita, I was being forced to let key people go that we could no longer afford. It was difficult and painstaking. Then, on a March Saturday, the bell tolled for me. Phil arrived at the office, we sat down, and I was fired. It was an experience I had never undergone before. He was as compassionate as he could muster, and it clearly was not in his comfort zone to be so. He told me I had done some amazing things and that he had always been impressed with my talent, confidence, and audacity. But he said something that was very simple but has had a tremendous lasting effect. It was, "As talented as you are you always have to remember that the Devil is in the details." Those words resonate with me now just about every day. He went on to explain that the tracks' failure to secure machine gaming made the ultimate operating life of the facility short-lived. He said they were going to stagger on, but they could no longer afford me. The same great deal that I had shrewdly negotiated was now an anchor firmly attached around my neck, dragging me down and out.

We had purchased a fabulous house at a spectacular country club in Wichita. Our run there had been miraculously blessed, but we were living above our means. Faced with the daunting task of staying afloat, I swung into action to market myself. A tremendous opportunity opened up in Iowa, and I seemed virtually assured of landing it. The job was to manage marketing and promotion of greyhound racing in the state. It was a perfect job for my skill set and the compensation was considerable. Two groups were vying to be recognized as the official representative organization of the state's racing participants. One offered me full control and immediate compensation to prepare their presentation to the racing commission. The other, the existing group, also offered me the job, but I would be reporting to their board of directors. Further, I would not be compensated until the contract was secured. Immediately needing income, I opted to go with the upstart group. It proved to be a good stopgap measure for the financial crisis but a disastrous decision long-term. Despite my presentation being literally 1000 times superior in every aspect, far more thorough, comprehensive and impressive than the rival group's, by a 3-2 vote, my organization lost out. It would not have mattered if I had staged a presentation narrated by Morgan Freeman with a troupe of Cirque de Soleil performers dazzling the audience to emphasize my points, the fix was in. The existing organization had some very influential political allies that pulled some serious behind the scenes shenanigans and powerful strings. The commission chairman, who had cast his vote for my presentation, looked at his dissenting colleagues and said, "I want it reflected in the record that in all of my years serving on this board, I believe this is the most baffling and disappointing decision in my tenure," His words were little consolation for me. The sure thing that I had been banking on had blown up in my face. I learned a harsh lesson that day, that merit is not necessarily the means that determine the ends. For me, the personal implications and cost would be enormous. No less than my marriage, the life I had built and my dreams and vision of the future, from that vote, basically received a death sentence.

Needing a job desperately, I accepted the position as general manager at Tucson Greyhound Park in Arizona. Just like in Kansas, the primary activity of the racing industry in that state was trying to acquire machine gaming. Slot machines were now seen as the eternal salvation for the racetrack industry. Tracks in states that had managed to secure it were flourishing; those without, were dying on the vine. My job in Tucson quickly evolved into primarily being a spokesperson and lobbyist for gaming. Native American tribes in the state had a complete and total monopoly. For the next year and a half, I spent a tremendous amount of time at the capital in Phoenix working on trying to convince legislators that the tracks, the state's licensed gaming franchises, needed to be granted the same opportunities as the Native Americans. Not additional advantages, simply a level playing field. I appeared at speaking events throughout the state to highlight the issue. Numerous debates and television appearances were also commonplace. When the referendums appeared on the ballot, the racetrack provision was soundly defeated. My sudden string of not so good fortune was starting to feel like a runaway train.

My total attention in Arizona was not on my job, something I regret to this day. Of course, it was unfair to the owners of the track that hired me. My wife had sued for divorce, and I flatly refused to participate. I did not open correspondence from her attorney and ignored all aspects of what was transpiring. No matter what my job was, to me, unquestionably my most important task was being a father. I traveled back to Wichita constantly to be with my boys. After only a year and a half in Arizona, I was let go.

Suddenly I was truly lost. I had nowhere to go. That's when my longest tenured friends, Jim and Craige, saved the day. They invited me to stay at their home in Atlanta to regroup, recover, and recapture stability. Jim owned and managed his company Specialty Fixtures, which produced custom-built counters for predominately retail businesses. I went to work helping him out that summer in a whole different kind of employment assignment. Two years before I was flying in corporate jets, sitting in and participating in meetings involving millions of dollars and potential acquisitions, and pursuing a career as a captain of industry managing hundreds of people. Suddenly I found myself behind the wheel of a giant Penske rental truck filled with massive photo processing counters produced for Eckerd Drug Stores. Loaded up with 16 to 18 of these monsters in the back, I was given a list of addresses in faraway places and sent off to make sure they reached their destinations. This was 2003, the introduction of GPS guidance was still several years from being unleashed. I had to drive to cities like Natchitoches, Louisiana or Watertown, New York, and wrestle one of these gargantuan wood and laminate beasts off the back of the truck to leave at the store to which it was assigned. Then the process of trying to figure out where the next stop was and how to get there would begin anew. Other than a few minor hiccups, the most famous of which is featured in these pages in a Keefer Story, I performed my tasks well. As I have stated many times, this kid can do it all.

That fall, I had the opportunity to go to Florida, back to the Melbourne track that I had helped launch 12 years before and work as event host and track announcer. My father lived in nearby Cocoa Beach, so I had a place to stay. That gig was short-lived because I received a major break at the beginning of 2004.

I became aware that another of my previous stomping grounds, specifically Birmingham, had an opening that attracted my attention. The director of the racing commission was retiring and I quickly applied for that position. I had departed Birmingham with very good relationships with several of these sitting racing commissioners and the track owner. Miraculously, everything fell into place, and for the first time in a long and diverse career in the racing and gaming industry, I was on the regulatory side. I inherited a tremendous staff that made the transition extremely easy. I had experienced such a miserable negative interaction with racing commissions in Wisconsin and Kansas that I came in with knowledge and expertise of exactly what I did not want to do. That has served me well.

The greatest blessing of my entire career path has been the ability in virtually every situation to stay involved in broadcasting and creative endeavors. The return to Birmingham was particularly gratifying as I hosted my own weekly sports show and appeared on other programs and numerous television features promoting the business. And for a brief time period, I had the ultimate opportunity for a sports broadcaster. a host gig on an afternoon drive show. As I've said many times and in many places across this great nation, "I have never met a microphone I didn't like."

I often reflect on the fact that there were so many things in terms of career opportunities that I probably could have/should have pursued. I have no doubts that I could have made a greater contribution in any number of areas and certainly a hell of a lot more money. However, the ride has been pretty remarkable for a guy who basically was just making it up as he went along. Without a proper starting point, lack of support and then approach of basically flying by the seat of my pants, I managed to accomplish a great deal. Hope springs eternal that I have one more great run still in me.

KEEFER STORY

High Profile Fan

A couple of years into my track announcing gig at Southland, a routine evening of calling the races turned into one of those nights that something extraordinary happens. Those rare moments that happen in life when seemingly impossible circumstances lead to amazing experiences.

It was about halfway through the racing card. I had just concluded wrapping up the results of a race on the public address system when there was a loud knocking on the door to my small broadcast booth. I worked high above the facility in a press box style area looking down upon the racetrack. The area was restricted to authorized personnel only. I had hosted visitors before, but to have someone knocking at my door was unusual. I opened it and immediately recognized one of our security sergeants standing on the other side in the hallway. He explained that the general manager had asked him to escort a guest up to my location who wanted to meet me. The guard step to the side slightly, and another gentleman who had been waiting just out of my sight stepped in.

This man was, to say the least, a sharp-dressed man. He was wearing what was obviously a very fine, meticulously fitting, expensive, navy blue suit. He wore a white shirt and blue tie. On his head was a white fedora style hat.

I had never met this gentleman, but that did not mean that I did not know his name and exactly who he was. You see, I left out one other distinctive description about his appearance, he had a long flowing, reddish beard that angled down his cheeks below his ears and extended to the lower third of his torso. It was trimmed in almost a triangular shape at its end. There was no doubt that the gentleman standing in my tiny announcer's booth was one of the world's most successful, recognizable music stars. He extended his hand and said, "Hey, I really wanted to meet you, I'm Billy Gibbons." I shook his hand and introduced myself.

OK, so let's reset this, the musical genius and driving force behind one of the most successful rock bands ever, ZZ Top, had expressed the desire to meet, me? If I had been thinking properly, I should have quipped, "I'd be happy to give you an autograph."

He may have sensed my confusion or perhaps he enjoyed the fact that I did not freak out or act beside myself with excitement from meeting him. He told me that he had come to the track that night with some friends and coworkers. He mentioned they had been enjoying the races in our exclusive clubhouse restaurant, then called Touch of Brass. He then told me how much he was enjoying my extremely colorful and entertaining announcing style. He was amazed that I could describe action moving at such a fast pace and be able to use so many creative descriptions. The track GM at the time, Chuck Clark, had stopped in to introduce himself and Billy had asked him about me. Incredibly, he told the Clark that he would really like to be introduced.

The really good thing about the whole encounter was that while I was amazed and tremendously flattered that a major star was complimenting my art and talent, I really was not the least bit star struck. To be honest, while I was certainly aware of the amazing success of ZZ Top, and certainly liked a few of their hits, I really was not a fan. We chatted a few minutes and I asked him why he was in town. He explained that the studio the band used for all of its recording tracks was in downtown Memphis and it was common for him to spend extended periods of time in the city. The track's new upscale restaurant had been suggested to him as a fun place to go, and now, here they were.

The greyhounds for the next race were lining up to be introduced, so I had to excuse myself and turn back to my work for a moment. He stood just on the other side of my small counter and observed me going through the introductions. I rattled off the names and weights of the runners along with a short breakdown of their records and running styles. When I finished, he remarked that he was amazed that I could relay that information without any notes. It was second nature for me, and I certainly was not impressed with myself; however, I certainly appreciated his continuing, unbelievably polite and flattering plaudits. He then asked me something that truly was a huge surprise. He asked if I minded if he stuck around and watched me work when the upcoming race was running. Of course, I assured him that he was certainly welcome to stay as long as he wanted. He settled into the extra chair as I took my spot at the window and described the action on the track. Of course, I pulled out all the stops and used some of my best "go to" words and phrases. A finish call such as, "It is all the 8, Nicky Finn ... He has huffed, and puffed, and blown this field away!" As the dogs crossed the wire, and I shut down the mic, when I turned around, he stood up and applauded. Talk about a surreal moment, but what an unforgettable experience.

It was not unusual on a busy night at Southland for me to be performing for 2500 to 3000 people. However, I was segregated from all of them in my solitary booth, far removed from the public areas. This command performance, for my celebrity audience of one, an individual used to performing onstage for tens of thousands of people, was a pretty staggering, unlikely event.

I wrapped up that race, and we continued to become acquainted. Amazingly, he was asking me questions about my background and aspirations. Of course, by this time, the word had spread around the officials' hallway, and a crowd started to mass of some of my coworkers outside my door. Judges, television technicians and cameramen, chart writers, photo finish specialist, lure operator and the runner, all were anxious to meet our celebrity visitor. Billy is an unbelievably gracious, kind, and polite man. He cheerfully shook hands with the unofficial receiving line of officials, and even indulged a couple of autograph requests. Time for the next race rolled around, and all of the intruders scurried back to their posts. I called another race with Billy standing by. At its conclusion, he told me he needed to get back downstairs to his party, but asked if I could stop by after the races to their table and meet everyone. Of course, I agreed and later that evening did just that. As the evening wrapped up, he thanked me again and told me he would be coming out as often as he could when in town.

About a week later, I received a manila envelope with a return address from Houston, Texas. It turned out to be from ZZ Top's management firm and was filled with a number of unusual promotional items, including some impressive looking stainless steel logo key chains. There was also a note thanking me for my hospitality and telling me how much he enjoyed the visit.

Periodically over the remainder of that season, word would reach me that he and his friends were at the track on a particular night. I always made a point to run down and say hello. On one such occasion, he mentioned they were having a big golf outing the next day and invited me to play. It was a great day of great fun, although a large number of participants were on hand. I played with a couple of guys that I had never met from the sizable entourage. Most were technical folks or musicians. Billy was not in my group, but in the bar afterward, he made a point to come over and talk to me for a while.

It was the following season when I next saw him. When booking his reservation, he had asked the maître d' to let me know that he was in town and coming out. I stopped by before the races and greeted him. Even though I had sent a note to thank him, I wanted to personally express my gratitude for receiving a Christmas present via mail from him several months before. It was a bizarre little voodoo looking doll that you were supposed to hang on your door for good luck. I thought it was pretty good to be on Billy Gibbons' Christmas list. He let me know during that conversation that he had made arrangements for booking the entire room two weeks later. He was throwing a big party, and the special occasion was his own birthday. He was insistent that I needed to be sure to come by. I asked him if it would be OK to name a special race that night in his honor. That would involve printing it in the official program, it being prominently featured on our television system and on our giant message board and, of course, become a prominent part of our track announcer's, yours truly, show that night. He enthusiastically embraced the idea.

When the night rolled around, I had two big surprises. The first, we ordered two very nice plaques commemorating the "Billy Gibbons Birthday Special Feature Race." Engraved also was a fully striding greyhound and an electric guitar. One of the awards was to be presented by Billy to the winning greyhound's trainer as they posed in the winner's circle. And he seemed greatly touched that the other was for him to keep in honor of the evening.

The second surprise, which I did not divulge to him at the time, was the fact that I had planned to do a highly unique specialty call for the race in his honor. My objective was to do a race description with as many ZZ Top song titles in it that I possibly could work in. He had already gone down trackside right before his race with a large accompanying group so they would be in position for their presentation and photograph. Just before the race began, I had instructed our director of marketing, who was in the winner's circle area, to tell Billy to be sure to listen to the call for the race because I was delivering something special in his honor.

Calling a horse or greyhound race is not something you can preplan or choreograph. What you describe has to be based on what you see occurring on the track. I knew certain parts of the call wouldn't make much sense, but that wasn't the point. Of course, I don't remember specifics, but the call went something like this ...

From the outside that's the 8 zooming to the front with such flash the others need "Cheap Sunglasses."

Next, it's the "Sharp Dressed Man" wearing the number 2, rushing up on the rail. The 3 is also making a big effort to stay in "Tush" with the leaders. The longshot 4 greyhound trying to award her backers and "Gimme All Your Lovin'" and a big payoff. And the six is last way back by that shack outside "Lagrange." As they approach the wire, it's the 5 taking charge. She has "Legs" and knows how to use them!

Billy told me later that he had absolutely loved my custom designed race call and told me it was incredibly creative. As I did all of his positive comments, that was particularly appreciated from somebody of his amazing talents. The night was a resounding success.

One of the last times I saw him during a later visit, we talked about how cool it would be if the band ever did a song about going to the races. He said we should name it, Dog Track Saturday Night. I later wrote some simple lyrics and sent them to him. I never heard a response of whether or not he liked it. Obviously the song never came to be.

Sadly, after three or four years of fairly close contact, my moving around and things changing in my life led to us losing touch. I still have a nice collection of things that he sent me and some notes he personally wrote and sent to me. Amazingly to this day, ZZ Top continues to be a force and has remarkably appealed to multiple generations of fans. Billy Gibbons was always the driving force and talented, creative genius that served as the backbone of the band. A brilliant worldwide star! And astonishingly, he was also something else, unabashedly, amazingly, a big time Kip Keefer Fan.

Close Encounter Of The Strangest Kind

I was wrapping up a 1987 season as Southland track announcer and director of publicity. Toward the end of the schedule, an announcement was made that our track would become a year-round operation for racing beginning the following April. I was a salaried employee, and the additional racing nights on the schedule would precipitate a significant amount of additional hours and labor. I requested and was granted a meeting with the track general manager Louis Derteen.

I explained my position and sought the information from him as to what my compensation adjustment would be with the change that was imminent. He informed me that perhaps I would get a small increase, but in his opinion, my compensation was " adequate." He informed me that for a young man, my $29,000 salary per year was "pretty damn good in West Memphis Arkansas." On that January morning when we met, I had recently turned 30 years old. My life had changed significantly since our last negotiation. I had been married just over year and our first child had arrived. And as unsophisticated as West Memphis Arkansas might have been, it certainly was not a Third World country. I also was well aware that the corporate entity and controlling stockholder of the business, a large conglomerate Delaware North Companies, out of Buffalo New York, had executives that had noticed my talent and proficiency. For the first time in my career, I was mindful of my worth.

I informed Mr. Derteen that by my calculation my workload was going to increase 30 to 40%. Based on that, I asked for an increase to $40,000. His reaction? He laughed and said, "And what happens when I decline?" To which I told him, "Then I suppose I have to quit." And he smirked and said something to the effect of, "Well, do what you have to do." So I did.

My father-in-law was a great man and understood the stand I had taken. He didn't think that bolting the course from my job was that wise since I had a family to take care of but was kind enough to offer me a job in his organization while I sorted things out.

He ran a home-based greyhound training farm adjacent to the family house in Proctor, Arkansas. I had worked with racing greyhounds previously on two occasions. My family had purchased a farm not far from the Blair compound where we operated a training facility and boarding kennel. And then, in the winter of 1986, I enjoyed a glorious year in St. Petersburg, Florida, as trainer for the Jenny Marriott kennel at the world-famous Derby Lane track. I had gone to work as trainer for Mrs. Robert Marriott's (Jenny) kennel. I had asked for and been granted a winter month's leave of absence. The experience was fantastic; all of my training cohorts provided one of the most entertaining periods of my entire life. At that time, and a big reason I initially I had wanted to go there, the legendary Keith Dillon kennel was racing my namesake, Keefer, and he was having a season to remember down south.

My first day at work, I was instructed to be there at 5 AM. That's right, in the morning! It was February, and it was freezing. The house and kennel were part of a large parcel of rural property. The grounds included a huge fenced pasture. Mr. Blair had a couple of cows and 20 to 25 goats running around out there. Well, not the cows so much, they were fat and almost immobile. Anyway, my career as a greyhound farmer got off to an ominous start. My first assignment was to take a shovel, go out into the pasture and locate an unfortunate goat that had passed away. I was assigned the task of digging a hole and providing for his burial. Now you have to remember, despite a very colorful and diverse employment history, the art of manual labor was not necessarily one of my most sparkling attributes. After locating the unfortunate deceased, I confidently plunged the shovel into Mother Earth in a spot that looked feasible. The handle of the implement reverberated in my hands as the steel point contacted and then bounced directly upwards in defiance. Not only did my initial thrust not initiate the process of digging a hole, it did not even make a dent. I redoubled my effort and after much determination had scooped out the equivalent of a tablespoon from a rock hard carton of ice cream. My hands were frozen, my spirits sagged. I had to trudge back to the boss man and report that I had failed in my mission. He seemed to take delight in the fact that the golden boy, master of the airwaves, highest IQ in the county, could not complete a mundane task.

That winter drug on slowly to say the least. Thankfully, racing season was coming up beginning in late March. The plan was I would handle the racing kennel until my colorful brother-in-law Rusty returned from the St. Pete season at the end of April. Then I would be his assistant throughout the summer and fall meet. That was a far better assignment than having to go to the farm every day. Still on Tuesdays and Fridays, my presence was required at 3:45 AM. Those were schooling days when the track was available for dogs to get workouts in. Schooling started at 5:30 AM and we, of course, had to be first in line. Days were long, but, at least, I was working around the track again.

It was a pleasant Wednesday morning, The day prior to the opening of the 1988 Southland racing season. After completing my Kennel work, I had one more assignment to complete my morning. Mr. Blair was a big believer in getting dogs out for additional exercise. That generally entailed walking them for about a mile. Sounds easy enough right? Well, putting a leash on the eight to ten dogs, weighing an average of about 65 pounds each, and then getting everybody moving in the same direction for these leisurely strolls, was a pretty significant challenge. Leads got crossed, feet became entangled, and suddenly movements proved problematic to the overall progress.

During that morning's dragathon, with myself, of course, serving as the drag-ee, the thought occurred to me as I walked along the back fence of the race track facility that I should be keeping an eye out on the ground for discarded items or anything of value. To this day, I don't know what triggered that notion, but just several steps later, lodged up against the chain-link fence, I came face-to-face with none other than the illustrious Ben Franklin. One of the slang terms for money is "dead presidents" and whoever came up with that was a moron. Ben Franklin is depicted on the $100 bill and that morning walking that group of dogs, that is exactly what I found. How could that not be an amazing day? Later on, I found out.

Kennel turnouts generally occur twice each morning, mid-afternoon and late evening. I had been issued one of the Blair fleet of trucks that facilitated transporting greyhounds. It was a modified pickup with a compartmentalized trailer mounted to the rear bed. That night, with only the task of letting the dogs out and putting them back up on the agenda, I opted to drive my wife Cathie's sporty RX7 to the kennel compound. it turned out to be a fortuitous decision. That proved particularly true for an inopportune crossing of paths with a stranger in the night.

I was cruising along down the service road that runs parallel to Interstate 40/55. Just a quarter-mile from the track facility, my melodious singing to whatever tune was playing was rudely interrupted. Suddenly, a sight that I can only describe as mind-boggling and incomprehensible. One second driving along, literally the next second, the indescribable visual of the seat of a pair of Wrangler jeans prominently was framed and displayed on the windshield directly in front of my face. It was so clear that I could see the stitching on the pockets and the product label. As my senses struggled to make some sort of sense of what was happening, all of a sudden, the vision disappeared. Dumbfounded, bewildered and visibly shaken, I quickly pulled over. Hopping out of the car on the dark road in the dead of night, I could see nothing wrong around me. I did notice immediately that the driver side headlight, a fancy flip up kind of deal, was missing. Additionally, there was a very large crack in the windshield. As I struggled to grasp what had occurred, suddenly the silence was broken by an audible moaning sound. I started to walk back toward the area of where the "incident" took place. That's when I saw him; about 50 yards further down the road, there was a figure laying in the middle of the street. Panicked, I dashed in that direction and came upon a bearded figure with a "CaterpillarTractor" hat still adorning his head (you can't make this stuff up), a flannel shirt and the blue jeans that I now could pick out of a lineup, having received such a thorough look at them in suspended animation previously. The gentleman was not very communicative and thankfully, heaven chose to dispatch needed reinforcements at that very instant. I was still basically in shock, and so it dawned on me that I had hit this fellow somehow with my vehicle. I had no earthly idea where in the hell he had come from and how his ass had come to rest on my windshield.

A man that turned out to be a guardian angel that night happened to have been outside the building checking tank levels at the Exxon station where he worked a couple of hundred yards down on the corner. He had jogged up to where I was standing with the unfortunate victim and immediately announced that he had seen the whole thing. He did not take the time to explain after determining that the gentleman was in need of attention. He asked him if he was hurt badly in any particular area, eliciting a response from him that his legs were in great pain. The gas station Saint, wearing his gray shirt with Jerry stitched across the pocket and rag hanging precariously out of his back pocket, turned and started jogging back toward the station. He declared he was going to go call for help and for me to stay with the beleaguered gentleman. I stood off to the side and continued to wonder what had transpired. Jerry's assurance that he had seen the whole thing had never been explained as far as the details went.

He returned in a short time, assuring me that help was on the way. I finally had a chance to ask the million-dollar question, "Who is this guy and where did he come from?" Gas station Jerry pointed to a big rig pulled up in the right emergency lane across the grass median just off the expressway. He explained that was his truck. Apparently the ill-fated driver pulled over, hopped down and set his sights on jogging across the access road to the Exxon for cigarettes or a bathroom break? The timing of his jog across the grass strip and entrance to the access road correlated precisely with my arrival in the Mazda. That resulted in us meeting at the precise instant that both of us arrived at that exact same spot. His leap from the shadows was something that I could not possibly have seen coming. His posterior appearing in the front window was due to the fact that the sports car was so low to the ground that when contact was made he was not slammed into as much as scooped up and hurled backward. Of course, the first contact was on the windshield and then he was lifted up over the top of the roof, clear of the back of the car, and flung through the air until he crashed back to earth on his concrete landing spot.

Ambulances, fire trucks, and police car soon rolled up. The injured man was 10 to 2, loaded in the ambulance and whisked away. A police sergeant pulled me aside, and I related everything I recalled. I've always wished I had a tape of that; I'm curious as to how I sounded and what I described. Once again, Jerry was huge in that process as his account before the authorities arrived had given me some solace and peace of mind. He had reiterated several times that it certainly was not my fault. Clearly, he told the police the same thing. After nearly an hour of questions, photography and report writing, I was told I was free to go. I also learned that I would not be charged with any wrongdoing.

Several days later, I learned from a friend of mine who worked at Crittendon Hospital in West Memphis, that the truck driver had been discharged. Incredibly, he had suffered no broken bones and no internal damage. He stayed several days with severely inflammation in his legs and a very sore back. As unpleasant as his experience that night was, and I opted for the keys to the Ford dog truck, the outcome would've been completely different. Had his clothes and counter been with the giant hood area and front fender of that vehicle, he would've been flatter than day old beer. He would've been smashed into and sent flying like a perfectly tossed bowling ball hitting a solo pin head on to pick up a spare. Two years later, I received a letter from an attorney in Virginia asking me to submit my recollections of the accident. Our family attorney told me I should wad up the letter and throw it away. He declared it a fishing expedition, hoping I would say the wrong thing.

In retrospect, I never felt guilty. The incident really did not bother me because replaying it repeatedly in my mind, I realized I was doing nothing more than driving down the street. I was not negligent or careless in any way. Certainly, I was relieved the man survived and miraculously was not catastrophically injured, but I never felt compelled to involve myself further in a situation in which I was also traumatized.

So, the next time that a big rig 18-wheel trucker cuts you off or blows past you doing 95, remember … One of them "crossed" Kip Keefer once and was lucky to live to tell the tale.

KEEFER STORY

Stuck!

The darkness had just begun to set in on the southwestern Louisiana night. I was diligently performing my tasks for my best friend Jim's business. I was delivering large photo processing counters to Eckerd's drug stores all across the fruited plain. On this particular night, I was down to my last stop of the day.

The vehicle I was utilizing was a large size Penske rental truck. It was certainly not a big rig, but I was hardly a highly-skilled operator. Oh, I was fine tooling along down the highway. Even in cities and towns, I had very few issues. However, to successfully execute my appointed assignments, I was always very careful not to put myself, more specifically my truck, in tight, challenging parking situations. For a task that required many stops and frequent unloading, meticulous thought and planning were required at each location. The primary thing that I desperately attempted to avoid at all cost was backing this monstrosity up. I had never earned my stripes as a "Good Ole Boy." I was clueless about how to fix things, had no acumen or interest in talking about or working on cars and, just as was the case with life itself, typically aspired to always be going forward and never in reverse.

I came to a major intersection off a state highway that led into the thriving metropolis of New Iberia. Now keep in mind, there was no such thing at this point, at least, it wasn't introduced yet, as GPS directions. I had a list of addresses and an atlas. Sometimes, there are hints at an intersection of which way would be most logical to turn in the search for the next stop. On this occasion, there was commerce visible in both directions. It was one of those times where I had to make my best guess. Of course, it usually turned out that my best guess was the wrong one. Unfortunately, this was one of those times. I made a right, and after just a block or so, realized the addresses were descending instead of ascending. I needed to turn around and head the other way. On the lookout for a suitable place to pull in where I would have enough room to maneuver my truck so I could pull out and proceed the other direction, I was not having any positive sightings. Soon, all signs of commerce came to an end. The road narrowed to two lanes, and soon I was completely out of town. Still going in the wrong direction on what suddenly had turned into a rural highway.

For three or four miles, there was nothing but pastures on either side and a few houses with small driveways. I had no choice but to continue on. Finally, on the left-hand side, there was a large structure at the top of a hill with a long driveway leading up to it. I could see a sign identifying it as a fire station. Excited at the prospect of finally being able to turn around, I pulled in and headed up the driveway. I was thinking how lucky I had been to come upon this; fire trucks were much bigger than my vehicle, surely the top of the hill offered an ideal spot to whip my rig around. As the drive came to an end, the dismaying reality set in. There was very little pavement at the end. The driveway turned straight into the structure behind a couple of massive garage-style doors. Fire trucks at the station were not turned around, they simply entered from the right and exited a similar door on the far left. I had no options; I was faced with the unthinkable scenario that I had so painstakingly tried to avoid in all my travels. I was going to have to try and back down the narrow space. And even if I was able to pull that off, I was going to be forced to back out onto the two-lane roadway, a daunting, dangerous prospect.

I began to slowly reverse the path I had just climbed. The first 40 or 50 feet seemed to go pretty well. However, there were subtle curves in the driveway, and suddenly I realized that I was in the grass a good six to eight feet on the driver's side. My efforts to straighten proved extremely difficult. I could see the front porch of the station, and a fireman had come out and was standing there watching me. I'm sure he was wondering what in the hell I was doing there and would most likely ask me himself what was I trying to do. It was a very dark night by this time, so I really could not see what I was doing. I finally made a fateful decision. The grass I was on seemed to be supporting the weight of my wheels. I decided to back up just a few more feet and then hopefully be able to cut the wheel to line up the truck back to the driveway in a forward position. It seemed like a good idea at the time; however, it went terribly wrong.

I backed up 10 feet until I was satisfied that I could now shift back to first gear and drive straight out to the pavement. When I hit the accelerator, it was clear right away something was wrong. The engine revved, the truck lurched forward, and I felt the sickening sensation of wheels spinning. Somehow, I was stuck.

Suddenly, I became aware that there were two gentlemen standing just by my door. I rolled down the window and said something to the effect that obviously I had a problem. One of them seemed highly agitated, the other slightly amused. Of course, they asked what I was trying to do in their fire station. I explained the situation of pulling in expecting to find a place to turn around. I then explained that in trying to back out I had gotten into the grass and thought it was solid enough to maneuver my way out. The annoyed firefighter looked at me with a mix of disgust and incredulity and said, "That probably would have worked if you had not backed into the chief's flower bed."

Of course, looking back in the mirrors and tentatively backing up on the grass, I had no idea of the presence of the flower bed. I hopped down from the cab and walked to the back. My two back wheels were clearly in some very soft portion of the earth. To make matters worse, even my front wheels appeared to have created trenches as they futilely tried to allow for my escape.

The nice firemen had a hopped into the truck and tried for a moment or two to extricate the vehicle but soon gave up. The angry fireman headed for the building declaring he had to go call the chief.

I stood around awkwardly talking to the civil fellow. He was quizzing me on my travels and what I was carrying and seemed to think it was funny that I was driving a truck and really had little idea what I was doing. He warned me that the chief was going to be pissed. His flower bed, which was a pretty good size, was his pride and joy. Now I had backed a rental truck right in the middle of it.

The scouting report on the chief proved highly accurate. He arrived with another fellow and after walking around to assess the situation came over to demand an explanation. I repeated the same sad tale that had precipitated this unfortunate mess. He began to complain vehemently about the damage to their grounds and what it was going to cost to repair. I assured him that I worked for a reputable company and that the owner/president was my lifelong best friend. I told him they had strong insurance coverage for anything and everything that might occur on the road. He did display a shred of a sense of humor at that point although it was totally at my expense. He cracked, "That's a good thing, with somebody like you driving his trucks, I suspect he needs all the coverage he can get."

By this time, I guess word was getting around because suddenly there were two more guys standing around in the group strategizing what to do. I had not even given any thought to what I was going to do if this problem could not be solved that evening.

A couple of the guys had gone into the station and brought out some kind of metal ramps. They were wedged under the back wheels but proved to be totally ineffective. At that point, this melodrama had been going on for nearly three hours. One of them finally said to the chief, "Do you want me to try to get Marvin over here?" The chief sent him inside to call Marvin. Before I could ask, one of the guys told me that Marvin operated a commercial towing service in the area and that he would be able to free the truck. The chief then chimed in that it was going to be expensive. I was forced to explain that I didn't have any substantial money or credit card on me. I had to do some quick negotiation and provide a lot of information before he was satisfied that I was not just going to be stuck, freed and dash.

It took more than 30 minutes to get the highly regarded expert Marvin there in this giant tow truck. That time was awkward because all the local fellows congregated in a sizable group while I stood dejectedly by myself leaning against my truck some 15 to 20 yards away. The tow truck driver was definitely a down-home Louisiana fella. He absolutely looked the part. With a cigarette hanging out of his mouth and a hideously bent up ball cap that had to have been first purchased during the Eisenhower administration, and almost all of his tease obviously a distant memory, he set to work. With his truck on the pavement, he stretched two giant chains a considerable distance and hooked them up to my beleaguered vehicle. He came back and pushed back some sort of lever and miraculously the yellow Penske started to lift up from its muddy entrapment. He instructed one of the fellows to get in the cab and told him what to do. Much to my astonishment, after a four-hour ordeal, Marvin the tow truck genius and his firefighting cohort had saved the day in less than 15 minutes. The rental truck was slowly eased down and positioned back on the driveway just beyond the point where the tow truck sat.

That was good news for me; I was in the forward position, thus, I would have to leave first. After this debacle sprinkled with large portions of embarrassment and humiliation, I don't think I was ever more anxious to exit a place than I was that night. I quickly reaffirmed that the chief was satisfied he had all the contact information he required and once again assured him that everything would be made right. Then, with no further delay, I beat a path down the driveway, climbed in my vehicle and left the preposterous situation I had created literally in my rearview mirror.

Shaken, exhausted, starving and most definitely kicking myself for my stupidity, I headed back up the highway and soon was greeted by commercial businesses. Passing through the original intersection where I had made the soon to be disastrous wrong turn, I drove another block or two and was flabbergasted when I saw the Eckerd store on the right. What a wrong turn it had been. I would've been finished five hours ago and avoided a ridiculous ordeal.

In retrospect, three or four months of transport yielded really only this one major faux pas. Factoring in my limited skill set in these pursuits, I suppose that was pretty good. Jim's company was billed for $800, which I thought was a little excessive, but he never made a big issue out of it and has enjoyed the story many times. I suppose the lesson from the eventful visit to the New Iberia transport Twilight Zone was really a microcosm of the role simple choices can make in the process of fate. Something as simple as a wrong turn can yield trying implications. However, it also seems sometimes turning in the opposite direction of where you intended to go works out. With all humility and respect, I'm due for a couple of those outcomes.

"You're the color of the sky reflecting in each storefront window pane,
You're the whispering and the sighing of my tires in the rain,
You're the hidden cost and the thing that's lost in everything I do,
Yeah, and I'll never stop looking for you,
In the sunlight and the shadows, and the faces on the Avenue."
— Jackson Browne

Star Crossed. It's My Own Damn Fault

Tennyson wrote, "It is better to have loved and lost than to have never loved at all."

Profound and poetic. I'm not so sure I agree.

The CSNY song used to say, love the one you're with. It was advice I should have adhered to, but I never could. I started out and always have been a Fixator! My focus and affections when fully activated, are pointed in one direction. The select group of extraordinary females to whom I gift wrapped and presented my heart, soul, and spirit, have sadly and devastatingly fallen into a classic Shakespearean quote, "Not To Be."

I want to set the record straight though in terms of my star-crossed romantic life. Some may be wanting to break out violins as they read some of the words of what has befallen me on my way to romantic versions of the re-creation of the Titanic's voyage. I don't recount the details of these experiences to elicit sympathy, quite the opposite. It is included to better define who I am, my story and everything that's resulted to add up to my modern-day realities. These occurrences all happened at key junctures, and all were defining, highly impactful episodes.

A dedicated, ardent mountain climber sets his sights on the ultimate achievement, reaching the summit of the peak he aspires to conquer. The task is not only daunting and ominous, it is fraught with innumerable pitfalls and dangers. And when the climber attempts to reach that lofty goal and fails, it is not the object of their desire, the mountain itself, that is blamed. The setting of sights on something that inspires awe by its very presence and is so majestic that it can't be resisted makes everything else seem ordinary and uninspiring. The failure to succeed can be attributed to all kinds of contributing factors and extenuating circumstances. However, regardless of the obstacles, the lure that makes it so desirable is the enormity of the challenge and incomparable euphoria of the prospect of success. The aspiring climber is not bitter over the inability to reach the summit, but heartbreak and disappointment certainly take a significant toll with each and every unsuccessful attempt. Regardless of intellectual capacity and logical analysis, there is one word that no true dreamer can ever accept or even acknowledge.... UNATTAINABLE

It is an apt comparison to the love life that I have pursued. My sights and goals always seemed to forcibly be hijacked and directed on the most magnificent, wondrous, seemingly unreachable heights. The thrill of possibly touching the sun or even coming tantalizingly close, has always overridden the fear of failure and the devastatingly painful fall back to earth.

People try to complicate a simple concept like love. I don't think it's confusing at all. There is one basic acid test that is the perfect measuring device of whether or not one is truly in love. It is unmistakably love when you emphasize the things that are most important for the happiness of the person who is the object of your affection. When their needs, completely supersede your own, that is the signal. In simpler terms, real love is when someone becomes more important to you than yourself.

First Love ... First Cut Always The Deepest

In every facet of life, getting off to a good start and being placed in positions which promote and enhance prospects for success, is always best. Or at least, finding the way or stumbling onto the right path, is critical. Sadly the pattern was set for me with a badly aborted launch that proved to be a setback that had reverberating implications for years to come.

Early in my sophomore year in high school, I was suddenly thunderstruck! I was like a duck that was hit in the head by a boat paddle, wandering around afterwards in a daze. She was a vibrant, personable thunderbolt in a cheerleader uniform. Short in stature but a giant in adorability and effervescence. Her brown eyes drew me in to the point of making escape impossible. Forcibly looking away after a short glimpses was imperative. It was much like avoiding staring directly into a solar eclipse. Those lingering gazes of adoration while worthwhile and wonderful, almost certainly would result in permanent peril.

Her most alluring charm, however, was not even her amazing beauty. It was a personality and the way of expressing herself that was irresistibly endearing. Over the next couple of years when I actually got to the point that I could converse with her, I was always struck by the relative ease of the experience. Despite her staggering beauty, immense popularity and vibrancy, she was not the least bit conceited or full of herself.

In our senior year, buoyed by modestly successful female encounters and experiences during the summer months, I realized the acquisition of some masculine confidence for the first time. I made a bold decision ... it was time to go for the gold. In the early stages of the football season, our conversations became lengthier and more substantive. There was a mysterious quality to her during that time. Of course, I wasn't sophisticated or skilled enough to actually mine and process that information. I found out much later that her family was dissolving at the time due to divorce. It was an experience I had already lived through. I could have been a tremendous asset to the struggle she was undergoing but failed miserably to recognize that. This was the first girl that I had ever been totally enamored with, and now I was trying to actually turn it into something. Deep down, I never really believed it was possible, to be perfectly honest. After all, sadly, I was woefully ill-prepared for the task.

Our fourth game that year was against a very good, state ranked, Tucker High School. That Friday morning, wandering around in the halls, I encountered her doing the same. We wound up spending an hour or so together walking around sitting in various places, etc. There was a dance schedule after the game that night, not really my thing, but I mentioned it and I asked if she was going. She told me that she may stop in but was ultimately going to another cheerleader's house whose parents were out of town for a party. She then said words that still ring in my head as so magical that I remember them clearly syllable by syllable:

"You should come over there."

I then shocked myself by immediately asking her if she wanted to get something to eat after the game and then I'd take her to the party. The fact that she readily agreed was probably a very good thing considering that I may have been unable to draw another breath until she answered. And so it was, I would be picking up the young love of my life, and we were going to have our first outing together. The 27th day of September in the year of the Lord 1974, it was going to be a night to always remember. Little did I know how accurate that would prove to be.

The game was a blur; obviously, my mind was on other things. So it's probably a blessing that I never saw the field that night. I stood on the sidelines and watched us build an improbable 6-0 lead against a team that we were not supposed to be competitive against. Our touchdown was a scoop and score by linebacker James Wagner followed by about a 70-yard run. The defense we put on the field week to week was awesome. Unfortunately, our offense was, well, not good! In the second half, Cinderella unfortunately turned into a pumpkin; Tucker scored twice, and we lost 14 to 6.

The plan was for me to sprint home right after the buses delivered us back at the school after the game. Then, jump in the shower, change, fire up our white Plymouth Satellite Sebring and speed the two blocks back to the school to the dance as quickly as possible to pick her up. I had done no running in the game as my number was never called but should've been wearing a track team uniform as I sprinted the block and a half to my house. That was where the first sign of impending doom immediately jumped up and slapped me upside the head. It was 10:45 on a Friday night and my garage was empty. I shared a car with my mother, and for the first time I could ever remember, at that hour of the evening, the car was not there.

Panic stricken, I entered the house and immediately demanded to know where our mother had gone to my brother and sister. Kristy was in eighth grade and in charge of my brother who on that fateful night was all of 11 years old. It was the first time that dynamic had ever been executed. My sister informed me of the devastating headline that our former next-door neighbor, professional baseball player Denis Menke, was in town with the Houston Astros for a late-season series with the Braves. He had called that afternoon and invited my mother to come down and meet him after the ballgame downtown. That night, of all nights? It was if God himself had risen up and thwarted me on the threshold of my greatest achievement. My mind was in a tumultuous frenzy, desperately trying to think of an alternative plan for transportation.

Remember, there certainly was no such thing as cell phones in this time. No pagers, and I have no clue where my mother had gone to meet Denis. Even if I could have gotten in touch with her and begged and cajoled her to come home, the drive from downtown Atlanta was still 20 to 30 minutes. And the fact they were meeting after the ball game, meant that their evening had basically just begun. A new plan was going to have to be put into place. Looking outside in my driveway, I noticed that the green Dodge Colt belonging to the illustrious Joe Lipham was parked there. Yes, the car was there, but there was no evidence of Joe's presence.

Joe had graduated from Peachtree the previous year. His pattern on game Friday nights was to hang with his rowdier crowd of friends, become comfortably intoxicated, smoke cigars, and yell and chant ridiculous songs and sayings during the game. His signature number bellowed along by his cohorts was a ridiculous little, screamed at the top of his lungs, ditty that went like this ...

I want to be a Texas Ranger,
I want to live next to death and danger,
Two old ladies lying in bed,
One turned to the other and said,
I want me a Texas Ranger,
I want me a Texas Ranger,
Black eye peas and chitlin gravy,

Damn I should have joined the Navy.
High brow, inexplicable stuff!

I went outside and heard the faint sound of singing coming from my brother's wooden fort 15 or 20 feet beyond the end of the driveway up in the trees. Lipham and a bottle of Boones Farm wine were present in the fort. I hollered at him to come out of there, and he stumbled down to greet me. Exasperated, I quickly apprised him of the situation. Gallantly, and the good true friend he was, he immediately offered me his keys to take his car. Problem solved? Not hardly. First, Joe was more impaired than I'd seen him in some time. It was basically fairly unusual for him to be that wasted. And, even if I could take him home and use his car, it was not going to work. At that time, I had not yet learned to operate a four-speed vehicle. However, the encounter with Joe did trigger an idea in my head. My brother's fort had been built by my mother's sometime boyfriend. His name was Dave Reagan; he was a teacher at Chesnut Elementary across the street. I had an idea for one last desperate act before I would have to face the unthinkable prospect of walking back to the school, finding my beloved, and telling her I had failed miserably.

Ironically, Dave lived in the same apartment complex where my prospective date resided. It was only about eight to ten minutes away. I dialed the number, and it was answered by a groggy, sleeping voice. I explained to Dave the situation, and he incredibly agreed to bring me his vehicle. I frantically tried to clean up best I could, deciding I did not have time for a full-scale shower. I completed a quick sink bath, brushed my teeth and tried to do the best I could with my short hair to make it look presentable. My biggest social opportunity ever, and I took a freaking sink bath. Moments later, still donning his pajama pants, Reagan pulled in the driveway. By the time I came out, there was no sign of Joe, but his car was still there. I remember thinking I was hoping that he was going to sleep it off in the tree fort. At this time, it was just before 11:30 PM. I had to drive Dave back to his apartment, drop him off, and quickly make my way back to the school. That was going to burn another crucial 20 minutes. Finally, around quarter to midnight, I arrived back at the Peachtree gym. Finding her was not a problem. She was not inside where the dance was going on; she was sitting expectantly out on the front steps. I apologized profusely and tried to give her a brief explanation as to what had occurred. She did vocalize the opinion that she thought I wasn't going to show and didn't know what she was going to do but quickly seemed relieved that we were finally underway. We both agreed we were starving, so we stopped at a little pizza joint that was open late on Friday and Saturday that was real close by. We had a slice or two and some nice conversation, and finally, my pulse rate leveled off a little bit.

We then drove to the party. The cheerleader hostess was someone I had known for many years as my parents and her folks had at one time been very good friends. There were still a good number of people there when we arrived shortly before 1 AM. Mingling with folks, I remember watching the replay of the local news which aired originally at 11:00. There was always a rebroadcast at 1 AM. Then, incredibly, the station would shut off for the remainder of the of the night/morning. I remember sitting next to her as we watched the highlights from our game on the sports portion of the show.

People were filtering out pretty regularly during the next hour or so, including my close friend who was there with his cheerleader girlfriend at the time. By about 2 AM, there were only six people left. The hostess and her boyfriend, one of the hostess' friends and her date and incredibly myself and my most cherished companion. I had asked her some time earlier if she wanted me to take her home when the party ended. She informed me that she was staying over. She had said, "Don't worry about me if you have to go. I can get a ride in the morning." I let her know that I would prefer to stay there with her.

I wish I could tell you that I had plotted this remarkable turn of events to take advantage of what seemed to be an incredibly fortuitous situation. But as I have already painfully admitted, I was so far over my head that for all intents and purposes I had already drowned. I did not have the confidence or experience to take any kind of initiative. Just to be where she was, that was far and away good enough for me at that point in time.

And then, the situation changed completely. All of a sudden, standing in the doorway was my ever present co-best friend. He had taken his date home and returned by himself. Suddenly, I was no longer alone with the love of my young life. In just moments, I would discover in a horrifying manner just how accurate the old saying, " Two's Company, but Three's a Crowd" truly is.

The other couples had retired to bedrooms, but the three of us sat in the living room listening to the Bread album that was playing from one of the rooms in the back. The conversation was comfortable, the three of us being good friends. While I thought his return was odd, I didn't really have a problem with it. Around 3 AM, we all started gathering up cushions and pillows and set up places to stretch out on the floor to catch some sleep. My friend's plans to go home or stay had never been discussed. But as the light went off, it was obvious what his decision was. After lying there for no more than a few moments, in the pitch black, just a few feet away, the unmistakable sounds of altered breathing and kissing was easy to discern. It seemed surreal for the minute or so that I endured it. However, it was all too clear, one of my best friends was topping off my evening by making out in the same room, 7 or 8 feet away, with the girl of my dreams. And it was on the night of our first ever outing. The cruelest irony was what I had gone through, just to tee this session up for the two of them. Suddenly, the impact hit me like a runaway truck loaded with grand pianos.

I literally slithered like a wounded snake on the floor quietly out of the room. I somehow managed to get to my feet, stagger to the front door, quietly opened and closed it and collapsed in a quivering, lifeless mass on the steps of the front porch. The realization and shock of what had occurred were a traumatic stimulus which manifested itself in a debilitating numbness that I had never experienced. I could not move; it was like being shot with a paralyzing elephant gun. I just sat there. David Gates, the lead singer for Bread, was still serenading the romantic hostess and her current boyfriend, a linebacker from our team, in the back bedroom. To this day, I can at times of great despair and disappointment, feel myself transported back to those brick steps, still sitting there listening to those love songs, ironically mostly about heartbreak.

"Used to be my life was just emotions passing by,
Then you came along and made me laugh and made me cry,
You taught me why."

At about 4:30 AM, I went back to Dave's car in the driveway and fell back to my house. It was much like General Lee and his devastated Confederate army retreating from Gettysburg back into Virginia following annihilation in an encounter that was supposed be their most glorious victory. I never even went inside my house. Instead, I sat motionless on the patio until sunrise. My feelings of numbness had turned to intense anger, frustration, and pain. I was consumed with feelings of complete and utter disillusionment and betrayal.

At around 7 AM, I took Dave's car back. He returned me to my house. I had still not slept and had no desire to do so. I told Dave and my social butterfly mother, who had set the chain of events in motion with her bizarre evening plans, briefly what had taken place. My mother's initial reaction was to impose yet another banishment of my buddy from setting foot on our property. That action had been taken three or four times previously for various offenses. Oftentimes, the crimes that were perpetrated that precipitated his expulsion were not even things that he directly did, yet he was always blamed. My feelings on the subject had already begun to transform. Yes, I was bitterly disappointed that she, the object of my affections, was callously capable of hurting me that way. Of course, I was furious with my friend, who had innocently returned after taking home his girlfriend. He of course, found himself in a situation in which he certainly could've reasoned that it was potentially a bad idea for him to stay there. In his defense, he didn't anticipate what was going to occur and the repercussions that resulted.

But most of all, the pervading feeling that was starting to consume me was complete and disdainful disgust and frustration with myself. Her agreement to go out with me and have me take her to the party was, in essence, an audition. I had climbed a considerable mountain to be put in position to actually spend time with her. However, it was clear to me that I had failed miserably. Of course, it wasn't all my fault, there were lots of extenuating circumstances that contributed to my derailment. I discovered that my feelings for her had not changed, but sadly after having lost the battle, which was predominately against myself, I had actually lost the entire war.

Predictably, I never asked for another chance. What happened on that fateful evening was never again discussed. I forgave my friend in a short period of time. After all do you blame a shark that bites a swimmer or a hurricane that devastates a coastal community? Females were always attracted to him, so his actions were more in order of the natural phenomenon as opposed to a conniving scumbag. He was just living in the moment and acted without thinking. And it was not him that initiated the session, he was just a willing participant. I also never have harbored blame on her. The final months of our senior year, she seemed more distant. There never was another opportunity. Poking around in the weeks before our prom, it appeared that incredibly she had not yet committed to going with anyone. I was attempting to muster up the courage to step forward. Then I was informed and witnessed for myself that she had cranked up a boyfriend scenario. It was a brief one, and with someone who absolutely didn't seem to fit, but it lasted long enough to throw cold water on any thoughts of one last try.

Almost immediately, after graduation, she left to go and live with her Father in another state. She was gone. I would not see her again for 34 years at a mini reunion in Atlanta. She is happily married and has two children. She lives in the northeast. Since I first saw her, over 15,000 days have come and gone. There is not a single one of those days that I have not thought about her. My love and adoration is ever present and that will never change.

Grown Woman

Love number two was a complete departure from my earliest forays. After chasing an abstract career opportunity in Jacksonville, on a whim and with next to no planning, I found myself back in Atlanta. Random had come to visit right after Hardy's wedding. The funny side story is, he had driven all night and finally exhausted, decided to pull over and sleep for a short bit before completing the journey. It turned out that where he shut it down to doze off was less than 10 miles from my apartment. After a couple of days of fun and frolic, he prepared to head back north. Obviously, things weren't going very well for me there, so I made the impetuous decision to hop in his VW Scirocco and go with him. I left behind possessions, mostly odds and ends. My bomb of a car had been towed and was impounded, so I left that behind too. I had rationalized that surely I would return in the near future and retrieve my things, but that never came to pass.

Back in Atlanta, Mark introduced me to his boss who had started several stores in local malls selling women's shoes. Random had worked for him when he was with Florsheim selling men's shoes. I was hired as a management trainee and assigned to the Perimeter Mall store for training. The store manager there was one year my senior. She had grown up in central Kansas and come to Atlanta several years before. She was stylish and elegant. She wore form-fitting dresses, hosiery, magnificent high-heeled shoes (of course she did, she managed a shoe store). Her hair and makeup were always immaculate. From the first moments that I saw her, I found it difficult to even breathe in her presence. My God, this was a grown up woman!

We instantly hit it off. Almost immediately, amazingly my highly animated mannerisms and antics entertained her thoroughly. And she was at a stage of her life where most of all, she wanted to have fun. But of course, there was a major obstacle and complication with those desires. What a shock, she had a boyfriend. And, she lived with him. Oh, and technically, they were engaged.

In a very short period of time, she started to describe all of the details of her situation. She complained he was completely insecure, constantly suspicious and incredibly possessive. She was the prototypical case study. Naturally she found him to be an extremely attractive man. It was appealing to her that he already had a decent income structure. He worked for his dad, and she felt like he had a very promising future. That provided for her need to feel secure and confident about her own future. On the flip side, she had already concluded that he was not blessed with abundance personality or charisma. She wanted to party and go out nights; he preferred intimate evenings in their small apartment enclosure. He had few friends and no desire to be very socially active at all.

I was able to deliver right away two things that she clearly really needed at that point of her life, ears and laughter. It was one of those magical circumstances where seemingly anything I said reinforced and enlightened or absolutely delighted and entertained her. Spending time in the Midwest later in life, and Kansas specifically, most people there are more understated and low-key. Perhaps my rather large, exuberant personality was something that she had not experienced a great deal in her personal relationships. The good news for me was, whatever was happening, it was tremendously gratifying that she obviously enjoyed my company.

After just a couple of weeks, on a late Sunday afternoon that she and I had worked together, we prepared to close the store. It had been really slow all day, so basically, we had spent the five or six operational hours just talking and laughing together. She was wearing a black dress that beautifully accentuated her incredible form. She was not fashion model type gorgeous. Her look and attractiveness were more of a natural essence. An endearing cuteness, out of the girl-next-door mode. But there was also a hint of untamed bawdiness. She was truly an irresistible combination of peaches and cream and a potentially lethal dose of sultry forbidden femme fatale fruit.

On our way out that Sunday, she noticed that one set of display lights had not been properly turned off. The switches were in the very back of the stockroom area of the shop. She headed back toward that area as I dutifully followed. It was dark as we made our way to the back. The memory of what happened next is so vivid in my mind; it's as if it came from a movie that I have seen repeatedly. The drama and intensity of the moment were certainly something that would have been very memorable in the film. For some reason, she slowed down suddenly and turned slightly to say something to me. I had to stop abruptly just in time to avoid slamming into her. Again, right out of a Hollywood script, we found ourselves in tight quarters and basically face-to-face. In that darkness, distinctive, undeniable electric intensity supercharged that narrow space. Suddenly, impulse and desire overwhelmed us both. A passionate embrace and frantic kissing ensued seconds later. It was unquestionably the most spontaneous, amazing exchange with another person of my life. It lasted four or five minutes, I can't recall the exact length. It did not go beyond some rather intimate touching. And I can remember it ending abruptly as perhaps some sanity was restored. Looking back, that was very unfortunate for me because something amazing happened in that exchange. If things had progressed a bit further, the course of history might have been seriously altered.

Romantic encounters have always been a very difficult mountain for me to climb. I am blessed with a very sharp and highly functional mind. Of course, that's mostly a blessing, but it has its downsides, particularly in the area of amorous activities. After all these years, I still do not know how to throw the switch to shut down the cerebral and activate the primal impulse sensory system. The act of physical love is not well served by thinking overriding sensation and feeling. That impromptu occurrence in the storeroom was one of the few times that the conversion mechanism operated properly. No planning, no over-thinking, just sheer unadulterated instinct and impulse. Had things progressed, I have no doubt to this day that something extraordinary could have occurred. But it was too soon, things were too complicated, and it was not really a blockbuster Hollywood production, it was real life. As minds were restored to previous capacity, we kind of stepped back and experienced an awkward few seconds. She turned and threw the switch that was the original mission, and we slowly shuffled back up the aisle toward the exit. Nothing was said as we walked to our cars. We stammered out our goodbyes, and I remember her stepping forward and giving me a quick hug. And then, off she went, heading home to her live-in companion.

In any other time or any slightly better circumstance, this could've been magic. However, at the time this was happening, I had no permanent place to live, very few clothes and possessions, and no real direction.

Mark was living platonically with two female roommates in a large apartment, and they were kind enough to let me sleep on the couch. If I didn't stay up there, I bunked down at the Heaven's. Jim and Craige's marriage was just a month or so away. They already had an apartment together, and that sofa was also a place I found myself on occasion. Had I been in a position to be able to offer her sanctuary, the stage was certainly set for that to happen. But, I was in no position to offer any such thing.

Fate also intervened the very next week following the storeroom encounter. I had been an instant success in terms of being able to sell effectively women's shoes and purses. It wasn't from great talents of salesmanship as much as effort and personality. And mainly it was because of her. As manager of that store, the better I performed, the better it was for her store in terms of credit and achievement. My training was deemed concluded. I was told to report to a new assignment at Northlake Mall. In a business decision that I would say would be filed under ill-advised, I would now be working as Random's assistant manager.

Suddenly separated, we talked daily when she was at the store. I missed her terribly and decided to make a bold statement. I sent her a dozen long stem red roses to the store and a card that simply said "I miss you" Love Kip. The fire was definitely ignited. Shortly before, her younger brother had come down from Kansas and had gone to work in some sort of warehouse job affiliated with the stores. He was a wild Indian, to say the least. His agenda was characterized by the desire to party at any and every opportunity. Excessive drinking and illicit substances were certainly a major ingredient in his desired equation. He also did not get along very well with the charming boyfriend. He basically had told her that her brother was no longer welcome to stay at their apartment. She called one morning to tell me that enough was enough, and that later that day, she and her brother were going to go out and see if they could find an apartment and move out.

Several days later, I was at Mark's apartment when the doorbell rang early in the evening. My love interest, flanked by her brother and his friend, stood at the door. She gleefully announced that they had acquired an apartment. She had come to retrieve me so I could see it. She and I rode in the backseat and sat closely together. She was excited and bubbly, and my head was spinning. The apartment was sparsely furnished, but earlier in the day, they had moved the bed and dresser she owned from the boyfriend's place to the apartment. With my vast experience, a.k.a. inexperience, it should have been pretty clear what was unfolding, but at that time, it was not apparent to me. I had assumed at some point that I would be returned to Mark's where my clothes and car were. She suggested the alternate plan of my staying at the apartment that evening, and she would take me back in the morning. Shortly thereafter, I found myself being led down the hall to her new quarters. I was elated, but I was also terrified. And even then, I still had not added it all up. Looking back on it now, I can't believe I was ever that ignorant. Unbeknown to me, I was at that moment an important part of this liberation strategy. This night, in her bed, was my moment to step up and shine. To reignite the emphatic spark and continuation of the unbridled, passionate storybook fireworks that we had shared at the store.

After a somewhat promising start, the progression to the next step was not a smooth transition. There was a significant degree of lack of confidence and uncertainty. And certainly there was a major dose of plain old inexperienced stage fright. Communication would probably have been a good place to start in addressing the unease I felt. The more I sensed her frustration that I was not more assertive, the more my cerebral instincts seized command and rendered me even more bumbling. At some point, she realized that she would have to take the initiative. With that realization, however, the fire of what was previously occurring immensely cooled off. Her expectation had been to be dominantly and passionately taken. To be able to do that was not remotely in my wheelhouse. My failure to complete that mission was not a physical malfunction but a mental and emotional one. I was too ignorant, unskilled and unsure of myself at the time. This absolutely had been an audition, and I was not prepared to seize the role. The implications of that night will forever resonate. Much like my failure at the slumber party years before with number one, history had repeated itself with number two. The circumstances were certainly different, but the root cause of what went wrong was basically the same. I simply did not have a clue. That night in her bed, was my first and last appearance there.

Over the next couple of months, we spent time together in group settings. She had begun to go back for a day or so at a time to her boyfriend's place. She would tell me that she did not love him but there was security and familiarity there that continued to draw her back. Right around the time of Jim and Craige's wedding, she told me she was moving back in with him.

It's hard to explain the emotional attachment that we had, but it was real. The sadness and resignation in her voice when telling me of her return to him gnaws at my soul even to this day. It seemed that her returning and reinstating her previous relationship status only reset the situation to where it had been originally and once again galvanized our bond. I was supposed to be the great rescuer it seems, but as a hero, I proved powerless. Despite everything that had happened, there was still something there, a resilient connection. But the timing couldn't have been worse; I simply had no resources to offer anything significant that could make it work.

We continued to talk, and as the hopeless romantic that I am, I continued to write her sweet notes and send flowers which she still anxiously and gratefully received. Then one Monday, I called her at the store, and she harshly began yelling at me, telling me I had lots of nerve to call after what I had done. Dumbfounded and in shock, I asked her what she was talking about. She shrieked in a haunting voice, "You know what you did." Then she slammed down the phone. I was beside myself; I had no idea what she was referring to. The next couple of days were absolutely hellish. Random finally called and asked her what was going on. She told him that her boyfriend's car had been keyed and two of his tires slashed at their apartment the previous Saturday night. He told her that he had seen me running away. It was so stupid because I did not know where they lived precisely; I had never actually met him and destroying someone's property is not something I would ever do under any circumstances. Sure, he was my rival for her affections, but what in the world would that accomplish? Besides, I had no hatred for him. Circumstances had beaten me, not that Jabroni. Even with his silver spoon set up, he had lost her before, and I was confident at some point he would lose her again. Of all the deficiencies he had that she had described to me over the last couple of months, if anything, I thought he was kind of a pitiful character. I did get the opportunity to speak to her shortly thereafter and made her see that that was a pathetic ploy by a guy who was seriously gripping to hold on.

A week later, life changed completely again as virtually all of us running the stores were fired. Admittedly, we had all gotten pretty fast and loose with the cash drawer. The paltry sums we were making did not support our very active lifestyles, and so there was a good deal of IOU presence in the till. On pay days we would reimburse the drawer, which created a vicious cycle because once again then we'd be broke and the borrowing would start anew. The store owner decided that that practice was not acceptable. Basically, all of our heads rolled at all of the stores.

I was staying by this time in the living room of the newlyweds, Jim and Craige's Buckhead apartment. It was obviously not an ideal situation. It was determined that I could live at the Heaverns' in Jim's old space for nominal rent. I secured a menial job at a close by shipping operation, but obviously that was not in line with my greater ambitions. My dad in Memphis had passed along that there were a couple of possible job opportunities if I wanted to go back there. I started to make plans to leave Atlanta once again.

I had completely lost touch with her since our connection through the store had been taken away. I was not even aware that during that same period of time that winter, she and her boyfriend had been involved in a serious car accident. She asked around and somehow tracked down the number at the Heaverns' house where she could reach me. I was shocked and surprised, and I'll admit delighted when she called. By that time, she had mostly recovered from head and neck issues from the accident. He was still laid up with some broken bones and internal injuries. I told her that I was moving to Memphis within the next week and was stunned when she was clearly upset at the news. She had just started a new job, once again in retail. She told me she was going for drinks the next night at Houlihan's, and she asked me if I would meet her there.

That next night, those couple of hours with her were some of the most emotional I have ever experienced. It was a contrasting blend of effusive praise and affection toward one another. We talked candidly about what had happened to us. We laughed, and yes, we cried. She told me she was once again engaged to him but would not be pushed into a hasty date. The accident had actually bought her some time while he recovered. Throughout much of the time, we held hands on top of the table. Despite her laments of me leaving Atlanta, the time with her that night was even more validation that I was making the right decision. I had to go build something, and clearly my best opportunity was in Memphis not in Atlanta. The heartbreak of falling in love with someone and not having anything substantial to offer them was a fate I had vowed never to experience again. Our final scene was appropriate for the cinematic type theme that our relationship had been from start to finish. We walked her friend to her car, and she set off. And then at her car, we stood silently for a long time in a loving, hugging embrace. There was no passion or other types of contact of any kind. I just held her. In that damp, cold February night, in that parking lot, directly across the street from the mall where we had met and experienced our most special of moments. Just before getting in her car, she became the first woman to ever say to me, "I love you!" I had said it to her before, but this was the first return of that phrase my way. I emphatically emphasized that my feelings would never change. The fact that it was so somber and sad as we professed our feelings for one another while saying goodbye at the same time is a deep emotional wound that has never healed. It was readily apparent to both of us what an extraordinary opportunity it was, but it just wasn't meant to be. We vowed to try to keep in touch, but of course, we never did. Since that night, I have never talked to her or seen her ever again. Unlike the others I have loved, I have no idea what became of her, where she is now, really nothing at all. I have done some searching in recent years but no results have been found. With all my heart, I wish every day that her life has turned out wonderfully and has been filled with happiness and contentment.

It would be three long years before anyone resonated on my radar screen. However, this time, fate was in my corner. My next love was the woman who would become my wife and mother of my children. Much more to come on that rise and fall ...

Lady Of The Lake

I absolutely love the story of King Arthur, Camelot and the Knights of the Round Table.

That story included so many incredible messages and themes, along with powerful visual images. One of my favorites is when Arthur believes he has lost Excalibur, the lady of the lake rises up from the depths and returns the lost sword, the symbol of his wisdom, power, virtue and claim to the throne, back to him. In what seemed to be a miracle, I found myself portraying a modern-day version of that very story.

In April 2011, I had driven down for a visit at my mother's. Case flew in a couple of days later from Las Vegas, and he and my brother were slated to head down to Miami. Case was playing in a poker tournament at the Hard Rock Casino there, and I always am anxious to visit fabulous Gulfstream Park for a day at the races.

The day before we were to head southeast, I awoke to a most distressing situation. Something was wrong now with my left eye. The one which had been so solid throughout my vision distress. In fact, up until that fateful morning, it had actually gotten stronger and even more functional with the failure of my right optic nerve in 2009; this incident was a bit different in its severity. However, the distortion of my eyes was undeniable. The first incident in 2009, revealed itself with a mysterious dark shelf-like effect on my right eye. This time, it was lack of focus and a fuzzy smoky essence. I hoped against hope that perhaps this was something else. After all, statistically, only about

12% of ischemic neuropathy patients have an occurrence in both optic nerves. Diagnosis, a couple of days later back in Birmingham, confirmed the worst.

My sister-in-law Terie, swung into action and her research yielded that a Dr. Johnson, at the University of Missouri eye hospital was a foremost expert on my condition. I flew to Columbia, Missouri and was given a treatment that had shown some promise in stabilizing an incident of NAION if introduced in its initial days. Unlike the right eye, which declined rapidly and almost totally failed, either the occurrence on the left side was not as severe or the prescription help stabilized it. Vision from my left eye remained in some capacity.

In the midst of all of this upheaval and chaos, something totally unexpected happened. It had all the appearances of a miracle from heaven; new love tracked me down for the first time in the seemingly forever. It materialized totally unexpectedly from a most unlikely source. She jumped in my life right off of my iPad.

I'm sure it will be a shocking revelation to all that she was a former Peachtree cheerleader. I had no relationship with her whatsoever back in those youthful days. She was a year older and the social structure was not set up where younger guys could interact with upper-class girls. This was particularly applicable in the event that the said girl was an absolute knockout beauty and immensely popular.

It started innocently on a Sunday evening as I perused my Facebook activity for the day. She had made a funny comment on a mutual friends post, and I followed up with some witty retort.

It didn't take very long in reflecting back as to how magnificent I had always thought she was, roaming those hallowed hallways of yesteryear. Her greatest attribute was the fact that she was breathtakingly naturally beautiful but not in a showy or magnified way. She carried herself in a rather understated manner. I remembered seeing her coming toward me back in those days and just freezing up in a basic sense of awe. I suddenly found myself doing something that I rarely if ever had done, I sent her a "friend request." Much to my delight, she immediately confirmed.

Buoyed by her quick acceptance, I typed out a couple of lines on the personal messenger function to thank her for coming aboard. I shared that seeing her confirm my request was a great relief. I told her I was having flashbacks from high school where I was petrified to even look at her much less have the audacity to speak. I wrote that if I had approached her in high school before being able to utter a sound, I was certain I would've internally combusted and burst into flames. Her answer back was so endearing that I was almost immediately smitten. She wrote that she was really happy that we had connected and that everything she'd ever seen me write had made her laugh. Now keep in mind, this is someone who I had always held in extremely high regard.

Over the next couple of weeks, the contact back-and-forth was conducted multiple times on a daily basis. The length and depth of the exchanges continued to expand. We cracked each other up, we analyzed one another's thoughts, and we shared our in most cases remarkably similar philosophies. In the midst of the greatest crisis that I have ever faced in my life, I had come to view her introduction into my life as the compensatory balance. The wonderful to cancel out the horrible.

After securing her address, I over-nighted a package full of a bunch of silly things that had emerged from online dialogue. The main items in the box were a half dozen fresh off the conveyor belt Krispy Kreme donuts and a shirt that I found in the back of my closet that featured a loop in the back. She had lamented that she never had easy access to her favorite donuts. And another time she mentioned how silly it had been back in elementary school when a girl liked a boy she would pull the loop off the back of his shirt. I also enclosed some candy bars because she had mentioned, and posted on Facebook, that was frequently what she had for lunch. It turned out her favorite, the Zero bar, was quite difficult to track down. Upon receiving the package, she wrote me a beautiful note thanking me for my efforts and praising effusively my creativity and thoughtfulness. In that message, she said that leaving the post office and thinking about the contents of the box, she had been momentarily overcome and found herself crying. She wrote, "The more I thought about it, the more touching it was. I mean I kept asking myself, who does this?" It was one of the most touching compliments I have ever received in my life. To think that I made someone so remarkable, so happy that she was overcome by it, was incomparably gratifying.

Our connection intensified. Amazingly, the same humble, unassuming demeanor that she had always displayed in her younger years was still the way she approached her life in this era. When I rattled on about fate and her being such an incredible gift, she uncomfortably deflected almost all praise. She lived in North Carolina and operated her own business. And it was just a short amount of time before we graduated to extensive nightly telephone conversations.

In one of those conversations, as we reminisced about high school days, she told me something that I absolutely could not believe. In her senior year, which would culminate in her being crowned Miss PHS, an honor that basically equated into her being tabbed the most popular girl in the school, she had not attended the prom that year. When I inquired as to why, she said simply, "Because nobody asked me." That discussion was late on a Friday night, and as I hung up the phone I was stunned at that revelation. We had been talking and laughing about the prospect of actually having to see one another sometime, and as I awoke that Saturday morning, I knew exactly how that had to happen. We rarely spoke during the day, but I had to make an exception call that morning. I asked her to be my date in the re-create of the 1974 Peachtree High School Prom. It was an idea that was so right. In one swoop, it could right a baffling historical anomaly that should never have happened. And for me, it was a chance to go back and perhaps correct some of my own haunting youthful chapters. For that one magical night, so many wonderful things could be accomplished.

The eventful evening was set for Sunday, October 23. As the days counted down towards our meeting, her attitude suddenly began to shift. Instead of the tentative, let's wait and see approach and demeanor, we began sounding very much like two people on the verge of a major step forward. Ten days prior to our meeting, on my 54th birthday, she called me several times, and each conversation was more special than the one before. She told me that she considered our intersecting lives to be an amazing blessing and then she could not believe how lucky she was. I had been caught up in the whirlwind of whimsical hope that maybe this miracle was something concrete. And then suddenly it all seemed like it was actually unfolding into a heaven-sent inevitable reality. In the final week leading up to our night out, she actually began sharing that information with her friends. Up to that point, we had not been public at all. I had not clued in my friends for fear that she would not approve and shy away. Incredibly, all of a sudden, she was the one who seemed excited at the prospects of what we had been building.

I had asked my brother to come up from Florida in those last couple of weeks to help me gather what I needed to make my event special. And, of course, it was his job to successfully deliver me to the venue. The plan was to check into the Dunwoody Embassy Suites. I had arranged a suite for her and one of my own. I spent the afternoon decorating the living room portion of my room with all of the items I had gathered.

The appointed hour was fast approaching, so I meticulously prepared myself. I was surprised at my lack of nervousness, but the foundation we had built over the previous 93 days was substantial. As I left my room down for hers, of course, I carried for her a prom corsage. I also had in my jacket pocket my iPhone, set to the iTunes function, and had the song we had adopted as our own playing for the crescendo of the face to face moment.

She had sent me the song, A Beautiful Mess by Jason Mraz, about a month earlier. Its lyrical content was a perfect match in my mind to the incredibly unique miracle we had found ourselves immersed in.

You've got the best of both worlds, 'cause you're the kind of girl who can take down a man and lift him back up again

You are strong but you're needy, humble but you're greedy and based upon your body language and shoddy cursive I've been reading,

Your style is quite selective but your mind is rather reckless,

Well I guess this just suggest that this is just what happiness is

And what a Beautiful Mess this is

It's like we're picking up trash, in dresses

Well it kind of hurts when the kind of words that you write kind of turn themselves into knives,

And don't mind my nerve you can call it fiction, but I like being submerged in your contradictions,

Dear ... cause here we are, here we are

Although you are biased, I love your advice, your comebacks they're quick and probably have to do with your insecurities,

There is no shame in being crazy,

Depending on how you take these .. words I am paraphrasing this relationship we are staging,

And what a beautiful mess this is,

It's like we're picking up trash in dresses,

Well it kind of hurts, when the kind of words that you say, kind of turn themselves into blades,

And kind and courteous is a life I've heard,

 But it's nice to say that we played in the dirt,

Dear....here we are, here we are, here we are, here we are, here we are, here we are, he we are.....

We're still here,

What a Beautiful Mess this is,

It's like, taking a guess, when the only answer is Yes!

And through timeless words and priceless pictures,

We'll fly like birds but not of this earth,

And tides they turn, and hearts disfigure,

But that's no concern because we're wounded together,

And we tore our dresses and stained our shirts,

But it's so nice today, the wait was so worth it.

She opened the door, and a vision of incalculable beauty and vibrancy stood before me. She was absolutely indescribable. She wore a fabulous black dress. I stood in the doorway for a brief instant and we had an amusing second to gather our senses as the moment incredibly had actually arrived. In that fleeting instant, my most powerful, electrifying exchange with another human being took place. It was just all too perfect and oh, so right. We stepped together and hugged. It is said when Mount Vesuvius erupted and its molten ash and lava rained down upon the villagers below, many were instantly vanquished in the very positions they had assumed seconds before contact. In that moment of holding her in that doorway, I would have gladly accepted that fate if that was the price of maintaining that embrace and that joyous time forever more. There were no volcanic abnormalities that day and the embrace eventually ended and our first words were uttered. She said to me, "How perfect, you're playing the song." She stepped back and invited me in. I had only covered four steps when she turned and I handed her the corsage and said, "This is for you." She took it from my hands, looked down at it and looked back up at me, then leaned forward and kissed me. It was like actually being awake during a dream. We had been together all of two minutes and the most beautiful woman in the world had already kissed me.

She presented me with a boutonniere to complete my outfit. We set off downstairs where I had arranged for a limousine to take us to dinner at Bones in Buckhead. The staff there was prepared as I had tipped them off as to the occasion. We were seated and treated like royalty. I ordered an expensive bottle of champagne to properly commemorate such a monumental event. We leisurely drank and dined. And for the entire 2 1/2 hours, our hands never separated. At one point, she even said to me, "I just can't let go of you." It was beyond astonishing; it exceeded any expectation I ever could've dreamed of. And the best way to describe it would be sheer magic.

When we finally rose to leave the restaurant, a table of six people who had been sitting adjacent to us was giving us a good-looking over. As we passed, the gentleman at the head of the table asked us to come over for a moment He explained that they had been wondering all evening what we were celebrating. They had tried to analyze all of the clues, the formal dress, flowers, champagne and constant holding of hands. They went around the table and submitted all of their guesses. Wedding, anniversary, special birthday, major celebration? When I explained that I was re-creating the prom from 37 years ago, correcting history, the women at the table gasped and sighed while the men smiled and nodded approvingly. We walked out toward the limo. Shortly before reaching the door, overcome by the experience we had just shared, we stopped and instinctively shared a kiss of immense tenderness, affection, and appreciation of the moment.

Back at the hotel, I told her I needed about 10 minutes to make sure everything was prepared. She went to her room to freshen up, and I went and fired up all of the props that I had brought to set the scene for 1974. I had the top songs from that year, a revolving glass disco ball, a giant banner I'd had professionally produced that displayed ... Peachtree High School Prom 1974, and a sizable supply of balloons all around the ceiling. The smile on her face when she saw all of the decorations was priceless. There were not very many songs in 1974 that were very good for slow dancing, but thankfully Chicago had come through with a good one. Our prom slow dance was to the following ...

If you leave me now you'll take away the biggest part of me,

Ooo No Baby please don't go,

And if you leave me now you'll take away the very heart of me

Ooo no I just want you to stay,

A love like ours is love that's hard to find,

How could we let it slip away?

We've come too far to leave it all behind,

Do you know to end it all

Then tomorrow comes and we'll both regret the things we said today,

After the dance, we toasted with champagne I had chilling in the room. And then I commenced the announcement for the 1974 prom queen. As I announced the winner, I unveiled the lower part of the banner which had her name and her new title. I produced a tiara and crowned her lovely dark haired head.

With the formal festivities over, she went back to her room to change into more comfortable clothing. For the next several hours, we cuddled on the sofa watching some classic TV episodes that she had given me that night for my birthday. She had curled up and fallen asleep; her head nestled comfortably on my shoulder. For the second or third time that evening, I was in a position that I would've been satisfied to remain in until the end of time. Sadly, eventually she woke and apologized for pinning me in what she perceived to be an uncomfortable position. I assured her that certainly was not the case. I walked her to her room; we embraced for a long while and shared a tender, goodnight kiss. The wondrous, perfect evening came to an end.

I was exhausted, but I could not sleep. I replayed every detail and actually wondered if she had found the night to be as perfect as I thought it went.

Before 8 AM, my phone rang and she was calling to report that she was up and preparing for her trip back north. We arranged to go down for the hotel's noted breakfast in half an hour. Immediately upon seeing her in her room, we joined hands, and just as the night before were reluctant to let go the remainder of our time together. We comfortably talked and laughed and ate our breakfast. Then we returned to her room with a cart and loaded up her considerable inventory of belongings she had brought up. We lingered for a long while after her car had been loaded, leaning up against the vehicle. Neither of us was ready for it to be over. She finally climbed into the seat behind the wheel where we continued to talk until finally she decided that she had to get going. Watching her drive away was devastating. All the buildup, the incredible evening we spent followed by the perfect morning, and suddenly, she was gone. Once again, we would be separated by considerable distance.

Returning to Birmingham, we spoke several times over the next couple of days. In our late night conversation on that following Tuesday, she had started the conversation by saying, "I miss my prom date." It was in response to that I posed a fateful question. I asked her what we would do as a follow-up if we lived in the same town. Logically, she answered, we would see each other again and do something a little more low-key. That is when I offered an idea: What if I was to come to her territory, check into a hotel, and we could do just as she suggested, casually follow up and see each other. After convincing her that I was just crazy enough to be driven up there to her area that very weekend, and following her realization that I was absolutely serious, her comment was, "That would be wonderful." There was no debate; if I had to ride a skateboard backward through blizzard-like conditions or a tropical rainstorm, come hell or high water, I was going to be in Western Carolina that weekend.

We were set to leave on Saturday after my radio program that afternoon. That plan was altered, however, upon hearing the heartbreaking news the next day that Mark's brother Gordon, also a long-time friend of mine, had passed away from pancreatic cancer. Of course, I had heard weeks before that he had been stricken, but the suddenness of his death was stunning and sobering. The funeral service was set for Saturday morning, and there was no way that I was not going to attend such an important event to honor his memory and show my support and sympathy for Mark and his family.

My brother and I arrived in Atlanta near the site of the next day's funeral service and checked into a hotel. Upon settling in, I made the usual late evening call to North Carolina. However, I also made something else, a terrible mistake. The fact that what I said was misinterpreted is little consolation or consequence now. In the course of our conversation, we talked about things we could do over the next few days when I was there. Our hotel reservations were in the closest town, which she informed me was about a 20-25 minute drive from her rather isolated place on a lake. The thought of her having to drive that distance was something that tweaked a nerve with me. Call it a feeling of emasculation or simply the impulse to feel uncomfortable with someone having to exert a great deal of effort to accommodate me, I suggested that perhaps it would make sense for me to stay at her house some nights to facilitate more sensible, convenient transportation arrangements. She informed me that she was not ready for that kind of plan. Stupidly, but certainly consistent with my glorious history of suicidal relationship sabotage, I did not realize I had wandered into a minefield. In no way shape or form was I inviting myself into her domain to attempt to accelerate events or force issues. I thought I was making a noble gesture. That wasn't the way she saw it, and she said so. Instead of recognizing the danger and apologizing while explaining myself, I actually allowed it to hurt my feelings. I expressed surprise and disappointment that she did not feel like we were at a point where inviting me to stay at her home was a viable option. When I realized that she had taken my suggestion as me pressuring her to move forward toward a potential physical relationship, I tried to clarify my position by saying what I was talking about was just a corner on the floor somewhere in the house She informed me that she had three guestrooms and that was not the issue. After negotiation worthy of resolving a world-class international crisis, I felt that by the end of the conversation some understanding had been reached. However, what I had trodden into was a poison pill of abundant magnitude.

After the funeral, my brother picked me up out front of the chapel, and we set off for North Carolina. We arrived late afternoon just in time for me to participate in my radio program by telephone.

My beloved who I had come to visit had long-standing plans that afternoon with a close female friend that was also in the area that day. However, she insisted that when she got home that night, she wanted to drive up to my location and see me. I assured her that the next day would be perfectly acceptable, but she said that I had made the effort to come all that way and it was the least she could do to come and welcome me. At around 9 o'clock, she arrived, and we had a nice, but rather low-key, initial reunion. She asked if I would mind riding with her in search of the special coffee that she absolutely loved and drank every single morning and sometimes throughout the day. Her supply was dangerously low, and she had to find some reinforcements. Game for anything and just thrilled to be with her, we set off toward local grocery stores that were still open at that hour on a Saturday night. The atmosphere was strange; I could tell that she was pretty tired from already spending a day at a campsite with her friends. I also wondered if the first less than perfect conversation we'd had the night before had diminished her enthusiasm. I have to admit, I felt awkward in the passenger seat, having never been in that position of not being the driver when out for a social engagement with a woman before. We went to several grocery stores, and her particular variety of coffee was sold out at our first three stops. She only knew of one other store in that area, a Harris Teeter grocery. It was a euphoric moment when we walked down the aisle and discovered that they had a stock of six Café Vienna's. The quest was a success, and oddly a great sense of relief came over me. In light of the previous night's difficult conversation and the bit of tension that evening, I certainly did not want to be associated with a run that was not successful.

She took me back to the hotel where we made plans to go out to lunch the next day at noon. The brief kiss goodnight, and once again she was off in her Volkswagen. I was worried about her driving back in a fatigued condition, so I called after about 15 minutes and talked to her for the rest of her drive to the house. I was surprised that it took 10 more minutes for her to arrive.

She picked me up around noon on Sunday; we went to lunch and then navigated the two-lane road for the 25-minute drive back to her place. The scenery was breathtaking from what I could enjoy visually, and it was a glorious fall day. When we pulled up to her lovely home on the lake, I had to laugh at my first glimpse at this beautiful woman's work pickup truck. It was all part of what made her so spectacular. The thought of her hooking up chains to the back of her vehicle and pulling out rocks or painstakingly lugging shrubberies or trees to her job sites was quite an image. Being the CEO and the entire workforce of her company, she had to do it all. Perhaps more than anyone I have ever met, she was up to the challenge.

I received the home tour. Next, we took advantage of the beautiful day and went for a long walk all around the area. I was rather relieved that we held hands much of that time, and some of the closeness that had seemed to be absent the previous two days appeared to have returned. She had asked me to bring a football along, and I had stopped at a store on the way up and purchased one to present to her. When we returned back to her house, we threw it around. It was a tad discouraging for me because the act of catching objects thrown my way is one of the more difficult aspects of my condition. That was particularly frustrating because my hand-eye coordination had always been unquestionably my strongest athletic attribute. The oddity of the condition was emphasized when throwing the ball to her. She started running funny little pass routes, and I was delivering ideal tosses to her, which incredibly she demonstrated her athletic prowess by catching virtually every one. We concluded those hijinks with me mapping out a play for her to run and doing play-by-play as if it was the final play in the Super Bowl. She ran her route and gathered in the aerial as I excitedly described the action. I then ran to celebrate our mythical championship-clinching play, and she leapt up for me to catch her and triumphantly hoist her into the air. It is a memory I will always cherish.

We went back into the house, down to her TV room and actually turned on a real NFL game. Moments later, she was curled up on the couch up against me and fast asleep as I lovingly stroked her head. It was the fourth or fifth time already in our very brief time together, but I just wished time could freeze right there and then. She woke up from a short nap and went and prepared us a meal. We watched some more TV and comfortably sat and talked. Finally, around 9.30, after a full day together, it was time to go back to the hotel. The drive in the dark on the two-lane road was lengthy as mentioned previously. I again expressed my discomfort, but she was forced to do this to facilitate our having time together. Unfortunately, that discussion morphed into the topic once again of where we were relationship-wise. I don't remember specifically what I said, but it was not well received, and her impression was that I was dissatisfied with her progress in the process. Looking back, the issue of her having to transport me and it's emotional impact on my confidence and manhood became blended with her perception that somehow I was pushing for more in our relationship. It's almost comical that the issue came to that. I was probably the last man on earth that would try and accelerate events to promote an immediate physical union. There is no question, I was all for it to be a gradual, naturally evolving phenomenon. And I know I tried to articulate that, but the message did not seem to be received. As amazing as our connection, or as we call it our wavelength, had been on all subjects, this one was not resonating. She had constructed formidable emotional walls after her heartbreaking marriage dissolution, and despite the fact that I had somehow managed to storm those fortifications, the terrain beyond was treacherous and fraught with danger.

That night, I logged on my laptop and searched to see if there was any place else I could stay that would be closer to her and more convenient for the final two days of my visit. I found a little, albeit overpriced, bed-and-breakfast in a little village just three miles from her house. I quickly booked it for the next two nights, packed up and had my brother drive me there. I had gotten him his own room in the hotel, and he was enjoying his stay doing what he liked doing best, sitting around alone, drinking and watching TV.

That afternoon, I informed her that I was now in a convenient location and thought that news would be received by her with appreciation. She agreed to pick me up so we could go out to dinner. It was obvious from the first moment that her demeanor had changed. Her answers were short, and there was little to no contact. We enjoyed dinner at a nice Italian restaurant, one that I had joked about in our conversations for seeming to be an unlikely business in a remote lake resort community. It was one week after the prom date dinner and an experience so unlike that magical first night; it was blatantly obvious something was wrong.

Early on she had told me about a movie that she absolutely loved. She did not have a copy of it, so I ordered it and brought it with me to give her as a gift. We returned to the TV room as we did the previous day and put in the movie. This time, there was no snuggling, she curled up on the opposite side of the couch. I was basically paralyzed from saying anything because the conversation on the way back to the hotel the previous night had turned in a negative direction. For whatever reason, I decided the best course of events that night was to simply weather the storm. She drove me the short distance back to the bed-and-breakfast and dropped me off with our goodbye just being a short peck on the lips. I knew there was trouble in paradise.

At 8:37 AM the next morning, the phone rang in my room. Her voice was distressed and agitated. She said that she had planned on working, but now she didn't know what she was supposed to do. While I probed to try and understand, she went on to explain that she felt responsible for my wellbeing that day. She asked if she needed to come over and make sure I had food and expressed concern about leaving me all day to do nothing. Originally, I had planned to stay on Tuesday because we had talked about going to many of her familiar spots and places we had talked about for all these months together. That obviously was no longer on the table. Then she uttered the phrase of doom that will haunt me until the day I die, "I'm sorry, but my heart just isn't in this."

She said she would get ready and drive up, and we could talk. We sat on the rocking chairs at the front porch of the establishment, took a walk down the street and then sat on a couple of big rocks at the far end of the parking lot over the next hour's time. She had written to me early on that the few times that a relationship had been started in her post-divorce era, she had found herself suddenly as she put it, " retreating back in my corner." I knew right away that was where she had gone now. It was soul emptying and devastating, but I think I was more in shock at first and unable to really mount a decent case for trying to counteract her hastiness. She asked me what I was going to do, and I said pack up, call my brother to come get me. She said she wanted to drive me back up to the original hotel and perhaps we could stop for lunch.

On the drive, my emotions and attitude began to shift from stunned bewilderment to frustration and anger. We had built such a foundation and gotten off to such an amazing start, for her to suddenly pull the plug was audacious and frankly almost cruel. You have to remember, right or wrong, I had associated this entire relationship with some sort of cosmic correction or divine intervention. She made reference to our "friendship" and I was immediately moved to start talking about being categorized. I reminded her that I had predicted early on that she would eventually drop me off at what I characterized as the "Swell Guy Exit," the place where I always seemed to wind up. The actual point of the end of the road, actually turned out to be, The Comfort Inn parking lot. After a jointly tearful prolonged hug, she was back in her vehicle and whisking away. The date was November 1, 2011. That was appropriate because in earlier conversations we had amazed each other by both referencing the fact that the time of day 11:11 we both frequently noticed was somehow relevant. She had made me familiar with the Bible verse, Hebrews 11:1 ... "Now Faith is the assurance of things hoped for, the convictions of things not seen."

11:1 will forever haunt me because, on 11/1, my faith and belief were destroyed in an instant. I have never seen her again.

The 30 days that followed were hellish. The second day I was home, I walked three miles to the closest grocery stores to my house. Between the two stores, they had 18 cans of her favorite coffee. I bought every single one. Carrying those back to my house proved to be a daunting challenge. After resting for a few minutes, I set off in the other direction to the FedEx Kinko's store, which was approximately a mile and a half away. I packed all 18 cans in a large box and over-nighted them to her. Even in my emotionally battered condition, nothing was more important than fulfilling her needs.

For the first time in my life, I suffered from severe depression, and my actions were inexplicably stupid. We had talked sporadically at first and then contact ceased after a couple of weeks. She felt that I was painting upon her a scarlet letter. I did write excessively about my pain and despair, but I certainly never identified her by name and never levied any criticism her way. I finally sat down and penned a heartfelt letter, and she began talking to me again. We vowed to start over, which basically meant friendship only. That was a role I was well familiar with. She thought it was important to initiate our new relationship by deleting all of the extensive messaging we had compiled over those months.

For the next year, we corresponded semi-regularly. There were times when I would send glum messages lamenting what might've been. She was always quick to say that she had not slammed any doors permanently shut, but I knew that wasn't the case. Not only had she retreated into her corner, where I was concerned, she had completely left the arena. Then suddenly, in the spring of 2013, she stopped responding. I noticed that two of her best friends, women who had routinely communicated with me over the previous couple of years, had suddenly de-friended me on Facebook. She remained on my roster, but obviously executed some kind of blocking mechanism so I no longer could see her thoughts and words that were routinely shared with everyone. After a period of time, she too jettisoned me.

Reading our last exchanges, there was absolutely nothing controversial or contentious. It's obvious to me that someone, and I suspect I know who, spread some sort of sensational falsehoods or concocted a story where I had made derogatory statements. If that was the cause for our complete cessation of relations, the disappointment I feel as a result is inconsolable. I have never had a single second of negative thoughts regarding her and still believe she's the most fiercely independent and admirable person I have ever met. It would be an absolute impossibility for me to say or do anything to criticize or hurt her. What I had believed emphatically was my salvation, instead wound up being the impetus that hurtled me into the deepest, darkest place I have ever been cast. However, the experience and memory of that one incredible, magical night, will never be diminished. There is absolutely no question that it was one of the most perfect, special things I ever was a part of.

I am hesitant to elaborate on my most recent loves. One is married, the other very recently divorced, and both, again, are far away.

Just weeks after the 11/1 heartbreak, through unusual circumstances, someone I had always thought a great deal of magically appeared in my life. Our relationship over the next year and a half would yield a different kind of heartbreak. This time, it would not be about what might have been, it was acceptance of what never could be.

She is a one in 100 billion unique creation. Breathtakingly beautiful, immensely complex, featuring vastly diverse, often conflicting, personalities, values, attitudes, and emotions. In the right settings and with her switch dialed into the whimsical/carefree modes, no one on the planet is more fun and freewheeling. She is easily the most fascinating person I've ever come across. Unfortunately, she is also married.

We partnered up on broadcasting projects and every moment spent with her was a joyride. It was the moments in between that were agonizing and empty. For a time, I was extremely important to her. I gladly was there whenever needed. There never was any inappropriate conduct. which was something I readily accepted. However, as a result of our deep connection and evolution of natural interaction, she psychologically was compelled to build an internal wall that served as the boundary that her feelings for me could not cross. Her actions were understandable, she was trying to protect her marriage and herself. My feelings had no such barriers resulting in me continuing far in advance down a solo path that most of the time was an extremely lonely place. Despite our immense enjoyment of our mutual endeavors and time together, the situation became intolerable for us both, for different reasons. It was not a crushing death blow when we could no longer continue, but it still was profoundly sad. This was due to the fact that there never was a realistic chance, or was any false hope ever implied that there was any opportunity for a relationship. The burden on her having to keep me at arm's length was painful to behold. The dehumanizing feeling that it inflicted on me was excruciating. Plus, understandably, her husband grew tired of our very close association. Despite all that, the unabashed and unfiltered honesty and intimacy of our conversations, was from day one until the end, astonishingly unique. The failure in that situation with a woman I loved thankfully did not result for the first time in an epic failure of my own. This time, it simply was never possible for it to ever be.

As I write these words, amazingly, a new love is firmly entrenched and completely owns my heart. Of course, it is incredibly difficult; seemingly impossible and vast distance challenged. It is an ill-advised attempt to reach the brightest star yet. She is so brilliant in every sense of the word that there is never the slightest notion in my mind that despite the likely prospect of more heartbreak and crushing disappointment, that an all-out crusade to reach this ultimate summit, is a mandatory quest. She is worth the effort and the risks, and a million times more.

The follies and failures have been gut-wrenching. There is irony in the fact that my earliest stumbles and shortcomings were brought about by lack of knowledge, experience, and confidence. Because of these deficiencies, I lost out to rivals, many who should not have prevailed. Now, armed with all of the things I was so severely lacking previously, I am still not successful. So many remarkable women have retreated into their own worlds as a result of being hurt and mistreated. Despite now featuring the expertise and confidence to flourish, the product has become a very tough sale. Structure, security and stability are the most sought after commodities. My approach and philosophy does not exactly fit that profile.

I do not pass the buck and assign blame to any of the women I've loved. The old saying, it's not you, it's me, in my case, certainly rings true. Undeniably, I have learned a lot of lessons and gained invaluable knowledge. That has not stopped me, however, from continuing to try to touch seemingly unreachable stars. After all, they are the brightest in the sky. So don't cry for me Alpharetta, my quest is a conscious choice. I may be insane, certainly stubborn and clearly delusional, but the day I stop reaching, will be the same day that I cease breathing.

Post 10

"There is a classic old saying, that every once in a while, even a blind squirrel finds an acorn. For me, that was certainly the case, but instead of an acorn, I stumbled upon a gold nugget."

Wedded Bliss

In the late spring of 1986, I returned to West Memphis from my incredibly enjoyable winter in St. Petersburg. The previous year, my father had invested retirement proceeds into buying a greyhound farm where I now resided. I had every intention of trying to make that business work as a sideline to my job at Southland. I also had started the promising Insider tip sheet enterprise. Later that year, I was going to turn 29. I had not had a serious relationship with anyone for a number of years. Now back in Arkansas, I had wandered back to the vast wilderness of no prospects. Early on that racing season, Jerry Catt, one of my coworkers at the track, was quizzing me about my lack of a social life. I explained to him that I had extremely high standards. He replied, "Your standards are killing you, son." Sadly, I knew he was right but there was no indication that I had any chance to change. Early in May, in a miraculous answer to prayers, the answer came calling one morning at our training track, and she did not come empty-handed in any sense of the word.

One of the first people I met when I first came to the Memphis area was Carroll Blair. I became acquainted with both of his sons, Randy, and Rusty, who became friends as well as his wife Jenneane and their remarkable youngest child, Holly. I had even met daughter Shauna that winter in St. Petersburg. After writing a feature story on Holly and her exploits in winning gold medals at the international Special Olympics in gymnastics, the Blairs invited me to their home for dinner. It was a delightful evening and an occasion where I got to know the family even better, even the eldest sister Terie. It was a classic American family atmosphere. I had met the entire group and immediately established a very good relationship with each and every one. There was only one member of the clan that I was yet to meet.

That changed one early morning as I worked at our greyhound training track. She appeared looking resplendent in the bright sunshine. This was middle daughter, Cathie. She had returned to Arkansas to regroup after experiencing the heartbreak of the dissolution of her marriage to her high school sweetheart. To say she made a strong first impression would be a gross understatement. And she left nothing to chance by presenting me a platter of home-baked chocolate chip cookies.

As it turned out, she was going to be working at Southland in the Kennel Club restaurant as a server. It became an eagerly anticipated part of my daily routine to see her and visit as she set up her station. She had told me that one of the things that had initially impressed her about me was the fact that the year before, following my dinner at the Blairs, her mother had told her how she could not believe that I had actually taken the time to write a thank you note and send it. Honestly, I had not done that to curry favor with anyone. I had written the note because I was greatly appreciative that they had invited me and very much enjoyed the experience. I also had written It because it was the right thing to do

That first month or so, I hemmed and hawed around and never asked her out. A lot of our conversations were dealing with her feelings about what had happened with her marriage. After a friend's wedding, we did end up spending a lot of time together at the reception. Afterwards, even though my brother and sister had ridden with me to the ceremony, I offered her a ride home. I made up my mind that I was going to ask her for a date. Too nervous to directly talk to her about it, I bought her a card and told her how impressed I was and that I hoped she would consider spending more time with me without accompaniment from others. To that, she responded in writing with a very nice letter that basically told me thanks but no thanks. She explained that she was still in too convoluted a place to think about a new relationship and though she was fond of me, she just didn't think it was a good idea. And of course, she played the dreaded ... " there is another guy I'm kind of seeing" card. She had met a local yahoo, a supervisor on a highway crew. No disrespect to the local residents of the area, but that was an ultra weak excuse. All it served to do was make me even more determined.

It's funny how instinctively there are just certain things that you absolutely know. That first day we talked, it was such a profound experience, an epiphany. It was crystal clear to me that destiny was not just knocking, it was kicking at the door. Here we both were, approaching 30, with similar goals and a great deal of commonalities. And where had we intersected? in the cultural and social wasteland of eastern Arkansas. I was such an admirer of her family and instantly was attracted to everything she was. Beautiful, elegant, classy, polite, athletic, personable and gifted with a wonderful sense of humor. In other words on that last point, she laughed at my humor and antics.

I knew her resistance was not just a deferment of my advances, she was obstructing fate itself. It's not nice to fool Mother Nature, and it's not wise to deny fate. This was too important, future lives were depending on my next move. I went to a local florist and ordered up a dozen red roses. They did not typically deliver out to the rural outlying area where the Blair house was, but the lady seemed to grasp the urgency. I wrote a personalized message on the card to attach hoping it would save the day. I basically said that I believed our meeting was not by chance, that it was orchestrated by none other than God above. I submitted my contention that if we did not give this a chance that we were making a horrendous mistake.

Later that afternoon, she called me and said we needed to talk. The rest is history. My action sent an effective message and relayed the right words. She embraced the concept. Things moved quickly after that. On the day prior to her birthday on August 14, I walked her up to my work area in the judges' stand/press box area. It was late, the races were over, but I had a surprise for her. We had a giant message screen outside above the dogs' board. I had programmed in a series of animations and messages to kick off her birthday celebration. This was high-level stuff back in those days when computers were still in their relatively early stages. The last message said, "Cathie, I Love You." There was never any formal proposal; I don't know how I missed that step, but apparently it wasn't necessary. We immediately started making wedding plans and the date was set for November 15, one Saturday after the closing of the track for the season.

Our families and closest friends were there on a bitterly cold weekend to celebrate our grand event. The gathering would certainly pay dividends for the illustrious Mark Random upon his return to Memphis. During our weekend what I'm gathering Mark was introduced to Cathie's lovely, talentedcousin Cindee. Within a year it would be their spectacular wedding we were attending in Cape May, New Jersey. Cathie and I were both Catholic, but with her being recently divorced, we chose to steer clear of church protocol after being told it would be a long drawn out process to be married in that faith. We ended up settling for a charming little chapel, designed our own unique ceremony and found a man of God willing to do the honors of joining us in holy matrimony. His name was Dub Marsh, and his church was directly next door to Graceland. Thank you, thank you very much, Pastor. We wrote and recited our own vows. She liked me to sing songs to her, and one of them was a John Denver tune called Follow Me. We decided that perhaps it would be too dramatic, and even nauseating, for some of our guests to endure my melodious rendition but decided that it would be very fitting for me to recite the lyrics to her during the ceremony.

It's by far the hardest thing I've ever done, to be so in love with you for so long,
Follow me where I go, what I do, and who I know.
Make it part of you to be a part of me.
Follow me up-and-down, all the way, all around,
Take my hand and I say you'll follow me.

It's long been on my mind, you know it's been a long, long time,
I tried to find the words that would make you understand,
The way I feel about you, and just how much I need you,
To be there when I come home to you with nowhere else to Ron,
Follow me wherever I go, what I do and who I know,
Make it part of you to be a part of me.
Follow me up-and-down all the way, and all-around,
Take my hand and say you'll follow me.

You see I'd like to spend my life with you, show you things I've seen,
Places where I'm going to, and places where I've been,
To have you there beside me and never be alone,
All those times you are with me, we would be at home.
Follow me where I go, what I do, and who I know,
Make a part of you to a part of me,
Follow me up-and-down, all the way, all around
Take my hand and I will follow you.

We whisked away the next morning on a fabulous honeymoon cruise to the Caribbean. It was magical, almost surreal, like living in some kind of storybook tale. When we returned, the first indication of something completely different happening set in. This was for real, this was forever.

Of course, there were adjustments. We had already initiated the building of a house that would not be ready for some months. So Cathie's brother Rusty, graciously allowed us to stay in his home while he and his family were in St. Petersburg for the winter racing season.

In mid-December, we traveled to Huntsville Alabama where Cathie was entered in the marathon there and attempting to qualify for Boston. As an athlete and a person very in tune with her body, she was detecting unusual feelings. We had not yet been married even a month, and yet there was suggestive evidence that something major may be in play. Before checking into the hotel, we stopped at a drugstore and procured a test kit. When she came out of the bathroom, her face said it all. It was positive, our newly-formed family unit's earliest stages was already expanding to include a third member. We were thrilled, we were exhilarated, we were flabbergasted. What about the race the next day? Do women run marathons when they're pregnant? After reaching her doctor and receiving his assurance that if she felt good that participating in the race was just fine, the true excitement of the news we had received took over. Months earlier in that same year, she had been reeling from a terrible divorce and was uncertain what her future held. I was feeling like life was passing me by, and my inability to make things happen was dooming me to a desolate future. In a veritable blink of an eye, everything had turned upside down, and in a very miraculous, blessed way. The next morning, with me scurrying from station to station and checkpoint to checkpoint, my new superstar wife, carrying her unexpected passenger, negotiated the hills and dales of Huntsville Alabama for 26.2 miles. Her time, which we tracked throughout to make sure she was on schedule, incredibly easily qualified her for participation in the Boston Marathon that was scheduled for April. Unfortunately, that was a race from which she was going to have to be scratched.

We settled into our new house that summer and on a scorching Mid-south August day, our little bundle of joy arrived. Well, not right on cue. He made his appearance about eight hours after we had gone to the hospital. Call it a rookie mistake. Cathie was overdue and feeling more miserable with every passing moment. Her wonderful, devoted sister, Holly, had stayed by her side much of the last couple of days leading up to the moment of truth. After attending a James Bond movie on a Friday night, signs of labor appeared in the wee hours of the morning that followed.

Describing that event is incredibly difficult to put into words and pay that miraculous experience proper tribute and reverence. Like the prototypical, mostly useless sidekick that a father in the delivery room is, I attempted to stay busy and provide whatever comfort and support I could as Cathie agonized to make her special delivery. She had read articles warning of possible detrimental effects of pain reducing drugs at birth and had decided that natural was the way to go. Her tiny body strained and struggled but just after 3 o'clock in the afternoon, Case

Blair Keefer made his initial earthly appearance. He was pink and perfect. I was so overwhelmed to have witnessed such a miraculous spectacle, I shed far more tears than my newborn son. I must've looked ridiculous in my absurd hospital cap and gown with my eyes watering like I had stuck my head in a sack of onions. Similar sensations to those that I had experienced at my wedding, honeymoon and initial days of marriage returned. I felt like an actor in a drama that the most wonderful writer in the world had authored. It all seemed too good to be true and that somehow I wasn't worthy to be in this position of such unbridled and unprecedented joy and wonderment. And Cathie, after the most heroic and harrowing period of hours, with pain and discomfort that I could not even fathom, she laid there all aglow beaming an incredible radiance. There has not been a moment in my life, before or since, that I have ever been more proud, awestruck and filled with love, admiration, gratitude and appreciation for another person. As we shared those initial moments with our new child, the overwhelming sensation was, this is the zenith. What could possibly ever live up to these moments. To this day, I'm proud to have those thoughts and relish the experience and every moment it involved as it was unfolding.

On Monday, we brought our new baby home. Despite not having parental experience on our collective resumes, we found being a mommy and daddy to be an extremely natural process that instinctively came easily for us both. I was more than anxious to help any and every way I could. More than anything else, I wanted her to rest and recuperate. I wanted her to understand the level of gratitude I felt. And I also was determined to be the best father possible for that wonderful little boy that had come into my life. I checked on Case constantly, and if he was unsettled in the least, I found myself letting him comfortably lie on my shoulder or chest while I rocked him in my lounge chair for hours on end.

The years that followed were extremely happy times. Cathie and Case bonded beautifully as well. I was the proudest daddy in history. The relationship between a father and his firstborn son is truly something extraordinarily special. To think back on those times, it is so humbling to appreciate that as he grew, I was his shining idol, and he was absolutely the center of my universe. It is so unfortunate when men that father a child, particularly a son, do not understand that this relationship is the most special and meaningful one they will ever have in their lives. I have incredible respect for single mothers who are left to handle all of the responsibilities and challenges of raising a child. And while it may not be a popular stance in this nontraditional day and age, but both parents, lending their invaluable love, support and guidance, are critical components to the development of children.

It would be four years and eight months before a glorious reprisal of the holiest, and most significant of experiences miraculously took place again. In the fall of 1991, Cathie told me upon my returning for my annual golf trip with my buddies in South Carolina, we were once again expecting. It was amazing news; we were both thrilled. She had convinced herself that surely, this time, it would be a daughter. A perfect little matched set, it all seemed so logical. In our little baby nursery, a tiny pink outfit and dress magically appeared. A month or so later when we set out for our ultrasound, we decided to find out what we were having.

That appointment went very well in terms of clearly seeing our newest addition. Technology had improved and as the enthusiastic nurse deployed the imaging equipment, she started describing in detail what we were looking at. To this day, her fateful words still resonate, " And we can see right here, it's a little man!"

Now for me, her gleeful announcement was magnificent. Not that I would have had one speck of disappointment had the proclamation gone the other direction. A second son, what splendid news. Cathie kept a brave face, but I could see her spirits temporarily sink. On the walk to the car, she was somewhat emotional. She was thrilled regardless, but I knew there were twinges of disappointment as well. Always prepared in these situations, I produced a blue card congratulating her on the wonderful news. She seemed baffled, wondering how I knew what the verdict would be. Of course, I had hedged my bets and bought a pink card as well. I was ready for either outcome.

I had also crafted a strategy to propose in the event that another male was coming aboard. Cathie's dad, my father-in-law Carroll, was a wonderful man and absolutely my wife's hero. I proposed that we name the baby in his honor. Of course, the idea of naming a boy Carroll was the source of some concern, but the plan was too perfect to concern ourselves with that. We had a party and presentation to make the announcement to the family. On April 4, once again a Saturday, Carroll Clayton Keefer made his debut at 7 o'clock in the morning. This labor had progressed rather quickly to say the least. This time, Cathie's older sister Terie, have been on hand and supervised the entire operation. There never was any question that she knew exactly what she was doing, but her insistence that it was not yet time to go to the hospital, despite the extreme discomfort of her sister, my wife, cut it shall we say, a little close. In the end, after a death-defying high-speed sojourn, we made it to the hospital with only less than 25 minutes to spare. I had made my delivery, and it was nerve-wracking and stressful. As soon as they had her settled in the delivery room, the combination of that pressure, a sleepless night of waiting, and no food for many hours added up to a most unique experience for the expectant father. As I stood by the bedside, waiting for the doctor to enter, I suddenly felt lightheaded and fainted right on the spot. My sudden thud upon hitting the floor caused quite a commotion just moments before the main event. Blessedly, I was quickly revived and back on my feet. Knowing more of what to expect, the second time around was far less overwhelming, but equally as amazing to behold. It's hard for me to imagine that for so many years, fathers nervously waited in an adjacent room and missed out on what can only be described as the most startling miracle you will ever witness in your life, participating in the birth of your child. As previously mentioned, true to his personality that we would later come to know and love so well, Clayt's first seconds would be very consistent with his life philosophy, he does things his own way. He wasted no time and was born in a matter of moments. When he emerged, he was a little bit on the blue side, which was attributed to him being cold. He was quickly wrapped up, and a baby blue knit cap was pulled down over his head and ears. It made a rather comical sight with that tiny little face peering out from under such a distinct fashion accessory. He barely fussed, just looked around with the puzzling expression that could best be described as slightly agitated. We had a new son, and Case had a little brother.

Clayt would be a different kind of child than Case. He was far more curious, much more mischievous and as previously mentioned, fiercely exhibited a mind of his own. Case was always totally trusting and dutiful with both Cathie and I. Clayt was loving and sweet, but his individuality and independence were ever present.

The nature of our family structure was determined almost from the very first day that Cathie and I were married. Parenthood arrived so quickly that critical developmental time for our own relationship was relegated to a back burner. So much of our time, energy, emphasis and attention were lavished on our sons. It was unspoken but clearly understood by us both that they were the two most important things in our world, and everything else paled in comparison.

It really is not important in the context of these pages to discuss in great detail what went wrong that led to the dissolution of our marriage. We were together for 14 wonderful years and a perfect storm of events led to our marital demise. Intense pressure from my career, overextension, and living above our means which created financial stress, the only brief period of career difficulty I ever experienced and unforgivably, decline of communication between the two of us, were all contributing factors. It should've never happened, we should've fought through it, there was a great deal of failure we both were responsible for.

After four years apart, we both had considerably wised up and developed a great deal of perspective. With Case in college in Kansas, Cathie and Clayt moved to Alabama to once again live with me. Having my son there through his high school years was indescribably gratifying. Cathie and I had returned to a very fulfilling relationship and once again lived under the same roof. However, the step was never taken for formal reconciliation. After five years, with Clayt off to college and just she and I living full-time together as roommates, it was time for us both to venture back out and find some kind of logical, sensible existence for the rest of our lives. It seemed to make sense at the time. Now days, I'm not so sure. She is now and will always be the mother of my children and the woman with which I shared so many incredible experiences. Our relationship now, despite her being remarried, is very rewarding. We share the knowledge that we did something absolutely fabulous together. Our two sons, both individuals of great quality and character, are our living legacies. No matter what the situation is in terms of where everyone winds up, the four of us will always be our family. Cathie gave me the greatest gift I could ever have received. Those gifts are not just limited to my sons, she granted me the amazing, powerful enabling blessings of purpose, commitment, and validity. For all of those things, I have always loved her and forever will.

"You've gone a million miles, how far'd you get?
To that place where you can't remember, and you can't forget,
She'll lead you down a path, there'll be tenderness in the air,
She'll let you come just far enough, so you know she's really there,
Then she'll look at you and smile, and in her eyes she'll say,
She's got a Secret Garden ...
Where everything you want, where everything you need,
Will always stay ...
A million miles away."

—Bruce Springsteen

Love Is A Many Splintered Thing

VALENTINE'S DAY Sucks

In this ridiculous modern world where everyone is offended by everything, let me throw in my two cents. The most exclusionary, segregationist BS day of the year, the one that I feel highly offended by my denial of access and participation, rolls around every February 14. My feelings are hurt watching it all unfold around me. Surely I must be able to file a lawsuit to make it go away.

Of course, I'm referring to Saint Valentine's Day! Consider this a friendly reminder to any of you dimwits, who somehow latched onto a woman and routinely forget that this day is vitally important to them.

I personally don't care for Valentine's Day and refuse to acknowledge it. There are a number of reasons, but predominately it is due to the fact that I am not in possession of the Golden Ticket required to participate, I have no sweetheart. That diminutive, cherubic, winged archer Cupid has certainly fired some of his magic little bolts into my heart over the years. Unfortunately, the arrows with my name on them don't seem to register in a beloved's soul or spirit. Instead, they appear to wind up behind those inspiring spots and instead lodge in an area that creates a pain in the backside. Chubby little Bastard never has my name penciled in on his list for a direct heart hit.

My irritation is only heightened when the same undeserving Don Juans, who forget birthdays, anniversaries and Valentine's Day, clumsily try and formulate a last second plan to appease their better half. Cheap flowers from the grocery store or the neighbor's rose bush, boring chocolates from Walgreens, a knockoff brand card that has "Grandma" crossed out and wife/girlfriend's name written in because the Dollar Store was all out. And my favorite, the hastily organized dinner outing to the China Buffet or Golden Corral ... All not good. Probably not a wise idea to give her a Dust Buster, George Foreman Grill or IHOP gift card either. And these aren't even the worst.

Oh, how I loathe the cheesy crap companies advertise as splendid Valentine's gifts. They suggest that if you call at the last minute and send her some footed pajamas, strawberries, or a stupid teddy bear, you are guaranteed to ignite her urges and be blissfully rewarded. What a joke! The worst commercial ever is when the gal, surrounded by her female coworkers, pulls from a box a goofy bear with a black mask on his eyes. She reads the card allegedly from her idiot of a partner, actually written by some schmuck in the Vermont Teddy Bear dynasty. "I sent you the Love Bandit Bear because you stole my Heart." Barf! Really? Of course, all the women standing around ooh and ahh, and are envious. Sure they are. Of course, the bear probably stacks up pretty good but up against a pair of Lottery Scratchers or a Shake Weight.

Me, well, I'm a Benched Romantic. An evening at a special or sentimentally significant restaurant or hotel that holds history and memories in your relationship, jewelry, a commemorative collectible, a full body deep tissue massage with oil and always some heartfelt words or verses actually written in by me on a mushy Hallmark card. Casanova Keefer can step up to the romantic dish and sock it out of the park. But alas, he has not been issued a uniform.

Not having anyone on Valentine's Day is like the opening scene in Animal House. When Kent and Larry visit the stuck up Omega Fraternity, for rush week, they are quickly labeled as non-desirables and ushered into a room of rejects. There is a complete nerd dressed atrociously in a way-too-short pair of slacks and white socks. His horn-rimmed glasses are taped in the middle to hold them together. There is also an Indian guy wearing a turban, a slightly built African fellow decked out in a suit and a blind dude in a wheelchair. Come on in Kip and all of you others with no sweethearts, you destitute misfits in the social stratosphere. Meet and join Sidney, Jugdish, Mohammed, and Clayton.

What a great day it is. You spend every day of the year hating yourself, and on this one date annually on the calendar, it's officially confirmed that all the world's women truly loathe, dismiss and reject you. In Chicago during prohibition, seven hoodlums were lined up and machine-gunned by Al Capone's rival gang on Valentine's Day. That Valentine's Day Massacre is forever infamous, but it is probably only slightly worse than eating a bologna sandwich by yourself on February 14.

So girls, put on your Hoody Footie pajamas, put your dime store flowers in water, cuddle up under your Hunk-A-Love Bear, that's if he remembered at all to get you anything. Be sure to fix that special fella a magnificent grilled cheese when he demands to know where dinner is. As for Cupid, I hope he collides at high-speed head on with an Amazon.com drone delivering some of that worthless garbage to an unfortunate lovely who's chosen a complete loser to be with. Love is in the air, so too are pathogens and contaminants. Happy Valentine's Day, Bah Humbug.

Cue Rod Serling

"Kip Keefer exists in a space somewhere between real life and a pseudo universe. Tread carefully if you ever find yourself aimlessly wandering near this ominous location. Heed this warning and do not suffer a similar fate.

Seemingly a real person and a quality human being, Kip may not realize it, but he is hopelessly, permanently entrenched in a place he willingly entered but unwittingly has been entrapped. You see while he thought he was embarking on a trail to joy and fulfillment, he was actually heading down a path that never leads anywhere. It appears there is no turning back; he now for a lifetime resides ... In The Friend Zone."

The Friend Zone, aka, Female relationship Purgatory. The problem is, regardless of the length of the stay, short-term or an extended period, the next stop is a certainty. The train out of this station never advances farther on; this is the end of the line. The cost of a ticket to be admitted here ... Being a "Nice Guy."

Entering the Friend Zone with any woman, particularly with someone you are attracted to, is an invalidating, futile, emasculating, ultimately fatal endeavor. The main requirement is being there to fill in cavernous emotional gaps and listen to real tales of woe about problems and challenges they are encountering. Most particularly focus on the transgressions perpetrated by the men in their lives, currently or previously, and all that these "jerks" are guilty of. Your sympathetic ear and wide shoulders are not offered shallowly or insincerely. You do become immersed and deeply do care. Once involved, you wait patiently, offering support, advice, reinforcement. The insane, misguided, unrealistic hope is that they will somehow realize the greatest guy imaginable is right before their eyes. But in the Friend Zone, your masculinity is invisible, checked, secured and locked away at the gate. There are moments that create incredible hope. "I love you so much" "You are an amazing person" "You have no idea how much you mean to me" "I don't know what I would do without you"... All of these are Emotional Mirages. Frequently, as you are riding high thinking that your sincere efforts, empathy and unyielding, legitimate concern is actually endearing you and magnifying your suitability, here is what ALWAYS comes next: "Nice to hear from you FRIEND." (The word Friend, strategically wielded in woman speak actually means ... You are a wonderful person, but I wouldn't sleep with you even if you were the last man on Earth not infected with the Ebola Virus.) "I guess I am going to have to start looking for someone" (meaning, you are certainly not a candidate or my personal favorite.... " "you are such a great guy, some woman is really going to be lucky to have you in her life."

Gee thanks. I don't have high hopes for that forecast, especially if they see me as a hideous, non-human Eunuch like you clearly do. I've invested countless actual communication hours and just as many thinking about you. It's nice I made such a great impression as you chastise other women for overlooking me. I have been sent that "great guy, you will find someone" message no less than five times by five different women in a time frame of less than a week. In a sad way, I know they mean well and are trying to be nice. However, they are anxious to pass that hot, unwanted potato that is you, to someone, anyone, besides themselves.

I am a Nice Guy. I don't know how to be anything else. I am a Sir Lancelot. I save Damsels In Distress and do good deeds. My reward is they stay with or seek another Black Knight, similar or exactly like the ones before who treated them so shabbily or even abusively. Sir Lancelot, the guy they couldn't imagine living without, his usefulness exhausted, is discarded and forgotten. My new title, Sir Shitouttaluck.

I concede, it's somewhat a product of the times and instant communication. It's a double-edged sword. As an Extrovert, Entertainer and Intelligent Person, I need interaction with other people. I am now and always have been a Romantic. Substituting this cyber existence for actual human contact sets this disappointment in motion.

This is a regular pattern phenomenon. I'm such a Swell Guy, I'm here for anyone. I want to help and feel confident that I almost always deliver. The syndrome is the same if you enter the Friend Zone. It only hurts when someone you really are excited to be in contact with delivers a devastating stiff arm. You would assume that an intelligent person would learn the lesson and steer clear of this soul sucking, dehumanizing wasteland. To date, this Moron, Yours truly, never seems to learn that obvious lesson. Now tell me all about it, what's the matter?

Not A Match

In the late summer or 2013, in an extreme moment of lunacy, loneliness, and sheer desperation, I did something that previously I would've assured you I would never ever entertain doing. I found myself filling out the forms, typing the words for the bio, assembling photographs and launching my own match.com profile.

This act of self-flagellation was prompted by my continuing belief, which turned out to be a pathetic, colossal miscalculation, that surely someone was out there who could make my life far more joyous, manageable and worthwhile. And as previously stated, I did not feel that this venture was in any way exploitive or selfish. I knew anyone who answered the call and rallied to Kip Keefer's side would be rewarded beyond her wildest imagination with incredible affection, admiration, appreciation, and attention.

My rationalization had led me to conclude that looking locally for someone was not a completely wacky idea. Further, I also viewed it as an opportunity to get to know some nice interesting women. I certainly did not view the expansion of my circle of prospects and friends to have any negative drawbacks.

Of course, for me, the major concern was the emasculating issue of my freedom of movement and mobility. Orchestrating dating maneuvers was going to be a difficult task. And of course, the biggest elephant in my prospective dating paradise was my lack of vision itself. Would women be receptive to dating interaction with me despite my sight limitations? I mean, let's face it, what I was attempting to do would basically be creating a whole new meaning for a common term around these circles, for the most part, I would literally be, "A Blind Date."

My initial days immersed in the murky wasteland that is the dating industry proved to be quite enlightening. Immediately, I was besieged by many contacts. I found it odd from the very beginning that almost every single one came from women who were far younger than me. Typically, they lived in major cities all around the country. The photographs that accompany their profiles usually reveal suggestively dressed, model type, gorgeous girls. Disguised in their bio would be various forms of writing out text numbers or emails to contact them. It didn't take Sherlock Holmes to figure out that these aspiring mates and dares, were most likely fat hairy guys sitting at a computer in their underwear smoking a cigar creating false profiles with an array of beautiful girls as the bait. The intent of their cyber fishing expedition, drawing lonely heart, moronic saps into trying to contact these mythical babes. Then the offer would be made to send pictures or arrange a rendezvous with the simple transfer of money. This big fish and had taken a lap or two around a number of oceans and never was stupid enough to bite on any of that nonsense. I did waste my time and file several complaints to the company for this appalling breach in their operation. None of those correspondences were ever answered. After all, the scammers are paying for pages to peddle their nefarious product, Match is benefiting, everybody wins. Even their sappy customers, after all, when a fifty-something-year-old man gets a provocative, suggestive "wink alert" from a 24-year-old supermodel in New York City, that's pretty heady stuff.

The fallacy of this dating site is, women members of quality can, but realistically do not contact the men. The daily matches are emailed overnight seven days a week. Many of the profiles and stories/photos therein feature seemingly lovely, intelligent highly impressive women. So of course, it is up to the men to select the ones they like and either send some lame alert to that fact or undertake the humiliating process of writing an email. As you can well imagine, especially in that early period of involvement in this, I deployed highly creative, oftentimes humorous, always extremely complimentary messaging strategies to try and impress the elite women featured on the pages. I figured that the best thing I had going for me was superior intellect to virtually all of my gender peer rivals. Employed, sober, sane, no domestic violence convictions, all my teeth, all seemed like major checkmarks in my column. I think there is little doubt that reading my bio would have distinguished me as someone refreshingly different. In retrospect, that probably proved to be detrimental. My determination to identify my dissimilarity to the standard issue, everyday guys these women were used to, did not lead to overwhelming support.

I should have recognized that lack of conformity was perhaps not the best route to go here in Alabama. Just reading the profile of just about every woman between the ages of 45 and 60 revealed that almost every single one highlighted the same things in describing themselves and who they were looking for.

It was amazing that every single, divorced woman on the dating site, and I'm talking 100% of them, always in the initial sentences mentioned their tremendous devotion and love for their close friends and family. I would think, this is just my opinion, that those things are certainly obvious. Their inclusion would be comparable to saying, I breathe numerous times a minute. There was almost always the insistence of powerful religious faith and usually highlighting of God coming first in their lives. Then the compulsory listing would begin. Common elements generally appeared mentioning, love of the outdoors, hiking, the beach and having sand between their toes, travel, dining out, curling up at home to watch a movie, dogs, and love of college football, usually Alabama football. Reading these profiles gave one the impression that all of these women had been raised in the exact same household. As I said before, being different meant being ostracized and rejected as some sort of bizarre freak show.

Despite my miscalculations, amazingly I had some initial success. A very attractive woman, who seemed very appreciative of my contact, indicated that she would like to meet. We had a wonderful time at a nice restaurant and planned a second get together. This time, she chose the venue, which turned out to be an even more expensive dining establishment. That didn't really bother me, I am not cheap in any manner. But the conversation that evening became very disturbing when her line of questioning seemed to be solely focused on my occupation and financial standing. She then shifted to tales of woe about how her fortune had been wrongfully seized from her by corrupt court officials who sided with her ex-husband in some Podunk county. It had left her with next to nothing. Hardly a mathematician, it was still not difficult for me to add up what this modern day Blanche Devereaux was looking for. So much for my initial Birmingham dating success.

However, it was my next experience that really proved to be educational about everything you should avoid in the treacherous jungle of online dating.

I received a well-written, highly enthusiastic match.com message from a girl identifying herself as Lily. She wrote a very flattering paragraph about how much she enjoyed my profile and how rare it was to find what looked like such a wonderful gentleman in the midst of "rednecks and ruffians." She went on to describe herself as someone who had been out of the loop for several years due to a serious injury. She expressed great interest in getting back into some form of social status. Unlike female counterparts on the site, when someone takes the time to write to me, my personal protocol and basic manners prompt me to always respond. I thanked her for her nice comments. I also politely asked two questions. First, why did she not include a picture on her profile?... and secondly, what was the nature of the injury that caused her to be shut down for that long a period?

Within minutes, I had an answer. She explained that she had fallen down steps and broken her neck. She said that initially she was not even expected to survive. She described extensive rehab and declared that she had miraculously after a long period of time sufficiently recovered. On the photo question, her explanation was that there had been no pictures taken of her in recent years. She only had older photographs and was not technically versed in how to display those. Plus, she explained that men had always flocked to her for her looks, and she did not feel comfortable on this dating site having that be the main point of emphasis. I knew that sounded suspect, but being relatively new to the online dating community, I did not press the issue. She concluded her message by asking me if I would consider meeting her for lunch whenever possible. She craftily led me in further by saying that this would be her first date in many years after all that had happened to her, and that she was so impressed with me that she was hoping I would agree to do the honors. I wrote back and said sure I would take her to lunch. I reasoned, what the hell, after all, what's the harm in that? We arranged the launch site near where she lived and convenient for me as I would be in transit back for my usual Thursday broadcasting gig. My brother at the time was providing driver services, for a salary, of course.

The big event was still two days away, but logging on I discovered that she had sent me six or eight messages overnight. They ranged from how excited she was at the prospect of meeting me, to what I thought she should wear, to hopes that our second date could be at her house because she was such an excellent cook. Then the messages on the day before became even more bizarre. That afternoon, I started receiving a series of virtually hourly updates on her deliberations about her wardrobe selection for the next day. Befuddled, I did not even respond, and yet they kept coming. The real tip off that something was wrong should have registered when one of the evening emails actually had a picture of a strange-looking black dress laid out side-by-side with a pair of slacks and some kind of blouse. Remember, this is a woman who claimed not to have the technical expertise to post her photo on her profile. Alarm bells should have sounded the liar-liar pants on fire warning. She asked in the email which one I liked better. I finally answered, "I'm not a great fashion expert; I'm sure anything you wear will be just fine." Then I concluded by telling her I would see her outside the restaurant at 12:30.

It was a very warm day that afternoon when my brother dropped me off at around 12:20. Since she had seen my pictures, I had told her that it would be up to her to spot me in front of the door. I told her I would be wearing a blue polo shirt and khaki slacks. From her description on her profile, she was allegedly 5'2, 54 years of age, with dark hair. From her description of herself, she was supposed to be very attractive. Various people approached, but none vaguely fit that profile. Soon it was 12:30, and I had to seek some shade to get out of the blazing sun but still maintain the position adjacent to the front door. Ten more minutes passed, now 12:40. The woman who had emailed me for 248 consecutive hours in anticipation of this major event was now officially late. We had not exchanged phone numbers, so there were no means of contact. When 12:45 registered on my phone, I started thinking the mystery woman had psyched herself out to the point where she chickened out.

I already had serious misgivings about this encounter and now was actually starting to feel relieved that it was not going to happen. Those thoughts quickly dissipated when my struggling vision in the midday glare detected a tiny figure walking straight towards me. When she came within arm's length, she looked up and asked if I was Kip? I did not answer wisely because I admitted I was indeed him. Cordially, I leaned down and gave her tiny frame a loose, congenial hug.

Let me attempt to paint a very clear picture for you of who stood before me. Five foot two was probably an exaggeration to start with, I would estimate closer to 4-10 or 11. To me, that really doesn't matter. And, I do believe she was once 54, sadly my best guess is that was at least 12, maybe 15 more birthdays, had come and gone since she sat on that mark. I can only speculate what she actually weighed, but I will say this. If she had applied to ride horses at the local race track, they would've sent her home and told her to put on some pounds. In other words, my best guess is she weighed less than 90 pounds. Indeed, her hair was dark, but it was also visibly wet and indisputably unstyled. Either she just emerged from the shower moments before or had encountered a spewing fire hydrant with her car window down as she turned into the parking lot. But it was the item perched on top of this damp mass that was by far the most disturbingly attention-getting. It was a hat, but not a hat that had been seen by anyone in civilization for at least 50 years. It appeared to be made out of some sort of silk-like material. The fabric and colors matched the pants she was wearing, which I will attempt to describe momentarily. The only thing I can compare this headgear to would be what badass bikers' girlfriends wore back in the 60s. It was kind of a puffed up, high rider, with the appearance of something that had been inflated. On the very front, protruding very slightly from the top of her forehead and the base of her hairline was a tiny, thin cap bill.

Now, the rest of her outfit, after all, it was equally a spectacular display. After the constant headlines of the day before, what she had settled on, or more likely just thrown on at the last possible second, can only be described as very original, but attire more suited for an appearance on one of the three rings of the Greatest Show On Earth, Ringling Brothers Barnum and Bailey Circus.

Let's start from the feet up. Her shoes were some sort of deep blue slippers. I noticed they had two silver buttons of some variety strategically attached just below the flaps of the shoe. The pants were easily the most unique garment of that variety I had ever seen. The closest thing that I could recall as to the form of these britches was the pants that Barbara Eden used to wear on the 60s sitcom I Dream of Jeannie. They were not made out of that frilly kind of material, however; more like that slick pseudo satin sweatpants material. They fit snugly around her tiny waist with an elastic presence, and from the top of her thighs to just below her knees, they flared out into a baggy lower formation that can only be described as puffed out. They were also striped, white, light lavender and green. I think they may have been ideal for lounging around the harem at any self-respecting sultan's palace. To this day, I'm not sure if they were actually sleepwear or some Middle Eastern imported pants that just never caught on here stateside. And despite the rather warm conditions, with the temperature in the mid-80s, her top was a tan mid sleeve, made out of some sort of sweater material. It had a rounded neckline that clung to her throat and seemed to me to be tight. The front of the shirt had these two raised fabric strip things that started up around each shoulder area, came down on both sides and intersected in the area of her abdomen. Again, my thought was, perhaps she had escaped from some sort of circus museum. Or maybe she was actually a genie who as a result of my correspondence, I had released from her bottle. I never had a chance to contemplate my wishes, but the first one would have been, me getting out of there. In retrospect, I am glad that I was not thinking up wishes because I was never going to be granted even the opportunity to ask for them. For one of the few times in my entire life, today I would not be doing very much speaking at all.

So we headed in to enjoy our fabulous lunch. It's a well-known fact that when you are accompanied by a dazzling, eye-catching, captivating woman, everyone takes notice. Well, the same thing is true of my companion that afternoon, but I suspect for completely different reasons. I have convinced myself that most people decided that I was doing a wonderful thing taking an eccentric coworker, or perhaps a bizarre aunt to lunch. Or horror of all horrors, could some of the looks have been accompanied by thoughts that we looked like an interesting couple? Perish the thought and shoot me now!

Finally, settled in at a table, one would think the situation would be a little less awkward. Nothing could've been further from the truth. In a creaky, slow-drawling, craggy voice, she immediately started talking as if she hadn't had the opportunity to talk in a very long time. And I concede, that very well may have been the case. Occasionally, I would try to interject a thought, but it quickly was swept aside as her rambling, unstoppable, surging train of thought roared onward. She talked about her accident and the hardships of recovery. She talked about her only child, a son, who was continuously in trouble and notorious for wrecking every vehicle he had ever operated. When she added that she had recently bought him a motorcycle, I knew I was in the presence of a true giant of judgment and intellectual capacity. She described in detail her five marriages and explained that technically she was still married. But the current husband had pretty much disappeared two years earlier, and she had no idea where he was. She gleefully told me that through his attorney, she received a check every month for her expenses. The other major topic she wanted to discuss was her pair of beloved dogs. One of them apparently a Great Dane. I had visions of the massive canine swallowing her whole if she ever crossed him. I politely listened to the diatribe; at least, my physical form sat prone on the chair listening intently. I realized at some point that my spirit had obviously had all it could stand and abandoned my body, leaving it to fend for itself. It had ascended upward and was looking down on the scene at the table below in bemused wonderment.

Around 2 o'clock as she rambled on, barely touching the tuna salad she had ordered for lunch, blessedly my phone rang. It was my brother and a rare occasion where I was actually glad to hear from him. He was asking about my estimated time of completion. I told him about five minutes. I turned back to the table and told her that I was needed at work and would have to leave now. We exited the restaurant, and I walked her to her car. During that entire walk, probably a couple of hundred yards but seeming to be the length of the New York City Marathon, she talked about wanting me to come over so she could fix me dinner. She was also excited about the prospect of me meeting her dogs. This was a woman who had not gleaned one fact and could not tell you one thing more about me than she knew almost two hours ago before we met. I literally could've said during the conversation that I was an axe murderer, and it would not have registered. But I offered no information because I never was granted the floor. I'm not exactly soft-spoken, but on this occasion, I was completely muted. She was very polite, thanking me profusely for a lovely time. It was the only time during the entire experience that I felt a twinge of pity for her. Conversely, I was feeling plenty sorry enough for myself. I gave her an awkward hug, and she stretched up to kiss my cheek. I spun away and realized my brother had been standing watching this entire spectacle just a few yards away. As I approached him, he could not contain a boisterous laugh. I was almost relieved that he had actually seen my companion for lunch so that in the future when I told the story, I had a witness to corroborate my testimony.

Later that evening, I typed out a very nice, complimentary message that let her know I had enjoyed meeting her, but I did not feel like we were very compatible. I would never hurt anybody's feelings so I also added that the fact that she was still married made me uncomfortable.

There is no question that the term, "sight unseen" is certainly two words that in the online dating game cannot be part of the vernacular.

I went on some more match dates, almost always from that point forward with women who were amazingly attractive, sometimes even somewhat personable. For whatever reason, none of those turned out to be successful romantic relationships. They did yield a pair of very nice friendships, which I'm sure will come as a big surprise to my readers. I wonder if any of them felt the time spent with me was like my time at the worst lunch date ever. I never got the sense it was that bad. Of course, in face-to-face meetings, I revealed my sight issue, and I'm sure that was a factor in some of the disconnects. There were also some that were interested, but in every case of those, I always felt they were just looking for someone to pencil into a spot that had been vacated. Almost your perception of, first decent guy to show up, first served.

My instincts have served me well throughout, and I should have stuck to them. Online dating is demeaning and humiliating for men. I knew it wasn't for me, and dammit, I was right. When it comes to Match, I am not a match.

A Touching Send Off

To wrap up this less than flowery chapter on love and romance, I thought it was important to go ahead and reveal that despite my jaded attitude and woefully less than monumental amorous achievement, in my heart will eternally reside a diehard romantic. So I thought I would include the words that I wrote to serve as the narration for my son Case and his bride Traci's rehearsal dinner party video. We hired a Morgan Freeman voice actor to recite it.

The journey on the path we call life is an experience common to us all.

There are those who choose to casually saunter, savoring the sights, spectacles, and scenery. Others move rapidly, forsaking the proverbial smelling of roses, determinedly aspiring to arrive at their desired destination with the utmost expedience. Regardless of one's pace or purpose, every story starts at the same place, the beginning.

The most blessed gift one can receive on their sojourn is the accompaniment of another. That person who is meant to be, who falls into perfect stride and harmoniously fits. One who joins you in marveling at the discoveries, reveling in triumphs, weathering storms and sharing seemingly ordinary moments ... that in fact, actually turn out to be some of the most profound and significant experiences in a lifetime

Finding someone you can live with is far less important than finding that person you can't conceive living without.

So what is the elusive secret of success? Well, it's simple really ... Place your emphasis, your energy and your total devotion in your partner as opposed to yourself. In a "What's In It For Me World," the concept of selflessness has become increasingly rare. This deference to one another is not a sacrifice of one's self, it's the key ingredient to the creation of something far more worthwhile, a miraculous, bountiful union. Far more than any Ghosts of Personal Glory, in the end, your requited Love is the Foundation for all the many Stories of Your Life.

Traci and Case, you are embarking on an incredible adventure. May the days ahead and all the chapters you will mutually author, be overflowing with enrichment, joy, and limitless memories.

Now ... Let this emphatic Celebration begin!

KEEFER STORY

Oh Brother!

In recent years, one of the central figures prominently cast in modern misadventures is my uniquely unusual younger brother Charles. Most people, including himself, refer to him as JR. Of course that is short for Junior. That designation was bestowed upon him 30 years ago when he and I were coworkers at Southland. The title was not issued as a follow-up to our father, it started off being Kip Jr. When he arrived on the scene, the guys we worked with swore that he was an exact replica of me from the standpoint of how he walked, talked and acted.

That phenomenon was not very difficult to figure out. When Bill Keefer flew the coop in 1970, young Charles Kerry was seven years old. Our father's ambitious social schedule and demanding career, which involves extensive travel, had provided little time for father-son bonding for Charles. With a five-year gap in age, Much of the focus of male role model responsibilities, fell on my shoulders.

Predictably, with me already in high school and pursuing my own interests, my mother doted over and spoiled my brother immensely. In 1977, my mother's company offered her a sales territory and good income potential if she would transfer from Atlanta to Norfolk, Virginia. She moved away with my sister and brother In tow. I was at the ripe old age of 19, and stayed behind.

In Virginia, the spoiling continued and was expanded. He was given a car and a boat and rules governing his behavior were very lax. He fell in with a wild crowd while still in high school. Drinking and smoking illegal materials became regular recreational habits.

When he did come to Arkansas to live with Dad and I, his long delayed bonding with Bill finally took place. Where it had been football and racing for me, the Bill/Jr components were drinking and partying.

Over the years, my brother had shown very little interest in anything interfering with his daily routine. Sadly, the dominant ingredient every day was alcohol. He is a very talented, thoughtful person, but ambition, career goals and relationships are in his world, obligatory impediments that he has chosen to deemphasize.

He worked for a number of years in the racing business, eventually heading back down to Florida where he was director of racing in Orlando. Following that, he moved to Tarpon Springs, just north of Clearwater, Florida, and took up residence with my mother in her condominium. He secured a good job at the Innisbrook Golf Resort, and did a very fine job running the customer service aspects of the property. The job was a good fit for him, as the manager he was able to make his own schedule and pretty much come and go as he pleased. He also had another great perk, access to all of the resorts golf courses for free. I was a great beneficiary of that arrangement. During this period, he also had a tremendous life highlight. At a Tampa Bay Lightning National hockey league game, the influence of his older brother, yours truly, paid off handsomely. In his early teen years, Following my lead and my friends, he had gotten heavily into hockey. We spent countless hours in our driveway "Pucking Around" as we called it. The night of that game, Junior was selected as one of the contestants in a promotion that allowed one shot from center ice. If the puck went in the net, the shooter would win a new truck. The catch was, that the entire goal was covered by a giant piece of wood and the only opening was basically the size of the puck itself. The tiny slot was just at the bottom of the covering in the center along the ice. Amazingly, Junior coolly executed a smooth shot that was dead on. It slid smoothly and went right through the tiny opening and into the net. The arena went wild, as Junior, standing as still as a statue, routinely raised his stick to the heavens in celebration. That night, his feAt, was featured on CNN/SI sports final as the play of the day. National television exposure for his moment of glory.

When the Innisbrook resort was sold to new ownership, Junior opted for a buyout and the severance package. For the next few years, he lived like a retiree. Without the annoyance of having to report to a job, or do anything else for that matter, he was free to pursue his passion of a stay up all night, sleep all day, cocktailing life.

At the point where my vision malfunctioned, was approximately the same time that JR's money ran out. Thoughts of him seeking a conventional job were out of the question. I concocted a win-win scenario that I thought would help us both. Basically it involved him coming to Birmingham, where he could work at the track as the announcer, and also help me with my mobility and earn some money doing that. The offer was enticing because I threw in free room and board, and provided the vehicles to drive. The arrangement went on for the next two years, but there was discord. His intentions were always good, and largely his heart was in the right place, but his availability as my driver and assistant was always based on his schedule that was determined by the ever present companion in his life, his alcohol. He was not a social drinker. An ideal evening for him involve sitting in his room alone, watching television and consuming a wide array of alcoholic beverages. It was not unusual in the course of one evening for him to down a considerable amounts of beer, wine and a variety of booze.

In December, 2014, he loaded up my car and headed to Florida for a six-week break at our mothers. He had developed another obsession in recent years, that being strenuous exercise, chiefly running. As his workouts increased in intensity, it provided a perfect rationalization that if he was in good enough shape to push himself in that manner, then surely his drinking would not be physically detrimental. I flew to Florida with my son Clayt and we spent a few days there for Christmas before heading on to Las Vegas to visit my older son. The plan was at the end of January, Junior would return to Birmingham with my car. It was a good plan, but it never happened

As he set out on that road trip, the beginnings of one of the stranger mysteries imaginable unfolded. He left on a Thursday, planning to stop on the way to visit a friend in Montgomery, which was on the route he chose. He was slated to arrive in Birmingham either Friday night or Saturday. Early that Friday morning, I received a call from my mother telling me that he had called Thursday night and reported to her that he had been involved in some sort of accident on I 10 just outside Marianna, Florida. She gave me a phone number to call which was a hotel in that town. I reached the groggy barely responsive Junior on the other end. His memory of what happened was extremely vague and even contradictory. He maintained someone had sideswiped him on the expressway. He could not tell me what kind of car it was or who was driving. When I asked did he follow the offender or did they make any effort to pull over, he responded that he was so shocked that he had lost sight of them. He was complaining about being banged up and his mouth being hurt. The way he was talking sounded to me like he might have had a head injury of some kind. Establishing that the car was still mobile, I urged him to go to an emergency room to get checked out. I told him to keep in contact with me and that if necessary, my son, one of his friends and I, would come down there on Saturday and drive he and the car back to Birmingham. I wish he had been cognizant enough to take that advice.

My sister in Florida had called to check on him Saturday morning, and was informed he had checked out. So now he was presumably on his way to Birmingham but as that day turned into night, there was no contact with him. The fact that he never touched base with my mother after Friday afternoon was a clear indication something was terribly wrong.

My brother is the ultimate mamas boy. He obsessively calls her every day to check in. She has been his facilitator and The privileged person on the receiving end of his endless lIsts of ailments and complaints during the course of his entire life. My mother is also a world class worrier. Anytime my brother had ever been on the road, he would be frantic in his anxiety to call her and update his progress. As Saturday transformed to Sunday, she had not heard from him.

When Sunday came and went, full-fledged crisis mode was implemented. To my mothers credit, she stayed relatively calm, but had not eaten or slept in two days. On Monday morning, I placed phone calls to police jurisdictions in Alabama and northern Florida and began the process of filing missing person reports. Several people had offered to drive me along the route that he would have taken. While all of those plans were being developed, I placed a call to my mother to assure her that I was doing everything on my end that I could possibly do. While on that call with her, my cell phone beeped indicating I had another call. That communication was from Jackson Hospital in Montgomery, Alabama. The caller identified herself as a representative of the hospital's financial office and prefaced her remarks with, as you know we have your brother Charles here. Of course I did not know, until that moment. And when I inquired as to his condition and other circumstances, she said she had no knowledge and was only trying to verify that he had insurance, which he did not. Finally she gave me a number to call and all they would tell me was that he had been admitted. I immediately made some calls and arranged for my invaluable office assistant Leda, to drive me to Montgomery. Within two hours I was there

Around midnight, Sunday evening/Monday morning, an ambulance was dispatched to a Salvation Army location to pick up my brother who was suffering from almost complete renal shut down and extreme delusion. According to the Salvation Army workers, he has been dropped off at their Shelter by police who had picked him up off the streets from an undisclosed location. The assumption of course was that he was a homeless, drug or alcohol addled Street person. There had been thunderstorms in the area that evening and when he was admitted he was absolutely soaking wet. He had no identification, nothing whatsoever on his person. He was diagnosed with severe kidney distress and hepatitis symptoms emanating from his liver. He could only mumble incoherently. After treatment, he stabilized but there was significant concern about his kidney's regaining full function. The only visible injury he sustained was a severe laceration of his tongue. It appeared he had violently bitten through it.

My first discussion with him was odd. He was able to communicate and had full recognition of who I was. In fact, as his condition had improved overnight, in the morning he was able to tell them his name and give them my phone number. However, he had no idea of anything that had occurred going back to when he had left my mothers place 4 days before.

His wallet and my keys were not with him. Also, $7000 in cash he had been carrying in a plastic bag also was not present. There was also the detail of my car and all of his possessions missing. He did not remember anything.

His condition improved over the five days of his hospitalization and he dodged a major bullet when his kidney function normalized. Still, there was no recollection as to what had happened.

I was in touch three times with the Montgomery police that week. They had no record of Junior being picked up and transported. They refused to issue a report that my car was stolen since there was no evidence a crime had occurred, let alone that it happened in their jurisdiction. That was bad news for me. A missing car is not covered by insurance. No police report, no claim. Supposedly they issued some kind of watch for the car but that lookout proved ineffective.

On the third day of his hospital stay, there was some brief comic relief to the tension. I had arrived at the hospital that morning to find him flat on his back sound asleep and snoring. I checked with the nurses who gave me an encouraging report on his overnight progress. I thought it was odd that he was laying there bare chested, sheet covering his lower half. I sat in the chair position at the top corner of the bed aligned with his head. He eventually awoke and seemed a little groggy during our conversation. He shuffled around a bit and raised his knees upwards resting the weight of his legs in the bottoms of his feet against the sheets. Suddenly, a nurse's assistant burst in the room through his open room door. Exasperated, she exclaimed, " Mr. Keefer, you can't be laying there Like that in all your glory. Everyone in the hall can see right into this room."

It took me just a second to process what she had said before it truly registered, leading me to ask in an incredulous tone, "Oh my God, he's naked?"

To which she replied, "Yes, you can't see that?"

And my comeback was, "thankfully no, I have severe vision impairment, and for the only   time since it happened, I'm so glad I do."

My brother meanwhile, lying there impassively offered up this gem of wisdom in response to the situation, "I don't know what all the fuss is about, everybody up here has seen everything I have."

Blessedly, the nurse quickly outfitted him in a new gown.

Later that day, a doctor had told me that the ugly injury to his tongue was consistent with someone who had a powerful seizure. His best guess was some kind of severe internal trauma, more than likely triggered by his drinking habits, and perhaps even exacerbated by his exercise schedule, had combined to basically shut down his system. He explained the memory loss was probably not that unusual in light of the circumstances. In severe trauma it would not be unusual for the brain to basically blackout as other systems were failing.

My sister and mother drove up to take him back to Florida to recuperate. After being released around noon on Friday, a tremendous struggle to load him successfully in the back of my sister's van finally succeeded and they headed south.

More than a year has passed, but my brother's memory of any aspect of those four days has never returned. He has basically gone into a shut in mode. He complains of constant aches and pains. Despite what happened, he continues to drink regularly, although he maintains he has cut way back. If there is a silver lining to the story, it's probably good that my mother is there to care for him, and hIm being there to look after her is also a good thing. They are both alarmists and paranoids, so on the downside they are sometimes negative enablers towards one another.

Some ten months after my brothers disappearance, I received a registered letter from an impound lot south of Montgomery stating that they had my car on theIr storage property. They had picked up the vehicle from a field behind a rural church in July. That meant that they had the car for four months before bothering to inform me. Supposedly they had notified the Montgomery Police Department, who of course have my car on their "watchlist." I was never informed that it had been found by either of those parties. And the really good news was included, that my daily storage fee, for them taking such great care of my vehicle in their 24 hour secured facility was currently standing at $3600. A week later, I visited this location which basically was a decimated, rundown, shithole junk yard. My car that they were taking such meticulous good care of, was parked amongst totaled, trashed, smashed out, rusting, decaying wrecks. There was significant damage to the front quadrant on the driver side, the windows were broken out and all operating systems in the vehicle were completely dead. My brother, the ultimate PacK Rat, had been hauling numerous containers and boxes of worthless crap, such as old newspapers, Books and magazines, canned goods and even a cooler with a variety of what had at one time been fruits. Needless to say after 10 months, that was an

unpleasant experience to open the lid of the container.
Everyone of his suitcases, bags and boxes had been turned
upside down and emptied. The car was literally filled floor
to ceiling with junk and refuse. Anything even remotely
usable or salvageable had been taken away. This included
a large portion of my brother's clothes. Clayt and I had
put some items in the trunk to be transported back to
Birmingham. Most of those items were also gone. We
did find a single sandal from a pair Clayt had received for
Christmas. We quickly deduced that the perpetrator we
were looking for was obviously a one legged man. With
the windows smashed out, all of this trash and abandon
contents, had been subject to the elements for months.
Of course that extended to the cloth seats and carpeting
within the interior. The smell emanating from what had
once been a very nice Honda Accord, was putrid. Bottom
line, the car was trashed. The disreputable, Scallywag
towing industry, is one of the most despicable, unethical
businesses that are allowed to operate in this country.
Basically they were demanding that I buy my own car
back from them. It had taken them less than a half hour
to hook it up and tow it in. Then, they dumped it in
their cesspool of wreckage and turned on the fee meter. I
had no intention of being victimized by this scandalous
extortion scheme. Recovering the vehicle was going to
be basically a break even proposition. Insurance would
fix the car of course, but I had my doubts that it could
ever be a decent vehicle again. I told the towing company
criminals where they could stick my Honda.

So the fate of the car was discovered, but the mystery of
what happened will never be known. There have been
those who have speculated that he had gone on some

kind of hellacious bender enroute which precipitated the events. Let me dispel once and for all that theory. The only things more influential in his personality than his drinking habits, are paranoia and obsessive compulsiveness. His fear of getting a DUI, even when he wasn't drunk, bordered on absurd. Add to that, his pattern of consumption never started before 5 o'clock in the afternoon it was virtually nonexistent during daylight hours, unless it was Sunrise and he had not yet gone to bed. After a great deal of time to reflect, Junior is convinced that he must've been somehow abducted or carjacked. I think physiologically his body finally had enough and one or more severe seizures were the result. It was a dangerously close call that almost resulted in the loss of my brother that did in the end cost me a car. I guess the glass half full way to look at it is if it had to be one or the other the best scenario prevailed.

KEEFER STORY

The Saga Continues

So, you have read the stories, shaken your head at the absurdities, laughed at the nonsense, been lifted by the triumphs and cringed over the heartbreaks. I would suspect, that more than likely it has not occurred to you dear reader, that this wildly swinging pendulum of twists and turns is not simply a look back, for it continues to this day.

As I write these words, my life and its day-to-day challenges are considerable. Not to brag, but I am proud of the resilience and strong sense of independence that I have maintained. Mobility of course, is a problem, but I am overcoming that with creative thinking. In fact, my capacity for thought is indisputably at an all-time high.

I hope people will not find what I'm about to say to be arrogant. When one of your senses is compromised, common knowledge states that compensations are made through enhancement and sharpening of other senses. In my case, I truly believe that the adjustment has occurred within the confines of my brain. As I explained earlier, my problem is not my eyesight. Instead, it is a neurological problem, basically faulty transmission of the images to my brain. It is really difficult to explain but I believe that everything I see is still transmitted. Like a television signal in the bygone era of transmission received by an antenna, the picture that appeared on the screen was often distorted, fuzzy or unclear. That is a very close description to what I experience. The transmission still arrives at the source, but the pictures are unclear. I firmly believe that a larger portion of my mind is called upon to facilitate that signal interpretation. And even though there is difficulty in viewing everything now, somehow there is recognition that allows me, in most everything, to be able to successfully function. It does require a great deal of concentration. When I have made mistakes, they can easily be traced To my temporarily forgetting my circumstances and not paying appropriate attention.

Another great example to try and explain this phenomenon occurs when I watch a game, show or movie intently. I find that after-the-fact, I have almost total recognition of what I saw. But that is not necessarily the case as I'm watching it. A movie scene that is significant, I may well miss a certain action or expression from a character that is important as it unfolds. But later, that image is clearly something I can summon. A great play in a game is another example. My recollection of it later seems more vivid than when I actually watched it.

I find my skills of perception and analysis are far more developed now. I theorize that it is this additional mental capacity that has been initiated by necessity, that is making it happen.

All the words in these pages indicate that I tick a little differently. I suppose it's appropriate that my life now is vastly out of the ordinary. On the one hand, it would be easy to throw up my hands and give up. I'm sure I would qualify for some sort of disability. But I have no intention of going quietly. I want to use the adversity that has intruded upon my existence as fuel and motivation. I am not ready to sit in a rocker and pass the time. The time is a too valuable commodity to waste. I am either going to do great things or literally die trying. I need to reintroduce myself to the world. I'm shocked that my family and long-time friends don't seem to grasp that I am in so many ways now a different person. I guess the longevity and comfort zone of familiarity is a difficult concept to recognize change and update. So hello world … I am Kip Keefer.

Post 12

"Close your eyes and think about all of the greatest moments of your life. Summon the images of the most significant highlight memories. Now answer this ... at any of these times, were you alone?"

THE MURAL ... A SHORT STORY

The final thought he had before drifting off to sleep after a long, listless, lonely day, was unsettling. The question had lingered on his mind before sleep mercifully was able to intercede.

"Is having to live this way even worth it any longer?" The posing of such a mental inquiry prompted in him a profound sense of futility, invalidation, emptiness and most distressingly, fear. He had never entertained thoughts of giving up. That would've seemed inconceivable, even a short time ago. His disillusionment and melancholy had rapidly mounted and suddenly seemed to be unbearable.

His eyes were still unopened as the first recognition of waking from a deep sleep occurred. In that instant, however, he instinctively knew something wasn't normal. He was immediately cognizant that he was not on his couch or in his own bed. The surface he was lying now was very soft and the feeling was a sensation of being immersed within it. There were no pillows or covers. His mind raced as to where he could be and how he got there. Then the realization, surely this must be a dream.

Sitting up, with no resistance, he slowly wedged open his eyes. He was immediately shocked to discover that his vision, which had severely been diminished for a number of years, was functioning perfectly. This had to be a dream. He was in a modest sized room with a brightness that was unlike any he had ever seen. It was accentuated by brilliant white surroundings. The walls on all sides, the soft carpet-like surface of the floor, and above, what appeared to be a ceiling awash in the basking glow of the room. It was strange, however, that despite the brightness there was no glare.

Any trepidation or anxiety from being in this mysterious room was negated by a feeling of tranquility prompted by the surroundings. Still assuming this situation was an elaborate dream, he tentatively started exploring the space. His first discovery, there were no doors or windows on any of the four walls. Despite the luminous environment, he could not see any source of that light. The temperature was comfortable, ideal actually, yet there were no vents and a flow of air could not be felt. He stood against a wall for a time, baffled and expecting to awaken from this strange dream. After several minutes, he was still standing in the same spot. He clapped his hands, lightly thumped himself on his head and even bent down to touch his toes. He shrugged and decided that while inexplicable, for now, this was his reality.

The thought emanated suddenly from the depths of his mind. Was this transition, was it possible, had he died? A chill of fast moving fear and dread consumed him. Then instantly it disappeared. This room eliminated fear and despair. Besides, he was aware of his surroundings and still fully aware of exactly who he was. The fact that he had no recollection of the previous day or night and no urgency or awareness of being expected or needed anywhere else, there was no cause for unrest. At this moment in time, he was assured by some knowing internal sense, he was precisely where he was supposed to be.

Gazing around the room again, there was an item he had not noticed previously. In fact, he would have sworn it was not there before. It was a small cabinet, white, of course. It was in front of the forward wall. He strode over to investigate. There was a closed lid across the top of the nightstand-sized item. He lifted the lid and slowly eased it back. Looking down, he was surprised to see an array of brushes and an artist's pallet. Below, there was one drawer. Opening it, he discovered it was filled with neatly organized markers of every color and description.

None of this made any sense. He was a writer and verbal communicator, he had no artistic ability whatsoever. The thought of painting or drawing was a laughable prospect. Not to mention the fact that there was no easel or canvas. And, there was no paint. He picked up the cloud-shaped pallet and examined it. The smooth surface was pristine. He picked up a brush and mimicked the process of dabbing it against the pallet to pick up some paint. He turned to the adjacent wall and wistfully brushed the blank space with a quick stroke. To his astonishment, a tiny streak of red, his favorite color, appeared. The pallet was still clean. He dabbed again and crossed the streak on the wall. It formed a perfect red cross-like symbol. He grabbed a different brush and thought about blue. The stroke along the wall appeared in that color. Suddenly, it was clear. This room was his studio, and despite it making no sense, he was placed there to paint. These brilliant, smooth white walls were actually the giant canvas for creation of a mural, his own personal creative gallery.

For a significant period of time, he simply stood staring at the vast empty space. While it had become clear that he was supposed to create some images, he still had no idea what was intended for him depict. He certainly could write, and there were markers. Impulsively, he suddenly found himself writing elaborate lists of names, places, events, memories, even dreams. Something intuitive took over. The names and places varied in size and style depending on their significance; family and closest friends were not only listed by name but also accompanied by a drawing of each person. He laughed at himself as the absurdity of his lack of artistic talent was so readily displayed. Still, he was compelled to grab a brush and diligently add flesh tones and he gallantly attempted to fill in features for each person. He worked for hours; there was no fatigue, hunger or thirst. He worked so feverishly, he did not even notice that he had transitioned to another wall to continue.

More lists, memories, names and faces, all of the places he'd been. He found himself intensely concentrating on the source of his life's greatest joy, his children. He chronicled and recreated every recollection of their lives, from birth to present day young adulthood. First words, first steps, school, programs, sports, graduations, arrears, weddings. He amazed himself, every memory was clear and concise.

On yet another wall, he recreated the great loves of his life. Again, he fervently labored on every word, each minute detail. The select group of the select few women he had unabashedly and unconditionally loved came to life anew.

It may have been hours, it could even have been days. He stepped back and surveyed his work. He was absolutely astounded. His endless lists of names and places, events and highlights, triumphs, and heartbreaks, were featured in a magnificent diversity of font styles, colors and calligraphy, the crude drawings of people had magically transformed into detailed, exquisite portraits. They were so vivid and lifelike, it was as if they were present in the room. Stepping back and standing in the center of this panorama he had miraculously created, he slowly rotated and drank in the words and images that surrounded him on all sides. The range of sentiments was overwhelming. He relished every moment; he relived every emotion. He reflected, laughed, sighed and cried. It was exhilarating and overwhelming to be inundated with the entirety of his personal history, the story of his life. Never had he experienced such extremely immense appreciation, comprehension, and perspective. And then suddenly, exhaustion came upon him. He dropped to the floor and instantly fell into a blissful, contented sleep.

When he awoke, he was surprised that he was still in the room. The light had not altered; the images surrounding him were still present. But then it became apparent, something was different. On each wall, empty space had opened in a variety of shapes and sizes. The images he had created had reshaped slightly. It seemed that these gaps were next to important people indicating perhaps that key information or history had somehow not been included. He pondered that thought momentarily, but then satisfied himself that his task had been executed thoroughly and nothing had been omitted.

On each of the four walls, the situation was the same. He wondered what he could have possibly added. He turned toward the supply cabinet only to realize it was no longer there. Where had it gone and why had it disappeared? Obviously, his task was completed after all. And then, at that instant, with the conclusion of that thought, it all became perfectly clear. He had been absolutely successful at completely chronicling and depicting the story of his life up to that precise moment. There was only one logical explanation. Those smaller spaces now empty on his mural represented stories and important moments involving those important people and places that were yet to come. The large spaces on the wall, many in the area of his children, made crystal clear sense. There was still so much more of their story to be authored along with his involvement in it. On the wall of his loves, a very large empty space was present. The thought of any further romance or matters of heart had long been abandoned. Could it be that there was more of a story ahead? The large empty void seemed to indicate the possibility that the unwritten chapters in that area, which had been a heartbreaking emptiness and disappointment, perhaps held the promise of the greatest blessings still being possible further ahead?

As he contemplated this revelation, he noticed in the low corner of the wall an image before him that he had not created. It was directly in front of where he now stood. It was a forked path. Just to the left, it diverted into a large gate, brilliantly illuminated with the lights so bright he was forced to shield his eyes. To the right, a continuing pathway leading to sunrise on a vast horizon. Instinctively, he was compelled suddenly to step forward toward the image depicted so realistically on the wall. He suddenly found himself seemingly suspended in there. Air was a comforting urge to veer to the left side and drift into the peaceful, basking, nurturing brilliant light. The feeling of comfort and peace it offered was incredibly desirable. But then he heard a sound that he instantly recognized, his own voice. It reminded him that he completely understood that the contents of his life mural were not completed. The powerful message that there was more to author, experience and give resonated. Resolutely, emboldened by the reassuring power of his own personal affirmation, he set his sights on the pathway with no hesitation.

Instantly, or so it seemed, he was sitting on the sofa in his apartment. The television was off, it was daylight. His first thought was his vision was again limited. He shrugged incredulously, contemplating the incredible, detail-laden dream he had just experienced. It all seemed so real. It was odd that he could remember all of it so vividly. He thought about the mystery of a person's subconscious mind and inner spirit. While pondering those marvels, he suddenly found himself wondering if it was something even greater that had choreographed this remarkable experience and epiphany. Could it be that he had been given a divine gift? One of enlightenment and perspective? He suddenly felt an incredible rush of gratitude and appreciation and vowed that he would devote all of his energies to making the remaining portions of his life mural inspirational, worthwhile, and uplifting. He shook his head slowly and said out loud, "What a dream!"

His thoughts were interrupted by a knock on the door. He rose and unlatched the lock and was pleasantly surprised to see his youngest son standing there. The young man stepped in and said he had worried after a number of unanswered calls and texts and had come by to make sure that everything was all right. Then, examining his dad, as if to reassure himself, with a quizzical look on his face he said, "What in the world have you been doing? You have paint all over you."

So I am continuing down the path and hoping to create the pictures, accounts and memories to paint more images. My hopes are unwavering that the masterpiece still to come will depict joy, laughter, fulfillment, and do I dare to dream it, acceptance, validation and love.